# LOST & FOUND
## LEGENDARY LAKE MICHIGAN SHIPWRECKS

**Cover**
Top Front: *Wells Burt*, C. T. Stone Family Collection
Bottom Front: *Carl D. Bradley* by Steve Witucki
Top Back: *Thomas Hume* by Robert Underhill
Bottom Back: *Rosinco, Ann Arbor No. 5, Three Brothers,* and *Alvin Clark*

**Photographs**
As credited and used with permission

**Published**
In the United States of America by In-Depth Editions, 2012
www.in-deptheditions.com
18 17 16 15 14 6 5 4 3 2
Second Edition

**Publisher Cataloging-in-Publication Data**
Van Heest, V. O.
Lost & found: legendary lake michigan shipwrecks/ V. O. Van Heest
304 p. : 192 ill., map ; 23 cm. (Great Lakes books)
Includes bibliographical references and index (294-302)
ISBN 978-09801750-5-9 (pbk: alk paper)
1. Shipwrecks—Michigan. 2. Shipwrecks—Wisconsin. 3. Shipwrecks—Illinois.
4. Shipwrecks—Indiana. 5. Shipwrecks—Great Lakes—Michigan, Lake.
6. Lake Michigan—History. 7. Shipping—Michigan, Lake.
I. Title II. Author

**2012**
G525.S5155 2012
910.452Van        2012914540

# LOST & FOUND
## LEGENDARY LAKE MICHIGAN SHIPWRECKS

V. O. VAN HEEST

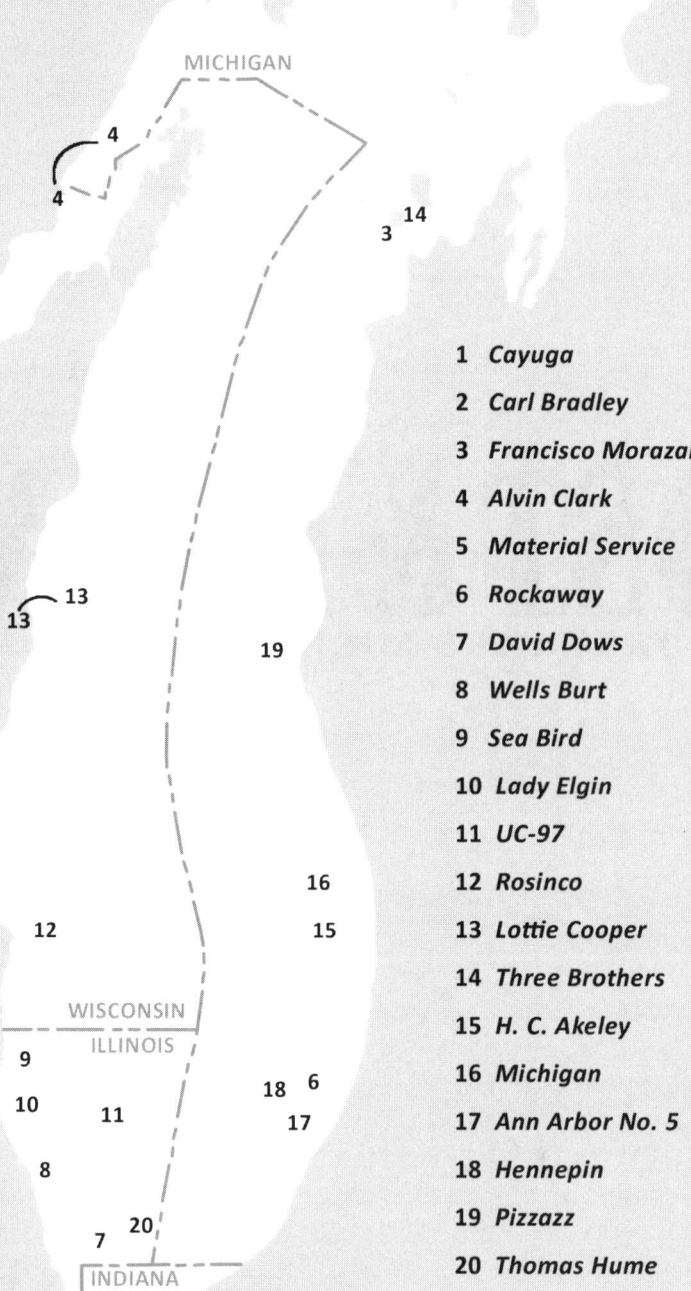

# LAKE MICHIGAN

MICHIGAN

WISCONSIN

ILLINOIS

INDIANA

1   Cayuga

2   Carl Bradley

3   Francisco Morazan

4   Alvin Clark

5   Material Service

6   Rockaway

7   David Dows

8   Wells Burt

9   Sea Bird

10  Lady Elgin

11  UC-97

12  Rosinco

13  Lottie Cooper

14  Three Brothers

15  H. C. Akeley

16  Michigan

17  Ann Arbor No. 5

18  Hennepin

19  Pizzazz

20  Thomas Hume

# TABLE OF CONTENTS

**The author prepares to make a dive.** *Photograph by Joseph Oliver*

# AUTHOR NOTES

The day my dad strapped a scuba tank on my back and tossed me into the deep end of his good friend Sam Davison's swimming pool in 1974, I began to see the world from a different perspective. After the initial rush of realizing I could survive in this foreign environment, I studied the new world around me. The drain, the skimmers, and the textured pool bottom appeared clear, but the world above me seemed blurred. I could hear nothing but a seemingly distant sound of my Dacor Olympic 400 regulator as I breathed in and out. At fourteen years old, I became hooked on the underwater world.

Two years later, Sam offered me a summer job at Dacor Corporation, the manufacturing company he had founded. There, I began assembling depth gauges and regulators, and Sam soon promoted me to a position in the repair department where I began to understand the inner workings of these complex devices. Sam encouraged everyone at Dacor, whether top management or assembly line workers, to become certified divers. So it was that in the summer of 1976, I earned my open water certification alongside other employees.

The next summer, my dad introduced me to another friend, Tom Coyne, the owner of Scuba Systems in Skokie, Illinois, who hired me to work at his dive shop. There, I sold gear, learned more about repair work from another employee, Larry Bouche (who years later would come to own the store), and swapped stories with the customers. A dive that fall with my pals from Dacor to the site of an old shipwreck just off Greenwood beach in Evanston, Illinois, just north of Chicago, would shape my life.

I found it amazing to explore that shipwreck—the *George Morley,* a steam-powered propeller that burned and sank on December 5, 1897, after an oil lamp explosion—even though the sinking event and a century underwater had reduced it to rubble. I rooted around piles of twisted metal and wood searching for clues that might offer a vision of what these ships looked like when they sailed and what the passengers and crew might have experienced in the final moments before the ship plunged beneath the waves. I found myself wanting to know more about that shipwreck and how it came to be in twenty feet of water off a popular swimming beach where, ironically, Sam Davison and my dad first experimented with homemade diving gear. It would take several years, after graduating from both high school and college, where I earned a degree in interior architecture, before I had a chance to begin satisfying that curiosity.

When I was twenty-six, a serendipitous encounter with scuba divers from the Chicago Maritime Society reintroduced me to the history-steeped world of shipwrecks. I began diving the schooner *David Dows* and returned to the *George Morley,* where I felt transported back in time to the age of sail and steam on the Great Lakes. The people who sailed these ships became real to me. My life from that point on has been about telling the stories of these ships and their crews. In 1988, I, along with two other members of the Chicago Maritime Society, founded the Underwater Archaeological Society of Chicago (UASC), a nonprofit organization dedicated to documenting shipwrecks and sharing the results of our work with other divers and the public.

In 1994, while presenting the UASC's work on the wreck of the *Goshawk* at an annual shipwreck convention in the Detroit area, I met another diver who, one year later, I would marry. I moved east across the shores of Lake Michigan to settle in Holland, Michigan. However, I was disappointed to learn that very few shipwrecks had been located on the eastern side of the lake. To continue diving on and documenting shipwrecks, we would have to find them first.

I began working with Kenneth Pott, then curator of the Michigan Maritime Museum in South Haven, and a group of people organized as the committee to establish the Southwest Michigan Underwater Preserve. The underwater preserve system had been created in 1980 to protect clusters of shipwrecks throughout the waters of Michigan, and Pott's research indicated that dozens of ships had gone down in the waters off Southwest Michigan. Very soon thereafter, members of our committee discovered the wreck of the *Verano*, a pleasure yacht lost in 1946 off South Haven. The vessel was significant because it was one of the lakes' earliest luxury yachts. It sailed through the Roaring Twenties, the tumultuous Great Depression, and the war years, and then sank in mysterious circumstances. The discovery of the shipwreck provided the hook to mount a project and the Michigan Humanities Council awarded a grant to study the wreck, conduct research, produce a documentary film, and make numerous public presentations about the shipwreck and its place in Michigan's maritime history. The media coverage garnered by the project brought attention to the proposed preserve, which prompted the state of Michigan to officially designate it the Southwest Michigan Underwater Preserve in 1999. The *Verano* also drew divers from far and wide to visit the shipwreck, adding yet another tourist attraction to the small town of South Haven.

In considering how the discovery of the *Verano* had generated significant local attention—not unlike the discovery of the *Titanic,* a few years earlier, had fueled worldwide interest in history, science, and technology—I wanted to find more shipwrecks that could help draw attention to the rich maritime history of the Great Lakes. After the establishment of the Southwest Michigan Underwater Preserve, I cofounded the Michigan Shipwreck Research Association (MSRA) with my spouse and several other like-minded people to discover, document, and interpret Michigan shipwrecks for education and archaeological purposes. Over the next many years working with noted Great Lakes shipwreck hunter David Trotter, and later nationally acclaimed author Clive Cussler, we discovered more than a dozen "new" shipwrecks. These in turn generated the topics that I began to write and lecture about and, in time, served as subjects for museum exhibits I have designed though my firm, Lafferty Van Heest and Associates.

A number of other individuals and teams have been responsible for making extraordinary shipwreck discoveries in Lake Michigan. Some locations are kept secret and only a small handful of divers "in the know" ever see them. Others are shared and become diving attractions. Some have been salvaged, others battled over in court, and still others studied archaeologically. The seeds of this book grew out of my thirty-year perspective diving shipwrecks. Over that time, I saw significant change in the conduct of divers, ranging from stripping wrecks of artifacts to leaving the wrecks intact for historical and archaeological study. As I considered the many shipwrecks that have been found, several stood out as becoming more "legendary" for what took place after their discoveries even more so than the events surrounding their losses. These shipwrecks seemed appropriate vehicles to convey the changes that have taken place in both lake transportation and scuba diving on Lake Michigan.

I have told the stories of the *Lady Elgin, Hennepin,* and *Thomas Hume* previously in full-length books, but share them again here in abbreviated form for the role they play in the evolution of shipwreck discovery and for those who prefer their shipwreck stories as snacks rather than seven-course meals. Likewise, other authors have written about the sinking of several of these vessels, but I have endeavored to tell the tale from the perspective of those who lived through the ordeal as a new way of looking at the incidents. In recounting the events, I typically used only primary sources that often included survivor or witness accounts. As the title implies, this book also details the discovery and documentation of the shipwrecks, whereas most writers stop at the point a vessel slips beneath the waves.

Over the last three decades, I have been fortunate to meet a great many people who share my interest in shipwreck research, exploration, and documentation and who have, in various ways, contributed to the development of this book.

Sam Davison and my father provided the inspiration and guidance to make me a diver. Jeff and Gary Davison and Jeff Rice helped pull together the stories of Sam's early years that allowed me to share the origins of Dacor. David Lewis offered insight into Max Nohl's early career and his own daring and ground-breaking dives on the *Carl D. Bradley*. David Truitt mentored me in leadership during our work on the *David Dows, Wells Burt,* and *Lady Elgin* projects, and Keith Pearson was always at my side as a research and diving partner. John McManamon and Robert Gadbois, my friends and associates from the Underwater Archaeological Society of Chicago (UASC), shared their research on the *David Dows* and *Sea Bird*. Joe Oliver, a good friend I worked with in the UASC, allowed me to include several of his exquisite underwater photographs that grace these pages. Jim Jarecki, a UASC past president offered his insights on Indiana and Illinois wrecks. Kenneth Pott readily accepted me into the committee to establish the SWMUP and shared his research and images on the *Rockaway*. My husband, Jack Van Heest, and associates Craig Rich and Geoffrey Reynolds of the Michigan Shipwreck Research Association, worked with me to research and document the *Michigan, Ann Arbor No. 5, Hennepin,* and *Thomas Hume*. MSRA technical divers Robert Underhill, Jeff Vos, Todd White, and Tim Marr shared their observations, video, and photographs that allowed me to tell a number of these stories. MSRA member and author, Neel Zoss, proofread this manuscript. Larry Czackor shared memories and photographs and Allan Petrulus recounted his dives on the *Material Service*. Archaeologist Gary Ellis provided Indiana's perspective on that wreck and his site plan and underwater video. Bradley Friend shared his underwater photographs and video of the *Rosinco*, Steve Radovan told the story of its discovery, and archaeologist Jeff Gray provided insight into the legal case regarding that wreck. Melanie Clark shared her beautiful underwater images of the *Carl D. Bradley*. William Lafferty, my business partner, worked with me to research the *Hennepin* and *Thomas Hume* and in the process taught me a lot about writing. He also allowed me to utilize portions of his research and text from our book *Buckets and Belts* in order to recap the story of the *Material Service*. David Trotter, who has served as a mentor and partner for more than a dozen years, discovered a number of the legendary shipwrecks presented in this book and offered advice on the manuscript. Likewise, Clive Cussler and Ralph Wilbanks of the National Underwater Marine Agency have discovered, in partnership with MSRA, a number of shipwrecks in southern Lake Michigan, one of which is included here. John McGarry and Dani LaFleur of the Lakeshore Museum Center as well as divers Tom Palmisano, Jeff Strunka, and Bud Brain served as partners to document the *Thomas Hume* along with MSRA members named previously. Bud Brain also shared memories of his participation raising the *Alvin Clark*, and the discovery of the *Sea Bird*. Chriss

Lyon found historical and genealogical information that contributed to the telling of several of these stories. Chad Pelishek at the City of Sheboygan entrusted me with his documents about the archaeological survey of the *Lottie Cooper*. Ross Richardson located and transcribed several newspaper articles associated with the *Michigan* and *Hennepin*. Steve Witucki and Bob Underhill provided their incredible images for this book's cover and C. T. Stone shared his painting of the *Wells Burt*. Artists Robert McGreevy, James Clary, and Eric Forsberg provided some of their paintings for reproduction in this book. David Erickson offered insights on the *Carl D. Bradley* and organized the 50th anniversary event. Patti Montgomery Reinhart and Katie Bleil at the Michigan Maritime Museum helped me access their archives. Walter Lewis maintains a website of maritime news articles that was of great help to me, as it is to almost every other researcher. Barb Patchin helped unearth the story of her ancestor, Captain Edward Stretch, to complete the *H. C. Akeley* story. Robert Love and John Bultema Sr. and Jr. shared memories of the *Ann Arbor No 5* and Bob Vande Vusse, Jed Jaworski, and Grant Brown gave me insights into its career. Patrick Labadie provided historical images from his vast collection for the book, accessed through Marlo Broad at the Alpena County Public Library. Last, but certainly not least, is my editor, Ann Weller, who helped make the manuscript ship-shape.

*I dedicate this book in memory of my father, Robert Olson,
and his good buddy, Sam Davison, who both
cultivated my interest in the underwater world.*

The wreck of the *Thomas Hume* in Illinois waters.
*Photograph by Robert Underhill*

# FOREWORD

L ittered on the bottom of the Great Lakes are the remains of more than 6000 shipwrecks gone missing on the Great Lakes since the late 1600s when the first commercial sailing ships began plying the region, most during the heyday of commercial shipping in the nineteenth century. The vast expanse of these inland waterways provided a natural transportation system linking the Midwestern states and portions of Canada to the rest of the world. Unpredictable weather makes them some of the most dangerous waters in the world. Sudden storms, fire, and fog have resulted in the destruction of these many thousands of vessels. Just over twenty percent of those vessels have come to rest on the bottom of Lake Michigan, second only in quantity to Lake Huron. Heavy passenger and cargo trade to the cities of Chicago, Milwaukee, and the many small lakefront communities on the eastern and western shores, combined with the prevailing northwest winds that have the full 400-mile length of the lake to build, conspired to end the careers of almost 2000 vessels and the lives of thousands of people. Several hundred of these vessels—mostly hard-to-maneuver sailing crafts—have been the victims of the raging winds and currents that pounded them into kindling along shore. However, many hundreds more were lost in deep water far offshore. To date, only some 300 shipwrecks have been found beyond the surf line in Lake Michigan.

Historically, the search for a lost ship would begin immediately after its disappearance. In order to recoup a portion of their losses, vessel owners or insurance agents often sought out a wrecker to recover their property, either a floating hulk that could be towed into shore and repaired, or a wreck, cargo, or equipment that could be salvaged. But first, the salvor had to find the wreck. Sometimes the telltale tip of a sailing ship's mast protruding above the lake's surface would mark the location. If the ship was lost in deeper water, survivors—if there were any—might be able to provide information to narrow down the location of the wreck. Witnesses who may have seen something from on board another ship or from shore might have valuable insight. Wreckage or bodies, found floating offshore or washed onto beaches, might have offered a clue to a wreck's location. If the salvors were successful in finding the wreck, the discovery often received equal, or sometimes, more news coverage than the loss of the vessel. However, more often than not, the surface of the lake kept these shipwrecks well hidden.

While the passage of time obscured these shipwrecks, they usually were not forgotten. In some cases, the lure of potential profit from a valuable cargo or piece of equipment meant that the search never really ended. The *Pewabic*, which sank in Lake Huron after a collision in 1865, is one such notable case. Its owners mounted a search for it immediately after it sank, hoping to salvage the valuable cargo of copper ingots, but could not find the wreck. As the years passed, salvage efforts resumed. It would take until 1897 for some cargo to be recovered, then more in 1917, and still more in 1974.

A valuable cargo like copper is a rarity in the Great Lakes. After several decades underwater, most shipwrecks lose their commercial value but in time gain a new value as historical artifacts. When equipment for searching and diving became available and affordable following World War II, early explorers sought out these shipwrecks in order to recover artifacts for personal collections or to sell to others. The media regularly reported the feats of these diving pioneers and when the public had the chance to see shipwrecks brought up piece by piece, excitement and interest grew.

When underwater motion picture and still photography became available in the late 1970s, divers had the means to share their conquests through imagery in addition to the artifacts they found. A number of film festivals cropped up around the Great Lakes and the sport of shipwreck hunting and diving increased exponentially. More and more shipwrecks were found and many more artifacts were recovered. The pictures, worth the proverbial "thousand words," provided the media with even better ways to convey these exciting stories of adventure and discovery.

Although divers derived great enjoyment (and sometimes cash) for the artifacts, archaeologists eventually took issue with the loss of historical data that occurs when an object is recovered without proper documentation or conservation and parceled out to private collections. The same technologies that served to make shipwreck diving possible also provided archaeologists the tools to work underwater. This generated a whole new movement in the Great Lakes. Soon, federal and state governments became involved in creating laws to ban divers from salvaging shipwrecks in favor of leaving the shipwrecks untouched for archaeological study and recreational pursuit.

Over the last several centuries in which ships have been lost on Lake Michigan and later found, a handful are notable both for the dramatic and often tragic circumstances of their loss, as well as for the considerable attention they received after their discovery. *Titanic* serves as an easily understood example: When the ocean liner sank in 1912, it became famous because of the stories of amazing survival and tragic loss. When Robert Ballard discovered the wreck of the *Titanic* in 1985—and brought back images of the bow, the pilothouse, and the dripping rusticles—the shipwreck became legendary. This book includes the stories of twenty Lake Michigan vessels that, likewise, became famous when they were lost and then legendary after their discovery. Selected from among shipwrecks in Wisconsin, Illinois, Indiana, and Michigan, and presented chronologically based on the dates they were found, these stories provide a look at the exciting and sometimes contentious evolution of diving activity on Lake Michigan ranging from salvage to archaeological study. The stories also put the readers on deck, so-to-speak, to experience the frightening ordeal of the sinking from the perspective of the crew and passengers, and offer a view of the fascinating evolution of commercial transportation on the Great Lakes from the earliest sailing vessels to the most modern self-unloaders.

There are certainly a number of other shipwrecks that could be considered legendary, but those will have to wait for another volume. Some may question why *Le Griffon,* the Inland Seas' most famous shipwreck, lost in Lake Michigan in 1679 and reportedly discovered in 2006 by explorer Steve Libert, has not been included. Although Libert filed for legal ownership of *Le Griffon* soon after he found a timber protruding from the lake bottom off the shores of Wisconsin's Door County Peninsula in Michigan waters, he has not proven that he actually found a shipwreck, let alone the famed *Le Griffon*. In fact, after receiving a permit to excavate in 2013, he found nothing buried under the timber. It seems more likely that a wreck, six skeletons, and artifacts dating from the 1600s, found in 1927 along the shores of the Mississagi Strait on Manitoulin Island in Canada were Le Griffon and its crew.

For now, the twenty stories included here must suffice. They tell of some of Lake Michigan's most famous, deadly, mysterious, and dramatic shipwrecks that have become legendary after their discovery.

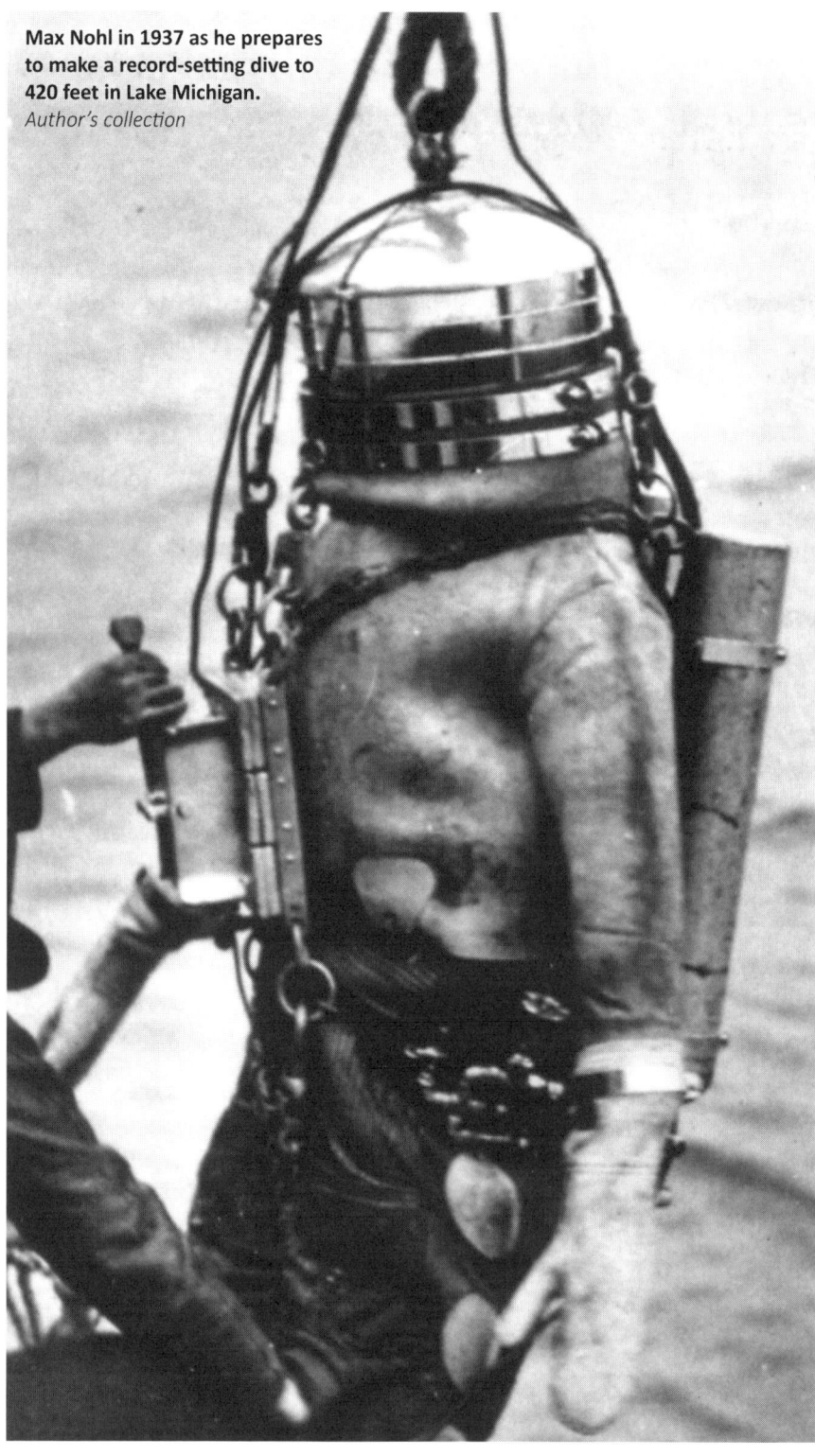

Max Nohl in 1937 as he prepares to make a record-setting dive to 420 feet in Lake Michigan.
*Author's collection*

# INTRODUCTION

The ability to breathe underwater was a prerequisite before shipwrecks in Lake Michigan could be found, explored, and salvaged, of course. Long before humans settled in the American Midwest, man searched for ways to break free of the limitations of breath-hold diving. In 1500, Leonardo da Vinci designed equipment for underwater exploration. It would take, however, almost two centuries before man could effectively work underwater. In 1691, physicist Edmund Halley designed a diving bell with an air hose tethered to the inside so that divers could explore short distances beyond the bell. In 1715, English inventor John Lethbridge used a pressure-proof, wooden barrel with a glass viewing porthole and watertight leather sleeves to conduct salvage operations in sixty feet of water. Expanding on this idea, British salvage operators John and Charles Dean developed in 1829 a diving rig made from a fire-fighting helmet into which air could be pumped continually. In the 1830s, German-born English engineer Augustas Siebe fashioned a helmet fitted with a watertight canvas diving suit and a valve in the helmet for an air hose. This dress, typically referred to as a hard-hat suit and continually modified, became the equipment of choice for the commercial divers who would work in the Great Lakes and oceans for the next century.

Lake Michigan boasted a particularly active commercial diving community from the mid-nineteenth to the early twentieth century. Every major port and most minor ports served as the home of wrecking companies that employed divers to perform underwater engineering and maintenance duties, salvage, harbor maintenance, bridge work, and other construction work, as well as body recovery. These early divers included the Falcon Brothers of Chicago; Charles Gunderson, Arthur Loeb, and Iver Johnsen, also of Chicago; Pearl E. Purdy of Sturgeon Bay, Wisconsin; and John Dodd of Manistee, Michigan, among many others. The famous Captain James Reid originally from Alpena, Michigan, who had relocated his wrecking business to Sarnia, Ontario, was one of the international salvors who would be called into the Lake Michigan region for specialized work. However, these pioneering divers understood little of the physics involved in breathing compressed air at depth, which resulted in many debilitating accidents and deaths. In 1874, Peter Falcon salvaged the machinery and boiler from the *Milwaukee*. Unfortunately, the work resulted in the death of one of Falcon's divers, who perished soon after he ascended from a particularly long dive. No one recognized the cause of his death. Accidents that occurred during the building of the Brooklyn Bridge in 1883 would lead to a medical understanding of the physics of diving. Many divers on that project became permanently disabled after they left the compressed atmosphere of the deep caissons and rapidly reentered normal atmospheric conditions. When doctors and scientists began studying this problem, they coined the term "caisson's disease," which later became known as decompression sickness. By 1908, techniques to avoid this affliction had been developed. J. S. Haldane, a Scottish physiologist, prepared the first dive tables that outlined decompression stop durations to provide the right amount time to dissolve compressed gas back into the bloodstream and avoid a build-up of bubbles in the joints.

Even after the physiology of diving started to be understood, commercial diving still relied on surface-supplied air. The seeds of self-contained diving, free of a tether, began in 1860 when Frenchman Benoit Rouquayrol set about developing and constructing an apparatus that permitted rescuers to penetrate mines while being able to breath normally. He first invented a demand regulator, which he later adapted with the assistance of French naval officer Auguste Denayrouze, that could be used as a self-contained underwater breathing unit. In 1878, English merchant seaman Henry Fleuss invented a device for breathing compressed oxygen. These innovations laid the groundwork for equipment that would be used during World War I. However, expelled air bubbles from these self-contained units posed a problem.

In 1911, the Germans led the development of a rebreather that recirculated and cleaned used air to avoid discharging gas bubbles that could alert the enemy to their position. This was certainly revolutionary for its time considering that similar units did not become available to recreational divers until the early 2000s. Although Jacques Cousteau is universally recognized as the father of the self-contained underwater breathing apparatus—which spurred the acronym SCUBA, now recognized as an actual word—in 1925, Yves Le Prieur, a French naval officer, designed and built an open-circuit compressed air respirator. According to Cousteau's first book, *The Silent World: A Story of Undersea Discovery and Adventure* published in 1953, he started diving with the self-contained underwater breathing apparatus invented by Le Prieur. However, he was not satisfied with the length of time he could spend underwater with that unit, and improved it by adding a demand regulator invented in 1942 by Émile Gagnan. His new Aqua-Lung, as it was known, hit the market in France in 1945 just after World War II. By the early 1950s, the Aqua-Lung could be purchased worldwide.

Because Cousteau was a consummate marketer, few people realize that individuals residing in Lake Michigan region played key roles in expanding the sport and the limits of diving. They helped establish the foundation for wreck hunting and diving that is still flourishing today. A review of the contributions of these early pioneers is warranted before delving into the many shipwreck discoveries they helped make possible. Without their efforts, the sport may not have taken off so quickly and may not have evolved into such an active diving community.

## MAX NOHL and DESCO

Ironically, the man who would pioneer underwater breathing apparatuses and specialized gas mixtures for deep diving had a near-drowning experience and suffered through the drowning death of one of his good friends. Consequently, Maximilian Eugene Nohl, a Milwaukee boy born in 1910, became fearful of the water as he grew up along the shores of Lake Michigan. However, he convinced himself to overcome his fears when he began reading stories about sunken treasure. He experimented with an inverted five gallon paint can as a dive helmet and soon thereafter decided to make diving his profession. With this goal in mind, he headed off to the Massachusetts Institute of Technology to obtain a degree in engineering. In 1933, a few years after his graduation, Nohl became intrigued with the Bathysphere that he saw on display at the Chicago World's Fair. The spherical, deep-sea submersible had been designed in 1928 to be used by the naturalist William Beebe to study sea creatures. Nohl took note that it could not maneuver on its own and designed a unit that could. The following July, he and fellow diver Jack Browne, also a marine inventor, explored a sunken steamship off Milwaukee. This dive solidified a friendship that would extend later to a business relationship. Brown, incidentally, came from a maritime background, his father being an executive with the Goodrich Transportation Company in Milwaukee that operated a line of steamships.

In 1935, Nohl planned to salvage the sunken steamship *John Dwight* off Martha's Vineyard in Massachusetts. The lure of possible bootleg liquor from the Roaring Twenties, Prohibition-era ship that sank in mysterious circumstances in 1923 caught Nohl's attention. He knew from newspaper accounts that one month after the sinking, salvers had attempted to find the wreck to no avail. Later, Navy divers found contraband liquor and dynamited the wreck in order to prevent salvage. A decade later, Nohl hoped that the dynamite had not damaged all the cargo, and that he might find the ship's safe. Treasure was, after all, what initially sparked Nohl's interest in diving.

Max Nohl was so renowned in Wisconsin and representative of the quintessential "man's man" that several liquor companies used his image to promote their products. *Author's collection*

Although Nohl's expedition was a bust because the *Dwight's* safe was empty and seawater had ruined the liquor bottles, the project garnered national publicity. Hollywood producer John D. Craig contacted Nohl about the possible salvage of the Cunard liner *Lusitania*, torpedoed during World War I, that lay in 312 feet of water off the Irish Coast. At that time, no equipment existed for diving operations at such a depth, but Nohl had already been working on deep-diving equipment and a special suit. Jack Browne worked with Nohl and Craig to get the equipment ready. In April 1937, Nohl contacted hyperbaric medicine expert Dr. Edgar End to explore the possibility of preventing nitrogen narcosis and caisson's disease. End helped him develop a mixture of life-sustaining helium and oxygen rather than air. Nohl again made the news in December 1937, when he made a record-shattering dive 420 feet down to the floor of Lake Michigan off Milwaukee, breathing this new mixture. After nine minutes, the surface support team brought him up slowly to fifty feet where he decompressed for more than an hour. He had no residual effects from the dive, which broke a record held by U.S. Navy diver Frank Crilley since 1915. Like the 1911 rebreathers, this technology was revolutionary. Modern recreational divers would not replicate the use of such a gas mixture until the 1980s.

The ground-breaking dive with new equipment and gas mixtures resulted in Nohl, Browne, and Craig forming Diving Equipment & Salvage Company (DESCO) in 1937, which took Nohl's focus away from a possible *Lusitania* dive. They set up an office on North 4th Street in Milwaukee. The firm sold product and continued to expand their line, but obtaining large Navy contracts during World War II positioned DESCO as the largest diving equipment manufacturer in the world. By 1945, Nohl left DESCO to pursue other interests. The sinking of the cargo ship *Prins Willem V* on October 14, 1954, after a collision with the barge *Sinclair XII* off Milwaukee, captured his attention.

The U.S. Army Corps of Engineers determined that the wreck extended up too close to the surface and would cause an obstruction for marine traffic. It sought bids for clearing the obstruction. Nohl entered a bid of $50,000, plus salvage rights to the vessel, and won the contract. In the spring of 1955 he began work. After just a few survey dives, he found that he only had to clear away a small gangplank to achieve the proper clearance. Although the Army Corps fought payment, arguing that the job was simpler than anticipated, it eventually paid Nohl $47,000 and allowed him to proceed with his salvage plans. Nohl hoped to raise the vessel and make more money selling it and its cargo. However, he experienced one problem after another and had not yet achieved his goal when on February 6, 1960, he and his wife were killed in an automobile accident that also took the life of R&B singer Jesse Belvin, co-writer of the 1950s hit "Earth Angel." Considering Nohl's ingenuity and tenacity, if he had lived, the *Prins Willem V* may not have existed as a wreck for divers to explore today.

Decades later, Max Nohl's feats would inspire many recreational divers to become certified in technical diving, allowing them to reach wrecks never before attainable. However, it would take almost sixty years for sport divers to break Nohl's 1937 record deep commercial dive. Terrence Tysall and Mike Zee used tri-mix gas, similar to the mix pioneered by Nohl, to dive to the *Edmund Fitzgerald* in 1995. However, most sport divers still use the more conventional compressed air to reach wrecks in depths not exceeding 130 feet, considered the limit of recreational divers. Another pioneering diver in the Lake Michigan region would be instrumental in developing recreational equipment that would greatly expand the sport of shipwreck diving on Lake Michigan and throughout the nation, as well.

## SAM DAVISON and DACOR

Sam Davison established Dacor Corporation in 1954 in Evanston, Illinois, to serve the equipment needs of a growing sport diving community. Following in the footsteps Max Nohl, who sold commercial diving gear through DESCO, and Jacques Cousteau, who sold recreational gear, Davison's first demand regulator would fuel shipwreck diving in Lake Michigan, making the acquisition of basic gear for sport diving convenient and affordable.

Born in 1925 in Pennsylvania to parents Sam and Thelma, Davison had little connection to the water as a boy. By 1940, his father, a salesman, had relocated the family to Atlanta, Georgia, another place with little access to water. However, during his four years as a U.S. Marine stationed in the South Pacific during World War II, he used Japanese goggles to see underwater, which exposed him to this fascinating world. After the war, he studied engineering at the University of Miami, then moved to Evanston, where his parents had relocated. There, he met Evanston-born Robert Olson who would plant the seeds for what would become a prosperous company for Davison. Olson had also just returned from the South Pacific where he had served in the U.S. Navy as a swimming instructor and later a member of an underwater demolition team. During the invasion of Saipan, he used a rebreather to position explosives to blast holes in the coral to allow boat access to the island.

In Evanston, the young adventurers fabricated a homemade diving apparatus from a five gallon oil can. They cut a hole in it, fashioned a glass faceplate, and added padded supports so that it could rest on their shoulders. A hose through the top allowed them to pump in fresh air. At the time, Olson worked as a lifeguard at Greenwood Beach near the campus of Northwestern University, and after his shift, he and Davison would launch a small boat and experiment with the homemade breathing device. It was thrilling to them to explore the bottom of Lake Michigan. However, this took a backseat to working and eventual families for both men. Olson became a salesman and married in 1949. Davison also married and soon thereafter had a son. The two couples socialized often, but the men rarely dived any more.

When Olson happened upon the July 1953 issue of *Poplar Science*, the cover story entitled, "How to Build Your Own Aqua Lung" caught his eye. Olson, who always lived by the mantra "find the need and fill it," saw the potential in the growing demand for scuba diving equipment. He knew that Davison had been

contemplating starting a manufacturing business of some sort, but had not yet settled on a product. Olson encouraged Davison to follow the plans laid out in the magazine and manufacture his own scuba gear. He even predicted that Davison could become quite successful in that new industry, at the time dominated by Jacques Cousteau, whose Aqua Lung products were being distributed in the United States.

Intrigued, Davison studied the magazine's plans and using his engineering ability designed what he considered a better breathing unit. He took his drawings to a local machine shop and had his unit built, finding that it worked well in water up to 170 feet deep. Davison's father, who had a business relationship

**Sam Davison is pictured in 1987 in Florida aboard his boat the Dacor Diver.**
*Photograph by the Author*

22

with the Montgomery Ward department store, arranged for his son to show the equipment to the buyer who was so impressed that he ordered ten units and shortly thereafter 300 more. Suddenly, Davison found himself in business. Davison borrowed money from his parents and rented a storefront warehouse in Evanston in 1954. He chose the name Dacor, using the first two letters of his last name combined with the first three letters of the word "corporation." In 1955, Dacor introduced its first two hose regulator, the "Dial-A-Breath, which restricted the flow of air until the diver demanded it. Davison believed this unit would limit air consumption and extend bottom time. Over the ensuing years, Dacor modified its original regulator design many times and expanded the line to include every possible item needed by a diver, including accessories and clothing. The company placed the distinctive black oval logo with bright yellow block letters DACOR on everything. As Olson predicted, his friend became quite successful.

By the 1970s, shipwreck diving had become a very popular sport in Lake Michigan. Several charter boat captains took divers to the wrecks, and many divers operated their own dive boats up and down the eastern and western shores. Shipwrecks were found each summer and the diving craze increased. Davison expanded Dacor, relocated the plant to an industrial park in Northfield, Illinois, purchased a house less than a mile away, and built an enclosed pool for employee scuba training and equip-

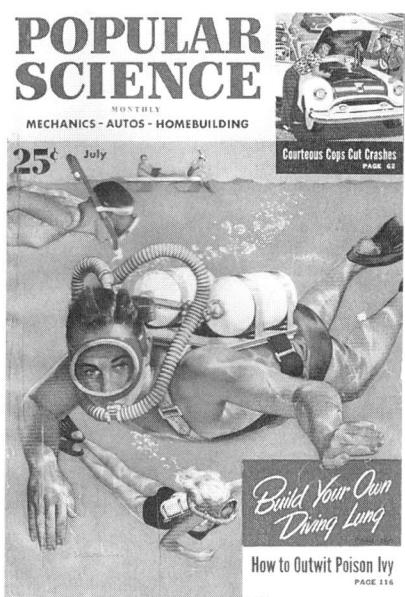

**POPULAR SCIENCE**

MONTHLY

MECHANICS - AUTOS - HOMEBUILDING

25¢ July

Courteous Cops Cut Crashes
PAGE 62

Build Your Own Diving Lung

How to Outwit Poison Ivy
PAGE 116

Robert Olson (above left) called the article "How to Build Your Own Aqua Lung" in the July 1953 issue of *Popular Science* to the attention of his fried Sam Davison (right), who would design and build his own diving equipment and manufacture it under the company name Dacor Corporation. *Photograph by Author*

ment testing. In time, he brought his sons Jeff and Gary, from his second marriage, into the firm. He treated everyone at the plant like family and provided the opportunity for his more than one hundred employees to become certified divers. Although by then several other diving gear manufacturers existed, Dacor remained the equipment of choice in the Lake Michigan region and for a time ranked as the largest manufacturer of scuba gear in the country. Divers knew if they had a problem with anything, they could mail the gear to the factory or show up at the door for service. Sadly, Davison did not survive to see some of the lakes' most legendary wrecks found. He died of lung cancer in 1987 at age sixty-two, leaving the company to his wife and sons to operate. In 1998, they sold Dacor to a rival diving gear manufacturer, Mares.

Two of Davison's local contemporaries helped in a different way to expand the sport of diving and make it more safe.

## RALPH ERICKSON, JOHN CRONIN, and PADI

Coinciding with the early growth of Dacor, Chicagoan Ralph Erickson, a World War II veteran who obtained undergraduate and master's degrees in physical education from Northwestern University, and John Cronin, of Niles, Illinois, who worked for U.S. Divers, would found the Professional Association of Diving Instructors (PADI) in 1966. This organization, established to promote the sport and make diving safer by developing standard methodologies for instruction, would have a profound impact on diving in the Lake Michigan region, and around the world.

Erickson began his career in professional education. He served as a swimming coach for over three decades at high schools and at Loyola University of Chicago and was the leader of many championship teams. In 1959, he established the Erickson Swimming School. Swimming on the surface naturally led to swimming underwater and by 1961, Erickson obtained basic dive training and went on to become a diving instructor. Through this process, he concluded that scuba certification agencies at that time lacked professionalism and made it difficult for people to enter the sport. While attending a diving banquet in December 1961, Erickson, met John Cronin, then a top Midwestern-based salesman for U.S. Divers, a scuba gear manufacturer in California. A friendship immediately developed, and over the next several years they developed a concept of a new, professional diver training organization.

As explained in PADI's corporate website, the organization was officially born when "Cronin brought a bottle of Johnnie Walker Black Label and thirty dollars to Erickson's apartment in Morton Grove, Illinois. They discussed what to call the organization; Cronin insisted that the word 'professional' be in the name. Erickson wanted to call it an 'association of diving instructors.' After a few scotches, the acronym PADI was born: Professional Association of Diving Instructors."

Initially, the men met at local restaurants. Then Cronin remodeled the basement of his home in Niles, Illinois, to become the headquarters for PADI. He hired a neighbor as their part-time secretary. His son, Brian—today PADI's CEO—stuffed and sealed envelopes. Their focus became to expand the sport of diving nationally and assure that people would be properly trained.

PADI grew slowly. By the late 1960s, the organization had 400 instructor members, yet still struggled. Cronin's move to California after a promotion to sales manager at U.S. Divers, and eventually president of the company, allowed him to reach a wider group of people. Meanwhile, Erickson expanded and developed a modular training program for the basic open water diver course. Then PADI began creating its own integrated, multi-media student and instructor educational materials for advanced and specialty courses. This development spawned an incredible growth period for PADI in the 1970s and made it unique from other agencies. By the late 1980s PADI had become the leading scuba diving training organization in the world. With so many new people involved in the sport having an impact on both sea-life and historic shipwrecks, PADI worked hard over the years to teach responsible and conscientious diver behavior and strived to keep the sport free from government legislation. Cronin was quoted as having said, "We want to feel that our children, their children, and generations to come will be able to enjoy the underwater world that has given us so much. If scuba divers do not take an active role in preserving the aquatic realm, who will?"

His words were certainly farsighted. Divers indeed would become both the finders and the caretakers of historic shipwrecks in the Great Lakes, where the fresh water maintains them in extraordinary condition. However, as the twenty stories that follow illustrate, the definition of "preserving" would be interpreted in a number of different ways.

Ralph Erickson (left) and John Cronin, the founders of the Professional Association of Diving Instructors. *Courtesy PADI*

A stunning before-and-after image shows the *Cayuga* as it sailed and how it appeared on the bottom in 2002 after a survey by divers and filmmakers, Jim and Pat Stayer. *Paintings by Robert McGreevy*

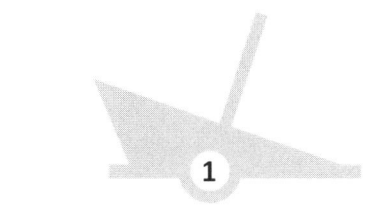

# 1

# DOUBLE TROUBLE

The massive steel-hulled *Cayuga* received considerable attention at the time of its build, heralded among the largest and most well-appointed vessels of its time. However, its sinking, discovery, and subsequent salvage effort received even more attention than its career. The vessel became legendary for the daring and groundbreaking attempt to salvage it. A century later, the wreck serves as a reminder that salvage was, and still is, the first and primary response of ship owners looking to minimize financial losses and divers seeking a way to earn money. The *Cayuga* sets the scene for how people would respond to shipwreck discoveries for more than a century to come.

A reporter from the Cleveland *Marine Record* witnessed the launch of the new steamship *Cayuga* on April 2, 1889, a mild day for early spring. He noted that although vessel launchings in Cleveland were becoming very common, the locals seemed especially captivated by this new vessel: 3000 people turned out for the ceremony. The reporter seemed impressed that the Indian name *Cayuga* was "purely American" and heralded the freighter as being "without a doubt, one of the finest built boats ever put afloat in the old Cuyahoga River." He gave Globe Iron Works Company credit for that accomplishment.

By that time, Globe Iron Works had been in business for several decades. The company was founded in 1869 when three businessmen acquired the Sanderson & Company foundry that had been in operation since 1853, and renamed it Globe. Three years later they purchased a half-interest in the wooden shipbuilder George Presley & Company. In 1880, the three investors started a new shipyard in Cleveland to build steel ships, calling it Globe Shipbuilding Company. Presley built the company's first three hulls even while the new yard was under construction. In 1886, the shipbuilding business was merged under the name Globe Iron Works. Globe bought out Presley in 1887 and soon thereafter two other local shipbuilders. By the time Globe built the *Cayuga*, it was the premier shipbuilder in Cleveland. (Eventually all of Globe's holdings would become American Ship Building Company, later known as AmShip Cleveland.)

Globe built the *Cayuga* under contract with the Lehigh Valley Railroad, which paid $250,000 for the new freighter. The railroad had been incorporated in Pennsylvania in 1846 by American businessman Asa Packard to transport the state's anthracite coal. It would operate for thirty years before branching into water-borne transportation. In 1880, the railroad established the Lehigh Valley Transportation Line to operate a fleet of ships on the Great Lakes as a way to extend its line. The company began with a tug and six barges and then started building wooden steamers, including the *Robert A. Packer, Oceanica, Clyde,* and *Tacoma,* and then two more, the *Harry E. Packer* and *Fred Mercur.* In 1888, the company began having its vessels made in steel, the first being the *E. P. Wilbur,* named for Asa Packer's nephew and personal secretary at the time, Elijah Packer Wilbur, who would in time become president of the railroad. Using these vessels, the line was especially successful in the movement of anthracite, grain, and package freight between Buffalo and Chicago, Milwaukee, Duluth, Superior, and other Midwestern cities.

As the line's second steel ship, the *Cayuga* was built as a sister to the *E. P. Wilbur.* At just over 300 feet long and forty feet wide, both ships were massive for their time, heralded as the biggest on the lakes. A triple expansion steam engine and two boilers, all of which had already been installed before the launch, powered the *Cayuga.* It was expected to run at about fourteen miles an hour, just as the *Wilbur* had been clocked. At the time of the *Cayuga*'s launch, Lehigh was so busy it already had another steamship in the works at Globe, the *Seneca,* which would be completed even before the *Cayuga* would make its first run.

The *Cayuga*, just before its launch in April 1889. *C. Patrick Labadie Collection - Alpena County Public Library*

The christening ceremony was performed by a Miss Ashburn and took place on time, apparently a rarity for shipbuilders in Cleveland, but something that had come to be expected of the prestigious Globe Iron Works. According to the *Marine Herald*'s reporter, the movement of the "grand structure from the ways was greeted with the most enthusiastic cheers from the multitudes and the whistles from many tugs in the vicinity." He complimented Globe for the fine, new steel steamboat equipped in first-class style. The fitting-out would take another six weeks, according to a Globe official.

The *Cayuga* sailed successfully its first season with no incidents that would call it to the attention of reporters. However, at the beginning of the next season, the *Cayuga* made the headlines when on April 10, 1890, a reporter for the *Buffalo Evening News* reported a "Queer Accident to a Quarter Million Dollar Boat." During a heavy gale near Buffalo the prior afternoon, while being towed into the harbor empty by the tug *Gee*, the *Cayuga* became so hard to control that the *Gee* had to cut it loose. Captain Edward Condon of the *Cayuga* could not keep the bow into the wind and the vessel drifted onto the shoal, scraped, released, and almost capsized. Finally, it grounded on the rocks at the foot of Georgia Street. The heavy sea made it impossible to get a line to it from tugs and it remained stuck overnight. In the morning, six tugs were employed to try to pull it off. At about 9 a.m., the tugs succeeded in slowly moving the big freighter, iching it along at about two boat lengths per hour. By noon the *Cayuga* could operate on its own. The owner remarked that the *Cayuga* was so well built, it was not seriously damaged in the incident.

In 1891, the *Cayuga* was outfitted with 300 incandescent lights through the installation of a Fisher Electric Company automatic dynamo for marine installations, which represented a radical departure for lighting plants. The system was promoted for its minimal maintenance needs because it had self-oiling bearings and did not have rheostats or regulating devices. Its operation was heralded as so simple, an oiler could handle it rather than the ship's engineer, freeing him up focus his attention on the steam plant rather than the lighting system. A number of other vessels received this innovation at a time when shipboard electric lighting was starting to become the norm.

**The Fisher Electric Company automatic dynamo installed on the *Cayuga*.**
*Reprinted from Beeson's Sailors' Hard-Book, 1891*

In mid-November 1891, the *Cayuga* would experience an accident that would ominously forebode the future. When off Cheboygan, Michigan, Captain Driscoll of the *Cayuga* spotted another vessel heading right toward him, signaled to it, and hearing no response, tried to steer out of its way. The other vessel, the *Delaware,* plowed forward, ramming into the *Cayuga*'s starboard side and twisting a steel plate. In this case, the damage was minimal. By the following year, the *Cayuga* still ranked among the three largest steam vessels on the lakes along with the *Saranac* and *Seneca*, all built by Globe and owned by Lehigh.

On May 5, 1895, on its first run of its seventh season, the *Cayuga* left Buffalo for Milwaukee to pick up a load of cargo for delivery back to Buffalo. With a crew of twenty-nine men, forty-seven-year-old Captain Graser commanded the steamer on what would be his third season sailing that vessel, his eighth year as a master, and his thirty-third year sailing. He had come up through the ranks and in 1887 was given the wooden propeller *Arizona* as his first command. He experienced his first calamity at the end of that season, when the *Arizona* burned off Marquette, Michigan, but he was praised with saving the crew and the ship by maneuvering it into shallow water. It was later salvaged by Reid Towing and Wrecking, a company tht would have a significant involvement with the *Cayuga* later.

The *Cayuga* reached Milwaukee by May 8 and loaded 1500 tons of flour, 38,000 bushels of oats, and other miscellaneous cargo. Wasting no time, Captain Graser began the run back to Buffalo at about 8 p.m. By 4:30 a.m. the next morning, the *Cayuga* entered the Straits of Mackinac, a tight passage where, true to the region's reputation, a dense fog hung over the water.

## LOST

At the same time the *Cayuga* steamed north, the *Joseph L. Hurd*, a twenty-six-year-old wooden steamer about half the size of the *Cayuga*, headed south toward Chicago carrying a cargo of lumber, under the command of Captain Charles E. Wilson. Both Wilson and Captain Graser kept a strict lookout from their respective vessels, but neither slackened his speed to the degree appropriate for such low-visibility conditions; instead both kept an eye on their schedules. Each expected that regular soundings of their fog horns would alert any other vessels to their presence. When opposite the Skillagalee light, the captains of the *Hurd* and *Cayuga* each heard the telltale blasts of another horn. Through open patches of fog, Graser saw a green light off his starboard bow and reversed his engines to avoid a collision. However, the vessels were too close for this maneuver to work. The *Hurd* struck the *Cayuga*'s starboard side just aft of the bulkhead. The collision was so violent it knocked overboard the *Hurd*'s steward George Johnston of Chicago, who had been standing on deck. He drowned in the frigid spring water before anyone could even try to save him.

The collision opened a huge hole in the *Cayuga*'s starboard side, six feet high and two feet wide, and according to accounts by the crew, knocked the vessel on its port side. The bow of the *Hurd* had been smashed in and water poured into the ship. As the *Hurd* began sinking, the *Cayuga* righted itself and for a moment appeared as if it might survive, but water rushing into the hole began dragging it down. The crews of both boats hurriedly began lowering the lifeboats. When they realized that neither vessel would sink immediately, they dared to return to their cabins to retrieve their personal possessions. It would take a full twenty-five minutes for the *Cayuga* to disappear beneath the surface in about seventeen fathoms of water, according to the captain. The *Hurd* remained afloat, buoyed up by its cargo of lumber. Safely in the lifeboats, the two crews remained near the scene for an hour, at which time the big steel freighter *Manola,* incidentally also built by Globe, came along, picked up the survivors, and transported them to Mackinaw.

Soon after arriving at Mackinaw City, Captain Wilson of the *Hurd* telegraphed the general manager of his company, a Mr. Austrian based in Mackinaw City, reporting that he had been in collision and that he had lost his steward overboard, and asking for instructions as to what he should do. "Our information is so meager," Austrian told reporters, "that we do not know what course we shall pursue regarding the *Hurd*." He supposed that Wilson would have thrown his anchor overboard before deserting the ship, to prevent it from drifting on a rocky shore in that region, and hoped a wrecking crew could save it.

The *Cayuga*'s captain and crew managed to catch a ride to Buffalo, but Captain Graser was immediately sent to Chicago to deal with insurance agents and commence work to locate the wreck. At seven years old, the *Cayuga* was still valuable, worth at least $200,000. Both it and the cargo, valued at over $100,000, were insured, but Lehigh Transportation wanted its vessel back. Officials began to make plans to raise it, but that would be considerably more of a challenge than raising the *Hurd*. The day after the collision, the wrecking tug *Favorite* towed the *Hurd* into Harbor Springs. Witnesses reported that it looked "a sorry sight," but it remained afloat. The wreckers had been unable to find the body of the steward.

From this point on, the *Cayuga* would be in the news almost weekly for the balance of the year and then often in the years to come.

## FOUND

In June, just weeks after the sinking, a New York underwriter sent Captain Wilbur of the steamer *City Of Grand Rapids* in search of the *Cayuga*, but he was unable to locate it. Just as Lehigh began making plans to build a replacement freighter, in late June the Chicago underwriters hired the wreckers C. A. MacDonald & Company to undertake another search. MacDonald put his

**The *Joseph L. Hurd* as it looked being towed into Harbor Springs, Michigan, the day after the collision with the *Cayuga*.** *C. Patrick Labadie Collection - Alpena County Public Library*

captain, C. H. Sinclair, in charge of the work, but really did not expect him to be successful. He bet Sinclair $50 that he could not find the wreck in two days. Perhaps inspired by the challenge, Sinclair did his homework. He charted the bearings taken by Captain Wilson at the site of the accident, Captain Martin Swain of the tug *Favorite*, and the keeper of the Skillagalee lighthouse. All three coincided at one spot. Working out of Cheboygan on the tug *George W. Cuyler*, Sinclair set out on Sunday, June 30, and within a couple hours had set a buoy at the prescribed spot. Then, he lowered the tug's anchor and started dragging, hoping to eventually hook the wreck. The fifty-dollar bet would be his because within five minutes he found the wreck just 450 feet from his buoy.

Insurance underwriters wasted no time in soliciting bids for the raising of the vessel, making the deadline the end of July, but had concerns that it could prove impossible to raise a 300-foot-long steel ship from 100 feet of water. Since the mid-1850s, numerous hard-hat divers, using the rig designed by Augustus Siebe in England in 1839, had established businesses around the Great Lakes. Called "submarine divers," these daring men, who knew little of the risks of breathing compressed air at depth, had been successfully salvaging grounded and sunken ships. However, at the time of the *Cayuga*'s sinking, the largest vessel yet raised had been half the *Cayuga*'s weight and that had been accomplished within protected waters. Captain James Reid of Reid Towing and Wrecking did not let that daunt him. His bid of $100,000 won him the job. His groundbreaking plan caught the attention of maritime men around the country. The fact that he would not be paid unless successful intrigued many people who would follow his efforts with great interest.

James Reid had humble beginnings in Canada. At nineteen, he moved to the little town of Alpena, Michigan, where great stands of trees provided a decent living for him and his wife in the late 1860s. There, they raised a family, and in time their oldest sons, James Thomas (Tom) and William, would join their father in the lumber business. In the mid-1870s, the Reids moved up to St.

Ignace in Michigan's Upper Peninsula to continue in the lumbering business. In just a few years, Reid found himself in the wrecking business quite by accident. He owned a tug used for rafting logs that had been sent downstream and when the barge *Plymouth* went on the rocks in the Straits, he was summoned to help pull it off. Improvising a crude salvaging outfit, Reid succeeded in saving the barge and was given a nice fee for doing so. This gave him the idea for a new business venture. The grounding of his own tug *Burnside* gave him more experience. Soon thereafter, he was hired to replace the propeller of the wooden small freighter *Algomah*. At that point, salvage work supplemented his lumbering income, and by 1885, provided his fifteen-year-old son Tom a career. His salvage achievements gained him notoriety and financial backing to incorporate and expand his new business. In 1888, the Reid Towing and Wrecking Company received $25,000, a huge sum, for his salvage of the barge *Minnehaha*, which went ashore at Drummond Island. A decade later, with numerous such successes under his belt, Reid began his work on the *Cayuga*.

On September 6, it was announced publicly that Reid had won the salvage job. Maritime enthusiasts waited with great anticipation for progress reports. Reporters did not disappoint, doling out the saga piece by piece as it unfolded. The *Marine Record* reported on September 12 that Reid had already been down to the wreck and found it lying on its side in 101 feet of water in good condition, with only its upper cabins gone. Reid expected to raise it "without any difficulty." W. H. Manlon and George Reynolds would serve as his divers.

The very next day, the same newspaper reported that Reid intended to use four large steel-plate pontoons to raise the vessel. The thirty-foot-long, twelve-foot diameter pontoons would be manufactured by the McKinnon Company of Bay City, Michigan, for $15,000 and would be complete in about two weeks.

By early October, Reid reported that he intended to get the job completed that fall. He planned to recover the 18,000 barrels of flour from the upper hold and drain out the bushels of oats onto the lake bottom. He carefully studied the hole in the starboard side and felt sure he could easily patch that and intended to bring the vessel into Harbor Springs, just like the *Hurd*.

Meanwhile, local inspectors investigating the accident found both captains guilty of the collision and revoked their licenses, declaring that they had violated rule 15 pertaining to the requirements of two vessels passing. Captain Glaser of the *Cayuga* thought his ship could have been spared if only the *Hurd* had reversed its engine as he did, but his comments did not matter in the decision.

By the end of 1895, Reid had recovered the flour, but had not yet pumped out the oats or raised the *Cayuga*. Reporters at the *Marine Review* and other more local newspapers continued to follow his efforts in 1896 at the rate of about one article per month. Readers learned of the difficulties that plagued Reid, but were not surprised, because from the beginning most people were skeptical that the job was even possible. By June, Reid had pumped the oats out of the lower hold and patched the hole. In July, he set several cables under the hull and positioned the four pontoons in preparation for the lift. They had the lifting power of 500 tons, but when his divers filled them with air, the weight snapped the cables. Reid ordered more pontoons. By late July, his comments to reporters were not filled with nearly as much confidence as before. He indicated that he would not be ready to try again until autumn, regarding the work as the "greatest piece of wrecking work ever attempted on fresh water." Bad weather that late summer slowed the work down even further. Then in November, disaster struck. Although they had been working underwater successfully for months, one diver must have come up too fast. As reported by Mary Donner, biographer of the Reids, the diver's "head became so full of blood that they had difficulty in removing his helmet." Although the term did not exist at the time, an air embolism caused by a rapid ascent while holding his breath may have led to his death. Reid said little to reporters about that, and instead expressed hope that the next summer he would raise the *Cayuga*.

In February 1897, Reid tried to shade his failures, telling reporters he had not yet even attempted the lift, but expected to raise it before the winter set in. He admitted he had spent $40,000 so far on labor and equipment. That summer he was able to break the wreck free from the suction of the muck, but failed to lift the wreck as anticipated and lost one of his work barges in the process.

The start of both 1898 and 1899 saw Reid hopeful, but by the end of each year, newspapers reported his failures. In 1900, he set upon using rubber bags to raise the vessel, but nothing came of that. By the end of the first year of the new century, he finally gave up the effort, after having lost almost as much as he hoped to earn. Although the *Cayuga* was his only failure, the proud Reid did not take it well, especially considering how publicly it had all played out. He disappeared for a while to deal with his disappointment. His son, Tom, by then a husband, father, and business partner, carried on in his absence.

**Engine room gauge panel recovered from the *Cayuga* by an unidentified diver in the 1969 or soon thereafter, and later restored by collector Steve Gronow.** *www.lighthouselens.com*

It would be almost seventy years before anyone would see the wreck of the *Cayuga* again. Divers and wreck hunters John Steele from Waukegan, Illinois, and Gene Turner from Indiana located the *Cayuga* in the spring of 1969, perhaps by using the same bearings that had led to its original discovery in 1895. They were among the first generation of Great Lakes shipwreck hunters and were responsible for many of the earliest modern discoveries in Lake Michigan as well as some in Lakes Superior and Huron. Steele and Turner and the other intrepid early shipwreck explorers had the same goals in mind as the famous wrecker James Reid, although on a smaller scale. They worked to recover interesting artifacts from the vessels they found. This was a standard practice among those early divers, who felt that the effort to make a discovery gave them the rights to a memento of the accomplishment. Among the artifacts recovered from the *Cayuga* was a panel of brass engine room gauges, which has now, years later, been restored. At the time of this book's publishing, it was being offered for sale.

Today the wreck of the *Cayuga* displays the failed efforts of James Reid. His work barge lays just off the port side of the wreck in full view. The pontoons, long heralded as the inventive devices that would succeed in raising the vessel, are still secured with thick cables to the port and starboard sides of the wreck near the stern. The presence of these salvage tools and the absence of certain fittings and equipment serve as reminders that salvage was—both for commercial and recreational divers over more than a century—the primary reason to go in search of shipwrecks. With this in mind, the efforts made by divers described in the next several chapters will seem more understandable.

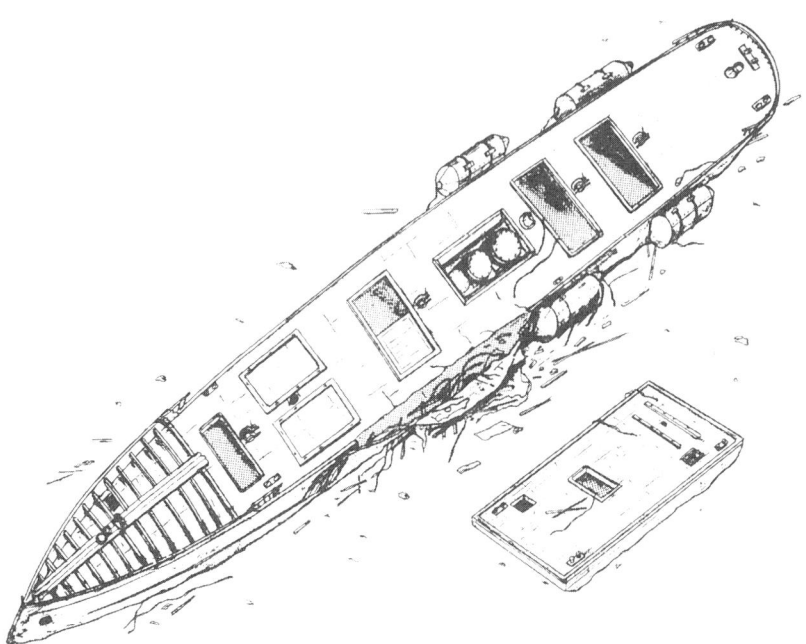

**Drawing of the wreck of the *Cayuga* from the book *Shipwrecks of the Straits of Mackinac*, copyright Dr. Charles & Jeri Baron Feltner 1981. The Feltners spent considerable time diving and documenting the *Cayuga* in the late 1970s and early 1980s, as well as many other shipwrecks in the Straits.** *Used with permission*

A spectacular rendition of the *Carl D. Bradley* before and after its sinking.
*Painting by Steve Witucki*

**2**

# TRAGEDY AND TRIUMPH

The 639-foot self-unloader *Carl D. Bradley* is famous for many reasons. For twenty-two years it held rank as the largest vessel operating on the Great Lakes. Its tragic loss in 1958 was among the most recent major commercial sinking incidents and it resulted in the deaths of thirty-three men, most residents of the same small town in Michigan. It is the largest vessel residing on the bottom of Lake Michigan and among the deepest yet found. The *Carl D. Bradley* has become legendary, of late, because it marks the earliest planned expedition on a Lake Michigan shipwreck, having taken place in 1959, barely six months after the vessel sank. Knowledge of that dive, however, did not come to light until almost fifty years later.

The *Carl D. Bradley* was launched in 1927, joining the Bradley Fleet of Rogers City, Michigan, as the Queen of the Lakes, the biggest and most powerful vessel. Its construction was the latest in a series of events that began with the discovery of a of massive wealth of limestone near the shores of Lake Huron just south of Rogers City, a small town in the northeast corner of Michigan's Lower Peninsula. In 1910, a group of New York businessmen formed Michigan Limestone and Chemical Company, after purchasing 8000 acres of that limestone-rich land. The company hired Chicagoan Carl David Bradley to oversee construction of the facility that would eventually become the world's largest limestone quarry and processing plant. Bradley hired 1200 Polish, German, and Italian immigrants to work at the plant, which quadrupled the town's population in just a few years. United States Steel Corporation, the world's largest producer of steel products, became the company's biggest customer, purchasing its limestone as a fluxing agent for the manufacturing of steel.

In 1912, Bradley founded the Bradley Transportation Company to control the company's shipment of limestone, building a fleet of self-unloaders, including his namesake, the *Carl D. Bradley*, equipped with conveyor belts to automate the unloading of bulk cargo. Although registered in New York City, the *Bradley* would operate out of Rogers City. The Bradley Transportation fleet primarily employed crewmen from Rogers City. Many of the crew were friends, neighbors, or relatives. Because the boats returned every few days to reload, the crew members could easily raise their families in Rogers City.

U.S. Steel purchased a controlling interest in Michigan Limestone in 1920 and promoted Carl D. Bradley from general manager to president of Michigan Limestone. Upon Bradley's death in 1928, just one year after the launch of his namesake massive ship, U.S. Steel took full control of Michigan Limestone and Bradley Transportation. The *Bradley* operated for the steel conglomerate for almost thirty years but with age came problems. The crew regularly joked that the boat was being held together by rust. Sailors reported finding sheared-off rivets by the bucketful following storms, due to the *Bradley*'s excessive twisting and bending in heavy weather. The company began planning an overhaul of the hull.

In April 1957, the *Bradley* sustained damage from a collision with the *White Rose* on the St. Clair River. It spent a week in dry dock in Chicago being repaired. Then, in the spring of 1958, it grounded near Cedarville, Michigan. Although the Coast Guard conducted an inspection of the *Bradley* on April 17, 1958, and found it seaworthy, the steel industry was experiencing a downturn and the *Bradley* was laid up from July through October that year. Put back into service in November, it grounded again near the same spot off Cedarville. Since U.S. Steel had scheduled the overhaul for the upcoming winter, but still had to fulfill stone orders, it quickly repaired the minor damage and put the

**The *Carl D. Bradley* in the 1940s.** *William Lafferty Collection*

*Bradley* back in service without reporting the grounding to the Coast Guard. U.S. Steel took pride in an award it had received the prior year for 2,228,775 injury-free man hours from April 1955 to December 1957. In addition, since the founding of Bradley Transportation in 1912, the company had never lost a ship. However, that would soon change.

## LOST

The *Bradley* departed Gary, Indiana, on November 17, 1958, after delivering its last load of limestone for the year. Captain Roland Bryan directed his wheelsman to head north to Manitowoc, Wisconsin, where he ship would be laid up for an $800,000 replacement of its rusting cargo hold. A powerful low-pressure system had formed over the Pacific Ocean and reached the Great Lakes region by the next morning. However, in running along Lake Michigan's western shore, the *Bradley* would be protected by the shore, taking the building southwest seas on its stern. A radio call from headquarters that morning must have surprised Bryan and annoyed the crew, who would have been looking forward to getting home in time for Thanksgiving. The company ordered Bryan to return to Rogers City for one more load of stone before the lay-up. Despite reports of gale force winds and thirty-foot seas that compelled many other freighter captains to take shelter along Wisconsin's shore, Bryan, known as a "heavy weather man," decided to proceed as fast as possible to Rogers City. He headed northeast across the lake from the Door County peninsula toward the Straits of Mackinac. That decision would be fatal. Seaman Frank Mays, twenty-six years old at the time, recalls the tragic night with clarity, "I was in the dunnage room when I heard a deafening thud. I rushed on deck to see the stern flapping up and down, whipping like a dog's tail."

Mays had been born in Rogers City, attended Rogers City High School, married a woman he met while in the Navy, moved to Iowa, had three beautiful boys, and returned home to take up a life on the boats—a life that would change completely during the next, agonizing fifteen hours. Mays climbed up to the bow and onto a raft secured on the upper deck and waited for the boat to sink beneath him. From that perch, he watched in horror as sparks flew when the huge steel deck plates began tearing apart. He could see his crewmate, John Fogelsonger, running toward the stern, then suddenly disappearing as the deck beneath his feet ripped open. Seconds after that, Mays was pitched into the air and landed in the icy water. He struggled back onto the raft as the *Bradley* upended and began its plunge to the bottom of Lake Michigan. By morning only he and First Mate Elmer Fleming were alive. They had spent a perilous night aboard a raft with two other men who had died overnight, and were rescued by the crew of the Coast Guard vessel *Sundew*. Their thirty-three shipmates, including two of Mays' own cousins, had perished, leaving behind twenty-five widows and fifty-four fatherless children. The loss devastated the people of the small town. Few other wrecking incidents had taken the lives of so many from one community. To add to Mays' grief after the accident, U.S. Steel and Bradley Transportation officials never acknowledged his eyewitness account of the freighter breaking apart before it sank, and instead insisted that the *Bradley* sank in one piece.

"Have you heard of the *Carl D. Bradley*?"

That question was posed to the author in early 2008 by seventy-four-year-old Georgia resident R. David Lewis. Of course, every Great Lakes wreck diver has heard about the tragic sinking of the 638-foot self-unloader in northern Lake Michigan on November 18, 1958.

Lewis continued, "Well, I probably shouldn't talk about this, but I'm the only diver who has been down to the *Bradley*." Apparently he had not heard about the recent dives to this wreck. In 1997 "Deep Quest" expedition leaders Jim Clary and Fred Shannon took Mays down to the wreck in a submersible and became the first team to record images of both halves of the ship and to prove that Frank Mays had been correct about the ship's breakup. Following that, at least three teams of technical divers, beginning with Mirek Standowicz in 2001, had made the 350-foot deep dive to the *Bradley* on both the bow and

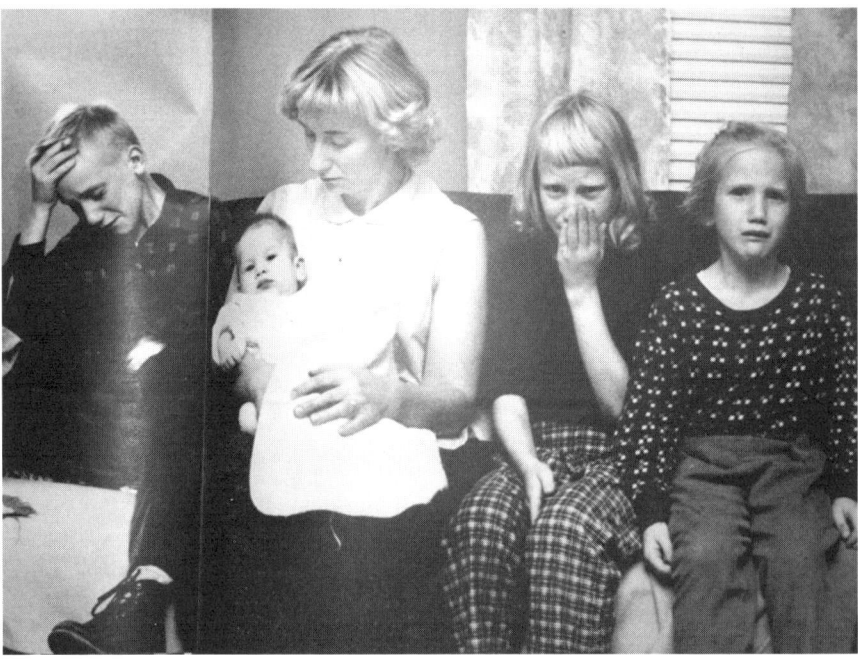

The December 1, 1958, *Life Magazine* included this heart-wrenching photograph of Cecelia Krawczak with her two-month-old baby, Jo Lynn, the youngest of six children, and siblings Ronald, Jacinta, and Rose Ann, that was taken soon after they learned that the body of their husband and father, Joe, had just been recovered. *Author's collection*

stern sections. Surprised to learn that it had become common knowledge that the wreck of the *Bradley* is in two pieces, Lewis also seemed relieved. "I should have realized that in the last fifty years others would dive it," he said. At first, Lewis seemed hesitant to provide any details about his dives to the *Bradley*, but, he finally decided to share his story.

"In December 1958, I received a call from a man who had just heard that I was involved in raising a sunken dredge. The man said, 'I need an accomplished diver for a difficult job.'" If Lewis would agree to meet with him, he would explain the job. Even at twenty-five years old, Lewis was, indeed, an accomplished diver. Born in Chicago in 1934, he grew up on the water, literally. The depression hit his family hard, forcing them to sell everything except their forty-two-foot Alden schooner, *Fairmaid*, which became their home as they hopped from port to port over the next four years. They eventually settled in St. Joseph, Michigan, along Lake Michigan's eastern shore. His parents' love of the water defined Lewis' life. "For as much time as I spent *on* the water, I was immensely curious to learn what was *under* the water." Because of his family's meager shipboard existence for so long, Lewis learned how to scrounge or modify everyday objects to accomplish his goals, and he needed something to help him get underwater.

At the age of ten, Lewis designed and built his first open helmet, made of an inverted, cast-iron cooking pot into which he drilled viewing portholes with a circular saw. Using scavenged Plexiglas scraps from Truscott Boat Company (makers of PT boats for the war effort) he heated the material, curved it, and used a gasket made of inner-tube rubber and machine screws to seal the windows. A junk yard, gas-powered, washing machine engine served as his air pump. A compressor from a scavenged refrigerator and a garden hose completed the air supply system. Lewis logged several hundred hours underwater with his homemade, surface-supplied dive system. At twelve, Lewis salvaged several aviator oxygen bottles from a military bomber that had recently ditched off St. Joseph. In time he realized these would make excellent breathing units. He constructed his first self-contained, air-demand breathing apparatus, but he preferred surface-supplied diving, which allowed him to stay underwater longer. He continued diving through high school, and took engineering classes at the University of Michigan until his funds ran out. He was hired by Heathkit Company in St. Joseph, later being promoted to project engineer in the Audio Engineering Department. He developed a prototype for a Scuba breathing apparatus in kit form, but product liability issues kept the company from producing it. To earn a little extra money, Lewis formed Meridian Divers Supply with fellow diver and businessman Jim Weaver to do commercial diving jobs, teach scuba at the local YWCA, and sell gear to the growing ranks of sport divers.

In late November, Lewis and another local commercial diver, Jim Brad-

**David Lewis' granddaughter Anya models the suit that Lewis wore to dive the *Carl Bradley* in 1959.** *Courtesy of David Lewis*

ley, were contracted to raise a dredge that had sunk at White Pigeon, Michigan. The successful completion of that job led to the phone call from a man calling himself Mr. Smith. Lewis explained, "The next night Jim Weaver and I knocked on the door of the seedy Buena Vista Motel on US12 (now Red Arrow Highway) near Stevensville, Michigan, and were ushered into the sitting area of the unit. The man introduced himself as Mr. Smith, and explained that he was acting for someone else who wished to remain anonymous. The door to the adjoining bedroom was cracked open and I was sure there was someone in there listening."

Smith questioned Lewis and Weaver at length about their diving qualifications. Finally, satisfied with their answers, he told them he needed an inspection of a ship that had recently sunk in northern Lake Michigan. Lewis explained that although they had the ability to make an inspection, they did not have the necessary boat and equipment and Lewis suggested a larger local marine contractor. Smith showed no interest. "We need total secrecy on this inspection and that would be impossible with a large corporation," he said.

In that case, Lewis explained, they would need to obtain a suitable boat, crew, and equipment, and it would be very expensive. In addition, they would need more details on the ship. It was a Catch-22: Smith was not willing to provide details until they committed to the job, and the divers did not want to commit to the job until they understood what was being asked of them. Smith suggested they think it over. Returning to Weaver's house, the two men stayed up most of the night discussing what little they knew of the job. Intrigued by the prospects of a challenge and the opportunity for good money, they decided to pursue the work. Lewis and Weaver met Smith the next night at the same motel and accepted the job, explaining that weather precluded them from diving until summer and they would need that time to make arrangements. Only then did Smith reveal the job: "I need absolute proof of the present condition of the *Carl D. Bradley*." He provided an approximate location in 360 feet, and the divers realized that perhaps they had bitten off more than they could chew.

"We told him we had never been below 200 feet, and never used heliox," a special blend of gas necessary for such a deep dive. That didn't discourage Smith. "You have six months to prepare." Then he handed Lewis a wad of bills. "Will $10,000 get you started?" asked Smith.

"I had more than a year's pay in my hand," Lewis recalled. "It was time to learn mixed-gas diving." Lewis knew that twenty-two years earlier, pioneer deep-diver Max Nohl had set a record with a 420-foot dive in Lake Michigan breathing self-contained heliox. Completely unaware of the brewing controversy between Frank Mays' report of the breakup of the *Bradley* and U.S. Steel's insistence that its boat had gone down in one piece, he and Weaver discussed the project, deciding they would need a sturdy, well-equipped boat, a crew, a camera, dive gear, and the right gas mix. And they would need to arrange leaves from their jobs. First Lewis approached his friend and occasional commercial dive partner, Jim Bradley from South Haven, for advice on the job. Bradley recalls thinking that his friend was either concocting a publicity stunt or was suicidal: "I would not become involved in this wild diving misadventure, or worse yet, have another friend killed diving." Bradley was still distraught over losing buddy William Amrein in a diving accident just a year before. Lewis then turned to Max Nohl for advice, making arrangements to meet at Nohl's home in Milwaukee. Before the trip, Lewis and Weaver approached Ferguson Welding Supply in St. Joseph to purchase the helium they would need for the job, but the supplier only had a small tank for filling balloons and recommended hydrogen instead. Knowing that hydrogen had similar properties to helium but combined violently with oxygen if ignited, Lewis was hesitant. Nohl provided advice on gas mixing techniques, gas handling problems, and decompression tables. Since both helium and hydrogen play no part in respiration, Nohl felt the alternative gas would work, but he stressed testing it thoroughly before using it on the *Bradley* dive.

On their return trip, Lewis and Weaver stopped at Greer Marine in Chicago to lease an underwater, closed-circuit television camera and monitor that they had seen at the previous Chicago Boat Show. This system, developed for surveillance during World War II, had just recently become commercially available. It could not, however, record images. To do that, Weaver would have to remain on the surface and snap pictures of the monitor with a Polaroid camera.

Needing a boat capable of supporting the equipment and making the forty-mile run in open seas, they decided a fish tug would do the job. Since the lamprey eel infestation had all but destroyed the commercial fishing industry on Lake Michigan, Weaver found a father and son fishing company in Muskegon seeking an alternative way to make money. They owned a steel tug with a diesel engine and a late-model commercial fathometer. The tug offered an enclosed cabin and a broad open stern that would facilitate diving. Both father and son agreed to the job and the cover story that they would be testing new deep-diving equipment.

Lewis described the diving gear he designed for the job: "For a dive of that depth and time, the quantity of gas needed excluded self-contained equipment. I wanted communication with Jim on the surface for safety reasons, but I knew my voice would be distorted by the mix. Since we had a working divers' phone, I modified a Scott Hydro-Pak full face mask with surface-supplied air and a transducer for communications. I attached a receiver to the headband over the right ear. The tilt-valve demand regulator on the Scott made it hard to breathe, but the mask was comfortable. We bought 500 feet of three-quarter-inch, double-braided, twin welding hose to supply the breathing mix, coupled with 500 feet of quarter-inch hose to serve as a pneumofathometer so that Jim could keep track of my depth. For thermal protection I modified a Bell-Aqua front entry drysuit by rubber cementing the hood to the Scott Hydro-Pak mask. I attached the hood to a neck ring using the locking lid of a pressure cooker. The hood and the attached mask could be sealed to the suit, but separated for donning purposes. I also installed double mushroom-type exhaust valves at each wrist and ankle to allow excess air to escape on ascent. The double valve reduced the chance of leaking, which could sap enough body heat to kill me."

Testing would be accomplished in Lewis and Weaver's personal recompression chamber. A few years earlier they had built it using two high-pressure, steam-generating tanks salvaged from Heathkit Company during a plant renovation. They converted the eight-foot-long, three-foot-diameter tank into the chamber and the smaller one into air storage to operate the chamber. Lewis got into the chamber with all his gear and the air mix he would use. Weaver secured the hatch and pressurized the chamber to the equivalent of 350 feet. During weeks of trial-and-error testing, Lewis experienced how the mix would allow him to maintain a clear head at depth and, more importantly, learned that it would sustain his life.

## FOUND

In late May 1959, the divers took a leave of absence from Heathkit Company. They packed a leased step van with equipment including borrowed cylinder racks, mixing manifolds, and booster pump, and rendezvoused with the boat and crew in Charlevoix, Michigan. After a meeting with Smith in a local motel, where he reviewed their accounting and gave them another bundle of cash to cover the boat crew and work to date, the team headed forty miles northwest from Charlevoix to the approximate location given them by Smith. With no satellite positioning, they used dead reckoning. Once at the spot, they dropped an anchor connected to a barrel for reference, and then began running lanes watching the fathometer for a telltale lump. It would take over a week until they finally found a target that might be the wreck, five miles southwest of the position Smith supplied. After several tight passes they located two high areas about 500 feet apart, which they suspected were the two ends of the ship.

After several attempts to hook the wreck with a grapnel, it finally caught. Lewis suited up and prepared to secure a mooring line. Lewis recounted, "It was black when I reached the 150-foot mark. Despite mounting anxiety, I followed the grapnel line down deeper than I had ever been before." Only the light from his closed-circuit television camera illuminated his descent. "I had to keep hitting the purge button on the Scott Hydro-Pack Mask to add the hydrogen/oxygen breathing gas into the mask." At the same time, the purge button sealed the exhaust valve causing the extra gas to enter the hood of the drysuit. For Lewis, this was exciting—the real thing—not a test dive in a chamber.

"I was cold despite wearing two sets of thermal underwear. At about 300 feet my heart raced when I saw a reflection from the lights. I slowed my descent and my breathing rate. A minute later, I realized I had just reached the starboard rail of the *Carl D. Bradley*." Not knowing precisely where the grapnel had hooked, he secured a mooring through a nearby scupper, then directed the camera toward the rail and instructed Weaver to snap a few Polaroid photos to check picture quality.

Extremely cold, Lewis realized he had to complete over two hours of decompression. Weaver communicated with him through all his decompression stops. Lewis recalls his disappointment when he surfaced, "We had actually found the ship but couldn't tell anyone about it except Mr. Smith." His phone call to Smith resulted in a directive: "Get me images to prove it's the *Bradley*, and details about its condition." They knew the *Bradley's* name would be on each side near the bow, so they planned to try to capture a photograph of it on the next dive. Dead reckoning led them to within 1000 feet of their mooring.

They spent time affixing a mooring to secure the boat over the wreck. Then Lewis made his second dive. "I figured my down line was at least 200 feet back from the name, so I would have to cover quite a distance dragging the camera, my triple hose, and com line to get the picture and get back to the ascent line within thirty minutes. I found it easier to pull myself along the railing rather than swim. I passed what I assumed was the A-frame and continued forward and finally hit it. The letters were larger than I expected. I backed off until Jim said that he could make out the "C" and then he snapped a photograph. I had been down fifteen minutes and because I could only remain on the bottom for thirty minutes, I had to start back immediately."

Their plan involved surveying the entire starboard rail, so Lewis would need to secure new moorings along the way. "On the next dive, I headed aft with the new line. Just when Jim told me to secure the new mooring, I felt the railing cable go slack. I swam another fifteen feet and found out why. The rail

**Mel Clark composed this amazing image of the *Bradley* auxiliary wheel at the stern.**
*Photograph by Mel Clark*

and deck and hull just ended in a ragged edge. I tied my line off near the break. Decompression seemed to take forever that time."

After that dive, they used the fathometer for a surface survey and found nothing for about one hundred feet aft of the bow section, and then discovered a thirty-five-foot rise from the bottom. "It appeared that the ship had broken in two," Lewis recalled. "We decided to anchor overnight at the site, get pictures of the break, make a quick check of the stern section, and then contact Smith." Looking forward to the possibility of several lucrative weeks' work in making a thorough inspection of both halves of the ship, the divers arranged a meeting with Smith at the motel to report their findings. Again, Smith ushered them into the unit and again they saw the door to the adjoining bedroom cracked open. They gave Smith the corrected position and their Polaroid photos, and described the break. "Are you positive that it's in two pieces?" Smith asked in an angry, disbelieving way.

"No doubt about it," Lewis told him. Smith excused himself to the adjoining room, returning fifteen minutes later with an offer, "If you swear never to divulge what you have done or seen, we will give you another $20,000 to cover your work and an extra $1,000 for the boat crew to keep quiet. We have connections that can make life difficult for anyone who breaks the pledge." Lewis felt insulted by the threat but also quite scared, so he and Weaver quickly agreed to maintain the secret. They told Smith they would need to go back once more to cut their marker buoys off the wreck.

On July 7, 1959, soon after Lewis wrapped up the *Bradley* job, the Coast Guard Board of Inquiry published their findings about the accident. The lengthy report conceded that "the vessel heaved upward and broke in two." The Coast Guard apparently believed Frank Mays and disregarded the Bradley Line claim they had located the wreck in one piece. Their final finding stated that "inasmuch as the exact location of the hull is unknown at this time…, the board may be reconvened should circumstances demand." After this finding, law firms for the Bradley Transportation Company made a $600,000 settlement offer to the thirty-three families of the victims. The offer was instead met with a $16 million lawsuit.

In October 1959, Global Marine Exploration from California surveyed the wreck of the *Bradley* with television cameras from their vessel *Submarex*. Hired by attorneys for U.S. Steel, their results indicated the vessel was in one piece. Attorneys asserted they had images of an intact hull, but none were ever made public.

In December 1959, survivor Frank Mays, who was given an administrative position with the company after the sinking, was told there was no more work for him. U.S. Steel president Christian Beukema, who always maintained the *Bradley* never split in two, would not respond to Mays' request for a reason for his firing.

Ultimately, the lawsuit was settled out of court for a sum of $1.25 million to be shared among the families, a small fraction of the original lawsuit amount.

"That job allowed me to buy my first home," Lewis recalled. However, he always felt that somehow he had been involved in something underhanded, but he never understood the ramifications of what he had observed. In hindsight, Jim Clary, who led the 1997 expedition to the *Bradley*, understands why Lewis was threatened to keep quiet about his findings. "If it had come out in 1959 that the ship was in such bad repair to have broken in two, its owners would have been liable for a lot more damages than the families actually settled for. While it can never be proven who requested the survey and paid for the divers' silence, readers may draw their own conclusions. For R. David Lewis, who had just recently started his own marine contracting business, this was a significant

**The new bell rests atop the *Bradley* pilothouse after the original bell was recovered for the 50th anniversary memorial and put on permanent display at the Great Lakes Lore Maritime Museum in Rogers City, Michigan.** *Photograph by Mel Clark*

job, but a job that nagged at his conscience for over fifty years. He broke no laws, and accomplished a milestone in the early years of diving but could never speak of it. Since sharing this story, Lewis has indicated that he is glad to finally understand the controversy surrounding the *Bradley*'s condition, why he was hired, and why he was silenced. "I never intended to talk about this, but I am glad to finally get it off my chest."

Lewis' observation that the *Bradley* had, in fact, split in two, never came to light and a big insurance payoff was never awarded to the families mattered little to those who lost someone on the *Bradley*. Money could never have taken the place of men they lost. Somehow, the families of the victims managed to move forward. Time lessened their pain, but they never forgot the tragic accident that forever changed their lives. A ceremony held on the 50th anniversary of the sinking reminded them that their loved ones had not been forgotten. At 5:30 p.m. on November 18, 2008, the Rogers City High School gymnasium brimmed with people—too many to count, but more than a third of the small rural community waited in anticipation. White-haired people dominated the room, but there were plenty of middle-agers, teens, and even toddlers looking around with expectation. Over the hum of the gymnasium lights snippets of conversations could be heard: "Never thought we'd be back here after all these years," "Elmer Fleming was my grandfather," "Bert's sailing so he couldn't be here tonight." The attendees smiled and waved to the people clustered in the

This haunting image inside the pilothouse of the *Carl D. Bradley was captured during a 2010 expedition to the wreck.* *Photograph by Mel Clark*

sea of chairs that filled the gym floor and to those sitting in the highest bleachers. One woman sat in a trance-like state seemingly unaware of her surroundings. Others rubbed eyes already red and wet, and still others clutched tissues in expectation of an emotion-filled evening. They gathered there to remember the thirty-three men who lost their lives on a cold and stormy night five decades earlier when Lake Michigan swallowed the mammoth self-unloader. Their thoughts were for their husbands, fathers, brothers, nephews, cousins, and neighbors whose lives were tragically cut short. Fifty years earlier, many of these same people filed by casket after casket to mourn over the bodies of fifteen hometown men during a mass wake in the high school gymnasium of the same school in the same town where little has changed in the last half-century.

Like the night the *Bradley* sank, it was biting cold outside on that early evening. A few latecomers dressed in camouflage gear with bright orange vests, probably just back from hunting, climbed to the top of the bleachers. As several dozen people took their seats on the stage flanking a worn bronze bell sitting on a cloth-draped pedestal, the audience began to quiet, but a wrinkle-faced woman could be heard murmuring, "Imagine those boys in the water on a night like tonight." A sturdy, robust man with a square jaw and glasses that were the only thing that revealed his age approached the podium and cleared his throat nervously because he was unaccustomed to the spotlight. "We're going to get started," he said, with little fanfare. An introduction was hardly necessary; everyone knew David Erickson, president and director of the Great

Lakes Lore Museum, the man who had organized the event.

Erickson was just seventeen when the *Bradley* went down. He remembered hearing the news of the sinking while listening to a ham radio at the hunting camp, just after the start of deer hunting season. Like everyone in town, he knew many of the men crewing on the boat that night, including school chums Bennie Schefke and Dennis Joppich, and was shocked when he later learned they and so many others had died. That didn't stop him from applying for his seaman's license the next spring. "What else could I do? My dad worked at the stone quarry, and my brothers worked on the boats," he told a television newscaster earlier that day. Like so many other local boys, Erickson knew job options in Rogers City were limited and college was not a consideration, so he signed on with the Bradley Transportation Company. Memories of the *Bradley's* sinking never worried him, because after all, it was a freak accident. Like most sailors, Erickson thought it could never happen again…until it did. Just seven years after the *Bradley* went down, in May 1965, while serving as a porter aboard the *Cedarville*, Erickson watched as the Norwegian vessel *Topdalsfjord* loomed out of the fog and collided with his boat as it was approaching the Mackinac Bridge. Minutes later he was thrown into the icy water as the *Cedarville* capsized. Fortunately for Erickson, he survived, but ten of his mates were not so lucky. Rogers City faced another heartbreaking tragedy, this one leaving ten new widows and thirty-three fatherless kids

Like Frank Mays, Erickson could never sail commercially again, but boats continued to dominate his life. He built model boats, sailed his own small boats, and stayed in touch with his buddies still working on the Bradley boats. Once retired from his maintenance job at United Auto Workers, he took over as the museum director. Embracing its mission of "Honoring Those Who Served," Erickson grew the museum in both membership and inductees into its honor roll, which now numbers over 380 sailers and is represented by personal plaques filling the walls of the museum. Erickson even has his own plaque in the room that honors the men who lived and died in the four most recent tragedies: the *Bradley*, *Cedarville*, *Daniel J. Morrell*, and *Edmund Fitzgerald*.

After opening remarks from the mayor, Erickson announced the start of the bell-ringing portion of the ceremony at precisely 5:35 p.m., the same moment the *Bradley* plunged beneath the waves. He invited an unimposing, youthful-appearing senior citizen to have the honor of ringing the bell for the first time. Frank Mays, known to all as the last living survivor of the *Bradley*, approached the bell in reverence.

Life in Rogers City had been difficult for Mays after the accident. Many of the locals sympathized with him, understanding that he too was a victim, but others were angry that Mays had lived rather than their loved ones.

Around every corner he saw the grieving faces of his friends and neighbors and it was too much for him. Mays took his family and left to make his way in the world outside of the Great Lakes. For the most part, he has carved out a satisfying life of rewarding work, love, and travel, but it is a life shadowed by being a survivor.

A projector displayed a large image of crewman John Fogelsonger in whose honor Mays rang the bell. Most people realized the significance that Fogelsonger was the first man to die that night so long ago, and so it was fitting he be remembered first. It seemed that the audience held its collective breath as Mays pulled back the clapper and let it go. The ring was strong and clear and ended the bell's fifty-year silence.

The bell was no ordinary bell. It is the very same bell that rested atop the pilothouse on the *Bradley* since its launch in 1927. In 2004, David Erickson had a special vision for the fiftieth anniversary. With the permission of U.S. Steel he set out to bring the *Bradley* bell home to Rogers City. When asked by Erickson to undertake the project, John Janzen, a forty-year-old, tall, wiry engineer and diver from Minnesota, felt honored and readily accepted the challenge. With a passion for history, his dive buddy, a stocky forty-year-old industrial electrician and fellow Minnesotan, John Scoles, was also more than willing. The complexities of the task, however, required nearly two years of planning and preparation. These experienced and specially trained technical divers had been to the *Bradley* first in 2004, then again in 2005, and were familiar with conditions at this deep and remote site, to which only a few divers have ever ventured since its rediscovery in 1995.

To safely accomplish such dangerous dives, they breathed a specially blended gas in which inert helium replaces a percentage of oxygen and nitrogen to reduce the toxic and disorienting effect these gases can have under extreme pressure. They wore drysuits with electric heaters in order to maintain body heat during the three-hour, thirty-minute dive, most of which would be spent decompressing on the way up. On August 7, 2007, they successfully removed the bell using a flame tube plasma torch in a complex and dangerous operation and later replaced it with a memorial bell engraved with the names of all thirty-three lost crew-

John Scoles (left) and John Janzen flank Frank Mays, sole remaining survivor of the *Carl D. Bradley*, when they returned to the dock after recovering the bell from the *Carl Bradley* in 2007. *Courtesy of John Janzen*

51

men. Frank Mays was aboard the dive boat and had the honor of lifting it safely into the boat. "I never thought I'd see that bell again," he admitted between wet hugs of congratulations with the divers.

"Being able to provide the bell to the families as a tangible connection to their lost loved ones is the greatest honor of my life," John Janzen humbly mentioned before the ceremony. And that evening it served its intended purpose. He was given the honor to ring the bell in memory of Captain Roland Bryan. As the ceremony proceeded, the faces of the victims filled the screen and their eyes spoke to the dreams they had never realized. Gary Orr rang for his dad, Mel; Gene Promo rang for his brother, Leo; and Tim Horn rang for his uncle, Paul. Their faces offered clues as to what their loved ones might have looked like had they had the opportunity to age, and their graying hair denoted they are now older than these victims ever were. Aileen Bauers rang for her husband, John, and showed how timeless love is: She never remarried.

For those who know the Krawczak family, the most poignant moment was when the baby, fifty-year-old Jo Lynn Zalewski, rang for her dad, wheelsman Joe Kwasczak. This family was traumatized when Joe died leaving his thirty-two-year-old wife, Cecelia, and six kids, aged two months to eleven years. All who saw the center spread of the December 1958 issue of *Life Magazine* (see page 42) cannot forget the agonizingly heartbroken look on their faces as the country shared their grief. Rogers City banded together for this family as they did for so many, delivering a semi-truck full of gifts at Christmas that

**Fifty years after the sinking of the *Bradley*, Cecelia Krawczak and her six children gathered to honor Joe Krawczak at the anniversary memorial in Alpena. Jo Lynn, second from left, never knew her father.** *Photograph by Christopher Winter, courtesy Michigan History Magazine*

year. Most of the kids remained in the town where their pain is remembered; elsewhere they might not be understood. And they attended the anniversary to remember. At Cecelia's side was her husband of forty-seven years and the man her kids now call Dad, Louis Dembny. Although she has had a fulfilling life, the anniversary was a very emotional day for Cecelia. It was her birthday and she was reminded of how excited she had been fifty years earlier in anticipation of Joe's return for her celebration. Instead her birthday has become a day of mourning.

After the ceremony, families were invited to the Rogers City Theater just south of the Lore Museum on 3rd Street in Rogers City, where the marquee announced "World Premier - *November Requiem,*" produced by siblings Brian and Anne Belanger in association with the Presque Isle Library." The hauntingly beautiful documentary explored how the small northern Michigan community came to grips with a disaster that even a half-century later remains vivid in the minds of those who lived through it. Interviews with surviving family members, maritime historians, the dive team, and Frank Mays provided perspective on this tragedy. If the ceremony did not elicit enough emotion, the documentary most certainly did. Tears poured from the eyes of many people exiting the theater, but they rolled down cheeks and over mouths curved with smiles elicited from knowing that, after fifty years, their loved ones had not been forgotten.

**Frank Mays, the sole remaining survivor of the *Carl Bradley*, at the time of the 50th anniversary of the sinking.** *Photograph by Christopher Winter, courtesy Michigan History Magazine*

Most people who visit South Manitou Island make the trek from the ferry dock on the southeast side of the island to the southwest side to glimpse the *Francisco Morazan* from the bluff. However, each year the wreck degrades further. One day it may no longer be visible above the surface of the lake. *Photograph by Enoch Haven*

## 3

# ACCIDENTAL ATTRACTION

The *Francisco Morazan* is unique because at present it is the only shipwreck that is visible above the surface of Lake Michigan. Hundreds of thousands of people have seen this shipwreck from their boats, from shore, or in the water exploring it—so many, in fact, that it has been included among Lake Michigan's many legendary shipwrecks simply because of its familiarity. However, few understand the long history of the vessel or the details of the accident that created what has became a tourist attraction in northern Lake Michigan.

Built in 1922 as the *Arcadia* by Deutsche Werft, of Hamburg, Germany, for German owners, the ship was 234 feet long, with a beam of nearly 37 feet. As built, the *Arcadia* had two steam turbines with a single-screw propeller. After a dozen years, which would mark the vessel's longest period operating under one owner with one name, in 1934 the *Arcadia* was sold to a party in Konigsberg, East Prussia, and renamed *Elbing*. A new four-cylinder compound steam engine was installed the next year. In 1940, the *Elbing* was requisitioned by the Kriegsmarine for use as a coal ship in Operation Sea Lion, Nazi Germany's plan to invade the United Kingdom, which never actually took place. In March 1941, it was set on fire and beached after being shelled by HMS *Tartar* during Operation Claymore, the British raid on the Lofoten Islands in Norway. Subsequently repaired, it sailed in Norwegian waters during 1942 and was returned to its Prussian owners in 1943.

The vessel was damaged after being shelled by artillery, then beached on Schweine Sand Island in the River Elbe, in Germany. Then England seized it and renamed it the *Empire Congress*. In 1946, England passed it on to the Norwegian government, which renamed it the *Brunes*. In 1947, a Norwegian party purchased it for use in merchant service and renamed it the *Skuld*. Ownership changed again in 1948 after a company merger, and the new owners renamed it *Ringas*.

**The *Francisco Morazan* is pictured when it was named the *Ringas*.** *Author's collection*

On June 30, 1952, the *Ringas* rescued the forty-six crew and three passengers from the *Mahenge*, which sank after a collision with another ship near the Channel Islands between France and England. In 1952, the vessel made its first trip into the Great Lakes delivering a cargo of china clay to Muskegon, Michigan. It returned the next year to Port Huron, Michigan, delivering pulpwood. In 1958, the *Ringas* was sold to a Greek owner and renamed *Los Mayos*. *Los Mayos* returned to the Great Lakes in 1958, but ran aground at Muskegon becoming damaged, but was repaired to sail again. In 1959, a Liberian business purchased the vessel, renamed it *Francisco Morazan,* and chartered it to the West Indies Transport Company of New York and Monrovia as well as the Interamerican Marine Operators, of New York.

The vessel was named for General Francisco Morazán, a Honduran general and a politician who ruled several Central American states at different times during a turbulent period from 1827 to 1842. He rose to prominence when he led liberal forces against the conservatives at the Battle of La Trinidad in 1827. Although he sought advancement and development of Central America, the means he used were not always moral and resulted in his execution in 1842. The country still shows great respect for him with statues and memorials and the owners may have named the vessel in his honor to attract crewmembers, many of whom they hoped would be Hondurans.

On October 21, 1960 Captain Eduardo Trivrazara, a Greek who had commanded the *Francisco Morazan* for the previous six months, began what was to become the last voyage for this ship. In Miami, Florida, he took on board a cargo of phosphates destined for Montreal and Toronto. Trivrazara brought along his twenty-nine-year-old wife, Anastasia, to serve as his assistant. The couple had one infant daughter at home in Greece, and another due in seven months. Twelve crewmembers served under him. After the Canadian delivery, the freighter sailed to Chicago, arriving there in mid-November to load over 1000 tons of mixed cargo including aluminum, baled hair, bottle caps, canned chicken, castings, chemicals, Gilsonite (an asphalt), hides, lard, machinery, phosphate, scrap metal, solder dross, tinplate, and toys destined for Rotterdam, Netherlands, and Hamburg, Germany.

The *Francisco Morazan* departed Chicago on November 28. Fog slowed its progress and a problem with the feed pump for the boiler required the ship to be stopped so that the pump could be worked on. Fearing the vessel and the crew would be trapped in the Great Lakes for the winter if they could not reach the St. Lawrence Seaway by December 1 when the locks shut down for the season, Trivrazara must have been relieved when the crew managed to get the pumps working again.

## LOST AND FOUND

Under way again on the night of Monday, November 28, the *Morazan* encountered a snowstorm, which greatly reduced visibility. Trivrazara pushed on trying to beat the lock closing and took a shortcut heading for the narrow passage between the Manitou Islands and the mainland near Sleeping Bear Point in northern Michigan. On Tuesday at 6.30 p.m., the captain and crew heard a terrible noise like metal scraping metal, and the ship suddenly ground to a halt. Sitting in her cabin at the time, Mrs. Trivrazara heard the noise and ran out into the corridor only to see crewmembers rushing around, packing their bags, and donning life jackets. Worried the freighter would soon sink, she dashed off to the pilothouse to find her husband in. Through gaps in the blinding snow, Trivrazara saw a small island just a few hundred yards in front of his ship. In time, he would come to understand that his ship had plowed right over the submerged remains of another vessel, the *Walter L. Frost*, a package freighter nearly the same size and build as the *Morazan*. In 1903, its captain had made the same navigational error, and the ship now lay wrecked in a mere

A ten-year-old snorkeler, Greta Davis, examines the wreck of the *Walter B. Frost* in fifteen feet of water on South Manitou Island's southeast side. The *Morazan* plowed right over its remains, which had lain there for fifty-six years at the time. *Photograph by the author*

A satellite image shows the *Francisco Morazan* visible above the water and the outline of the wreck of the *Walter B. Frost*, which it hit, just below and slightly to the left of the *Morazan*.

fifteen feet of water. Trivrazara's lack of familiarity with the waters of Lake Michigan and the storm undoubtedly combined to result in the grounding.

Although he knew his ship was taking on water through a hole in its lower hull and his wife was nearly paralyzed with fear, Trivrazara assessed that they were in no immediate danger. He tried to chart his position, then radioed his condition. "Mayday, Mayday, Mayday. This is the Liberian freighter *Francisco Morazan*. We have grounded in shallow water near South Manitou Island."

He immediately heard from a Coast Guardsman in the light station between the South and North Manitou Islands. Trivrazara could not report with any accuracy exactly where his vessel had grounded, so the Coast Guardsman radioed Wilber Moore, a state forest ranger and a winter resident on South Manitou Island, to walk its perimeter and try to pinpoint the location of the stranded freighter. Moore spotted it after a two-mile hike from his residence and through the night he flashed light signals to the stranded ship, assuring the crew the vessel had been spotted.

After consulting with Moore, the district Coast Guard headquarters dispatched the cutter *Mesquite* from Sturgeon Bay, Wisconsin, and the cutter *Sundew* from Charlevoix, Michigan, to aid the stranded vessel. In addition, the crew of a thirty-six-foot lifeboat from Frankfort, Michigan, answered the ship's first call for help. Aircraft from the Coast Guard air station at Traverse City attempted to reach the scene twice, but thirty-five-knot winds, severe icing conditions, and a six-foot swell forced them to give up. District Coast Guard officials called on the powerful icebreaker *Mackinaw* to pull the 2000-ton *Morazan* off the rocky shore, but a Coast Guard spokesman said they would not take the crew off unless it appeared the vessel would break up or capsize. On November 30, three representatives of the ship's insurance company were flown out to the ship. They determined that the *Francisco Morazan* could not be salvaged, but thought that the cargo could be recovered.

The next day, Thursday December 1, as the lake calmed a bit, Trivrazara arranged for his wife to be taken off the vessel. She had become ill because of the constant motion from the pounding surf, made worse because she was pregnant, and had stayed in bed since the accident. A tired and shaken

**The *Francisco Morazan* as it appeared just months after it grounded at South Manitou Island.** *National Park Service Collection*

Anastasia Trivrazara was transported by a Coast Guard launch to the *Mackinaw* late Thursday and then airlifted to the Coast Guard Station at Traverse City. The media converged on her when she arrived at 5:20 p.m. "I didn't want to leave him," she lamented in her lilting Greek accent. Reporters seemed fascinated, describing her as a raven-haired beauty, wearing a black sweater, black pedal pushers, and a grey checked coat. The next morning, she appeared in good health and spirits after getting some rest at a motel. She told reporters that she would remain in Traverse City until the fate of the *Morazan* was decided, then would fly to New York to stay with relatives.

A boarding party from the icebreaker *Mackinaw* stayed behind after Mrs. Trivrazara had been taken off the wreck. They examined the ship and found several holds flooded from a ten-foot hole, but they did not believe the crew to be in jeopardy. However, rising southwest winds and waves over Friday and Saturday pounded the freighter, making a salvage effort impossible. The Coast Guard told reporters that the continuing winds of twenty-five to thirty knots prevented a tug from putting salvage experts on board, but indicated, "Everybody's comfortable, and they've got heat on board."

Meanwhile, authorities had to consider the possibility that the crew, consisting of Spaniards, Greeks, Cubans, and Hondurans, would have to be taken off the stranded ship soon. An immigration department spokesman said six of the crewmen faced deportation if they had to be evacuated. Indeed, they would have to be. On Sunday, December 4, Coast Guardsmen plucked the captain, his crew, and three insurance officials from the stranded ship and transferred them to the *Mackinaw*. Around midnight, the *Mackinaw* anchored offshore in Grand Traverse Bay and waited until immigration officials decided what to do. After negotiations, Trivrazara, acting as agent for the ship's owners, assumed responsibility for delivery of the non-cleared seamen to New York and then back to their countries. They all left with Mrs. Trivrazara by bus the next Monday.

Roan Salvage of Sturgeon Bay, Wisconsin, was hired to try to dislodge the vessel but buffeting by a storm made that impossible. Fearing attempts to pillage the ship, agents for the vessel asked for law enforcement help. The Leelanau County sheriff's department arranged for Ed Riker, a permanent resident of the island, to watch over the vessel and its cargo. On January 3, just one month after the crew left the *Morazan*, Riker spotted a small boat and saw two men on board the wreck. He contacted the sheriff who was able to follow the boat in to shore to question the men.

In January 1961, the insurance company awarded a contract to Lake Michigan Hardwood Company to salvage the cargo from the *Francisco Morazan*. That company engaged George Grosvenor of Leland, Michigan, to assist in the operation. Grosvenor owned a small mail boat, *Smiling Thru,* which was able to operate in shallow water. The company planned to transfer the salvaged cargo from the *Smiling Thru* to the Lake Michigan Hardwood Company's larger boat, *Glen Shore,* for delivery to Leland. From there, it would be taken by truck to Chicago. By mid-February, the firm estimated that it had removed about half the cargo. By late March, the salvors had removed all that they could and the fate of the ship, which some estimated had weathered the winter well, remained uncertain.

During the summer of 1961, people flocked to the area to see the massive ship aground. There were so many, in fact, that police could not even attempt to keep tourists off the wreck. In time, all the loose or moveable parts were stripped off. In September, the ship's owners identified a Detroit firm to salvage the ship, but they never formally contracted for the work. Over the years, the islanders salvaged the remaining cargo for their own use. For years, they ate Blue Star chicken, washed their hair with Suave shampoo, and played with balsawood model aircraft kits.

Tragically, in August 1967, eighteen-year-old islander, Ronnie Riker, drowned while exploring the wreck. His death, reports of rotting cargo, and the potential of fuel leakage, prompted the Michigan attorney general in August 1968 to file a lawsuit to force the owners to remove the wreck. The day after he filed, a fire broke out on the wreck, which consumed all but the steel superstructure. The authorities suspected vandals but never apprehended anyone. Because the fire did not ignite the fuel oil, the court persisted in its demand that the wreck be removed. Yet by the following June, the owners still had not taken action, obviously to avoid paying the undoubtedly massive salvage fees.

Swimmers, snorkelers, and divers can easily access the engine room of the *Francisco Morazan,* once buried deep within the ship. The towering four-cylinder, compound steam engine and two boilers can be examined up close. *Photograph by the author*

A snorkeler's-eye view of the compartment just aft of the engine room, now exposed like a cavern. *Photograph by the author*

In text that accompanied this UPI photograph of the *Francisco Morazan* in 1968 as the fire burned out, the reporter pointed out the coincidence that only the prior week the attorney general had filed for removal of the vessel. *Author's Collection*

Over the ensuing five decades, the wreck has become the home of double-crested cormorants and seagulls that roost upon its many surfaces. However, the uric acid in bird droppings acts corrosively to break down metal surfaces. This and the action of the waves and ice has served to degrade it considerably over the years. In fact, the section between the engine room and bow has broken apart and lies in pieces below the surface. At the time of this book's printing, only about half of the vessel remains visible above the surface, but still draws boaters, snorkelers, and divers who enjoying exploring the remains

The wreck of the *Francisco Morazan* is a magnet for boaters, swimmers, paddleboarders, snorkelers, and divers who visit South Manitou Island, as well as cormorants and seagulls that call it home. *Photograph by the author*

from various viewpoints. Divers get a two-for-one treat: After exploring the wreck of the *Francisco Morazan*, they can swim about fifty yards south and dive on the wreck of the *Walter Frost*. This site continues to remain one of the island's most popular tourist attractions.

Soon after the *Alvin Clark* was raised, its masts were restepped. After it was pumped out, the schooner floated on its own. The diver who raised it had sails made and sailed it to other ports. *Courtesy of Dave Stevens*

# 4

# DEATH AND RESURRECTION

An ordinary workhorse during its nineteen-year career on the Great Lakes, the two-masted schooner *Alvin Clark* became legendary when it broke the surface of Lake Michigan 105 years after it sank, and floated on its own. In fact, the *Alvin Clark* lived to sail another twenty-five years in the twentieth century, six years longer than it sailed in the nineteenth century. After its resurrection, it was recognized as the oldest working schooner on the Great Lakes and was listed on the National Register of Historic Places.

## FOUND

On a cold November Wednesday in 1967, Dick Garbowski, a commercial fisherman from Menominee, Michigan, snagged a valuable fishing net on an obstruction northeast of Chambers Island in the Green Bay waters of Lake Michigan. After trying every which way to dislodge it with no success, he marked it with a buoy and called a friend, well-known wreck diver Frank Hoffmann, to lend a hand. The forty-one-year-old construction worker and owner of Anchor Inn in Egg Harbor, a motel and tavern in the small resort and fishing community on the Green Bay side of Wisconsin's Door Peninsula, quickly offered his help, especially because Garbowski told him that the net had probably become fouled on a shipwreck. Unable to find any divers to help on such short notice, Hoffmann prepared for a solo dive into the icy bay. On November 5, he arranged for a flight across the bay to Menominee, and from there Garbowski helped him load his gear on his fish tug, the *Dellie W,* and headed out to the net, sixteen miles away.

Garbowski had kept quiet about the predicament, worried someone might hear about it and try to abscond with the $1400 net. Hoffmann, too, had kept quiet because he knew that news of a new wreck could bring out other divers intent on looting. He suited up, strapped on his tank, and went over the side, then began his descent. He switched on his light at fifty feet because the water was so murky and began searching for the net. When he reached one hundred feet, he came upon the wreck and saw a row of deadeyes, blocks through which the shrouds pass to secure the masts. He began swimming along the wreck trying to locate the net, but suddenly his light began flickering on and off. Shaking from the cold, he finally encountered the net, which was hung up on another series of deadeyes farther forward on the ship. He reached for his knife, but was missing from its sheath. He grabbed for his spare knife and began trying to cut away the net. He freed it from one deadeye only to find it floated away and hooked on the next deadeye. Already down twenty minutes, he was ready to give up when his light went out completely and he found himself in utter blackness. He feared that one wrong move and he might become entangled in the net. Fortunately, the light popped on for a few seconds, and he backed carefully away from the net and slowly began his ascent not having achieved his goal. "I was never more glad to see the light of day as I was when I broke surface," he later recalled, and quickly sucked down the whiskey Garbowski offered him.

By the following weekend, Hoffmann had rounded up several dive buddies. They agreed that the first order of business would be to free the nets. Then, they agreed to salvage any cargo for Garbowski as a finder's fee. Since Hoffmann had made the first dive, he would determine how to divvy up the artifacts. Hoffmann and Bud Brain, a dive buddy from Chicago, made the next dive. They immediately swam to the net to try to work it free. When they could not loosen it, another pair followed them, until by day's end everyone had used up his allotted bottom time. Yet, the net remained fouled. There had been no time to explore the wreck, but the divers realized that it was nearly intact. Weather conspired to keep them off the wreck until late November when Hoff-

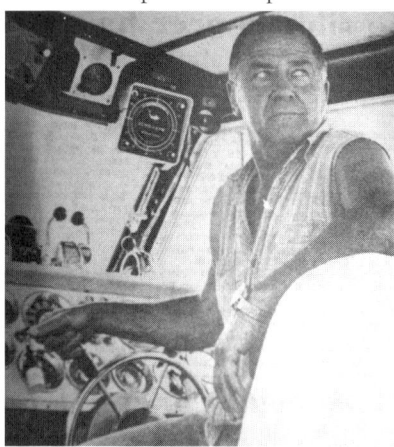

mann, Brain, and another Chicago diver, Bernie Bloom, tried to free the nets, only to fail once again. During that dive, they swam the length of the wreck and found the masts standing and the cabin intact. Although the cabin had filled with sand, they could see pieces of furniture poking through and became excited for what treasures might be revealed. The cargo hold had filled in with silt as well and so they could not see what, if anything, it had carried, but this was enough to really intrigue Hoffmann. He began scheming to raise it, something he had tried but failed to do the previous summer after he found the intact remains of the schoo-

**Bud Brain, nicknamed "iron man," was one of the very active members of the *Alvin Clark* dive team and is pictured around the time the schooner was raised.** *Author's collection*

ner *Jennie-Bell*. He undoubtedly would have heard about legendary Milwaukeean Max Nohl's plans to raise the *Prins Willem* back in the 1950s, and would have known about the successful recovery of the Swedish war ship *Vasa* from Stockholm Harbor just a few years earlier. These projects probably inspired him

Over the winter of 1968, Hoffmann applied for and received a salvage permit from the Army Corp of Engineers for the vessel that newspapers had begun referring to as "The Mystery Wreck From 19 Fathoms." Hoffmann and

**An artist's rendition of Frank Hoffmann.** *Reprinted from* The Mystery Ship From 19 Fathoms

the other divers planned to bring up the artifacts and agreed to hold them as common property until the ship came up, after which Hoffmann would split up the treasured items equitably. Hoffmann also began thinking about the possibility of raising the wreck and showcasing it for the public as a way to make some money off his claim. However, he still had to free the net.

The team was back at it in April 1968, but the divers found the visibility at the bottom even worse than the prior November. They could barely see two and a half feet in front of their eyes. It took six weekends of work before they could finally free the net, perhaps longer than necessary because during each dive the divers kept venturing off to retrieve some small artifact. At the stern, they found every diver's dream: the ship's wheel, still in position. Putting a hand on the wheel, Hoffmann gently moved it and found it still turned freely. It even had remnants of a canvas material wrapped around it, probably to avoid an arm getting entangled in the spokes. Most of the other artifacts, Hoffmann realized lay hidden away beneath the silt. To get at them, or to raise the ship, he would have to pump out the sand. This would be a colossal undertaking for a professional group, much less a group of amateurs. But once Hoffmann had the idea, he let nothing interfere with his vision of seeing the ship float again.

The crew began working on the design of a silt pumping system. Hoffmann became so obsessed over the project, he closed his motel to all but his crew and spent what little money he had to supply the operation, even offering the crew salary for their efforts. He purchased an Army surplus fire hose and motor to build his pump. The rig was so big he needed a different vessel to transport it and the divers to the site. He was thrilled when Harold Derusha of the Marinette Marine Corporation offered the use of *Cleo*, a sixty-foot military surplus landing craft as a work platform. All things seemed possible then. By

September they began making real progress pumping out the ship, but the stirred-up water and nearly pitch-black conditions made diving very dangerous. Hoffmann worried terribly for each of the divers, while all but forgetting about his wife and business. The project strained him emotionally and financially.

He perked up at the news that one of the crew had probably identified the schooner. An account in the *Green Bay Advocate* of June 1864 mentioned that the two-masted schooner *Alvin Clark* had sunk near Chambers Island. Hoffmann began researching the *Clark* and found that the dimensions and the fact it sank empty matched the Mystery Wreck. He hoped that the team could positively identify it once it came to the surface.

The *Alvin Clark*, had been the vision of an entrepreneurial fisherman, John P. Clark, who decided to try his hand at commercial shipping, a new venture that would require his own specialized vessel. In 1845, Clark commissioned the building of a two-masted schooner from the shipyard of Joseph Keating in the town of Truago, Michigan (later renamed Trenton). Clark named it after his son, Alvin. Launched in 1846 just as the Erie Canal was being enlarged to handle increased demands of shipping, the *Alvin Clark* served its owner well for five years, primarily carrying salt and fish on Lake Erie. But changing needs caused Clark to sell his schooner in 1851 to G. W. Bissel of Detroit, after which time the schooner began to sail on the upper Great Lakes, frequenting the growing city of Chicago quite regularly. It proved to be a sturdy, manageable sailing craft, but on one occasion, in May 1856, it ran afoul of the brig *Hutchinson* carrying away the brig's main rigging and chain plates. For the next five years, it carried such varied cargoes as barrel staves, salt, lumber, and package goods throughout the Great Lakes, wintering most every year at Racine, Wisconsin. In the spring of 1856, Racine sailor William Higgie took notice of the efficient craft. He and his brother John made Bissel a tempting offer. Higgie purchased the *Alvin Clark* and brought on his nephew, Francis Higgie, to work with him, planning to make a fortune in the lumber business. From that point onward, the *Clark* served in the lumber trade shipping product from Manistee, Michigan, as well as northern Wisconsin and Michigan's Upper Peninsula, to Chicago. The Higgies did earn a fortune, however, rumor held that they cut their product from public lands without making proper payments. Although the government tried to crack down on the shipments of these contraband cargoes, it would be the weather that put an end to the *Clark's* supposed illicit activities.

## LOST

On Wednesday, June 29, 1864, running light under full sail for Oconto, Wisconsin, a little port on the west side of Green Bay, to load lumber, the *Alvin Clark* was shorthanded, with only Captain Durnin, First Mate Dunn, Seaman

The *Alvin Clark,* fully rigged as it must have looked when it entered Green Bay. *Painting by Charles L. Peterson*

Michael Cray, and two others. With the War Between the States in full swing then, sailors were difficult to find. Cray, a twenty-one-year-old transplant from Toronto, had already served his time in the Union army and so was free to pursue his career. As they passed the entrance to Sturgeon Bay, called Death's Door, the skies darkened, but the seas remained calm. Cray and the other seamen were down below. They had removed the hatch covers and stowed them to air out the ship and were sweeping out the hold to prepare for the load. Durnin was in the aft cabin recording his noon journal entry. By about 4:30 p.m., when the *Clark* was near Chambers Island, a dark cloud bank appeared on the horizon, but neither Durnin or the crew were concerned, assuming they were in for just a light shower. They took note of two other sailing vessels and a steamer nearby and all continued on. When the rain hit, visibility became limited, but the wind was light, and since they were near their destination, Durnin decided to continue under full sail. This was a decision he would soon regret for, true to its name, Death's Door was not to be regarded lightly.

A powerful gust of wind hit the *Clark*, snapping the topgallant mast. Then the topmast fell, surprising the crew. Struggling through the tangled shrouds and sails, Cray grabbed an ax to cut the forward shrouds, but before he could reach them a second gust caught the sails broadside, capsizing the vessel. Amid a mass of tangled lines and wreckage, Cray found himself walking across the port side chain plates, the iron fasteners that held the deadeyes that secured the masts. Then suddenly, a wave forced him into the now-churning waters, where he thrashed about, clawing his way back onto the side of the schooner. Nearby he saw Captain Durnin struggling in the tangled rigging, and heard him beseech, "Oh my God, do I have to drown?"

Less than a mile away, Francis Higgie, coincidentally a nephew of the owners of the *Clark*, saw the whole event unfold from his perch on the brig *Dewitt*. He watched as the storm passed almost as quickly as it came, and in its wake the *Dewitt* made its way toward the scene, lowered the yawl and managed to rescue Cray and one other seaman, but the other three had already drowned. They took note of the wreck's position, still visible above the water and passed that information on to the elder Higgies so that they could salvage the ship. The Higgies hired the services of the tug *Sarah E. Bryant* and its crew to raise the vessel, but by the time they arrived, the *Clark* had disappeared beneath the surface. It would lie hidden for 105 years. Michael Cray soon gave up sailing and relocated to a farm near Benton Harbor, Michigan, where he married, had children, and spent the balance of his life.

In early 1968, Hoffmann began acquiring the gear necessary to raise the boat. The crew decided on a lift cable system that would allow them to hoist the schooner using *Cleo*. Then, while some divers continued to pump out the interior, others began boring tunnels under the wreck through which they would thread the cables. By November 15, 1968, the crew had set all the cables in place for the lift that they hoped would take place the following summer.

Hoffmann spent the winter trying to find a place for the *Alvin Clark,* once it came up. He also tried to find money to support the project, but little was forthcoming though interest in the project was high. Harold and his brother, Jim Derusha, offered the most support. In addition to the boat *Cleo*, he fronted Hoffmann the money to pay salaries and buy equipment and fuel. With the final tasks scheduled for May and June, Hoffmann targeted July 1 for the lift, but weather pushed the date back. On July 15, the crew unstepped and raised the two masts and transported them to Marinette Marine.

On Tuesday, July 22, the divers headed out to prepare for the lift, working nearly around the clock until Wednesday morning. *Cleo* anchored over the wreck, sporting a sign with Hoffmann's motto: "Faith can move mountains." Divers secured the lift cables to the barge. The next morning the twelve members of the crew began the slow process of cranking up the wreck using four hand-cranked winches. For every one hundred turns, the wreck raised five inches. Hundreds of boaters had traveled to the site that morning and Hoffmann allowed them an up-close look at the work barge if they agreed to take a turn at the winches. By 3 p.m., they had raised the *Clark* to within sixty feet of the surface when an approaching storm caused them to run for shore with the *Clark* dangling underneath *Cleo*. Fortunately, the storm passed quickly and they anchored in about fifty feet of water with the wreck nestled into the bottom to

**A few days before the raising of the *Alvin Clark*, the masts were unstepped and lifted to the surface.** *Photograph by Bernie Bloom*

wait out the night. On Thursday morning they started cranking again, winching the boat high enough to clear the more shallow river at Menominee. After two years of work, the bowsprit finally broke the surface just forward of *Cleo*, since the *Clark* was more than twice as long as the work boat. On Friday they began the run up the river to Marinette Marine. Thousands lined the channel to share in the excitement of seeing this vessel resurrected from the deep.

It would take until the following Tuesday, July 29, for divers to prepare, check, and recheck all the equipment for the final lift, working now in less than twenty feet of water in the river. If the lifting process didn't go perfectly, the ship could be ripped in two when pulled out of water.

Cranes were positioned to lift the wreck with strong cables to free it from the suction of the water, and the pumps were situated to suck out the remaining silt. On that Tuesday morning, a crowd of fifteen thousand people watched as the ship slowly broke the surface. After 3000 dives Hoffmann and his team could finally see the entire ship, which up until now they could only see a few feet at a time. After 105 years on the bottom of Green Bay, the *Alvin Clark* had finally reached port.

Little time could be afforded for congratulations. There was still a lot of

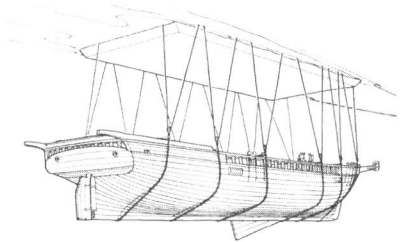

**The lifting cables in position on July 23, 1969, as the *Alvin Clark* is floated into Marinette/Menominee.** *Reprinted from Wooden Boat May/June 1983*

**This image captures the excitement of the moment when the *Alvin Clark* broke the surface after 105 years underwater.** *Milwaukee Public Library Collection*

work to be done. After pumping out the remaining silt, even employing the use of the *Clark*'s own bilge pump which still functioned, the divers carefully recovered the rest of the artifacts. They found the captain's writing desk, a brass locket, a wallet, clay pipes, a water pitcher, a clock, an oil lamp with patent date of August 11, 1863, tools, and three pennies, among hundreds of other things.

Even a crock of cheese—still full—was pulled from the ship, and deemed safe for human consumption. Although they found no markings on the ship to identify it, they did discover a metal bunk label in the fo'c'sle where the crew slept. It said, "Mich. Cray, Toronto, C. W.," probably belonging to one of the two survivors, Michael J. Cray, the only piece of evidence linking the ship to the *Alvin Clark*. With the help of Jim Quinn, director of the Nevel Public Museum, each piece was carefully cleaned and examined. The last effort was to restep the mast in preparation for the local blessing of the fleet. After more than a century underwater, the schooner actually floated on its own.

The divers enjoyed the attention that came to them after this amazing accomplishment. The public shared their enthusiasm for bringing this long-lost piece of history back into the world and had the opportunity to walk the decks of this time capsule and to go below to experience what it was like for the crew. Historians, artists, and engineers could study and document the ship without the constraints of low visibility, cold water, and scuba gear. Reporters told of the story in countless newspaper articles, magazine stories, and television documentaries. Frank Hoffmann's dream had come true: His beloved ship had been raised from the grave to have a new career as a tourist attraction, The Mystery Ship Seaport, along the new River Park near the interstate bridge joining Michigan and Wisconsin in Menominee, Michigan, supported by a $10,000 donation by the city to prepare its berth. However, everyone realized the ship could quickly dry out and decay without proper attention. Consulting

After the raising on the *Alvin Clark*, several members of the dive team pose for reporters. Left to right are Lyle Nelson, Harry Anderson, Jr., Bernie Bloom, Frank Hoffmann, James Quinn, and Gary Means. *Courtesy of Bernie Bloom*

The artifacts from the *Alvin Clark,* including the galley stove and the fo'c'sle box stove, were prominently featured in the Mystery Ship Museum in the 1970s and 1980s. After the vessel was demolished, many artifacts were parceled out to various people, but over one hundred items were donated to the Detroit Historical Society. *Milwaukee Public Library Collection*

with wood specialists, Hoffman applied a controversial steam treatment to dry the ship in a controlled manner. This helped slow the decay but would not serve to maintain it indefinitely.

The ship was designated a Michigan State Historic Site in 1972 and listed on the National Register of Historic Places in 1974. A few years later, the Coast Guard and the Smithsonian Institution acknowledged it as the oldest documented floating vessel. Hoping to cash in quickly on his efforts, Hoffmann

**An aerial view of the Mystery Ship Museum in Menominee, Michigan.**
*Courtesy of Joyce Hayward*

attempted to sell the *Clark* for a quarter million dollars to pay off his debt and make a profit. In early 1975 he began accepting bids on the ship. The City of Menominee showed interest as did the City of Trenton, Michigan, where it had been built, but neither made an offer. Hoffmann tried not to show his disappointment. He carried on with his museum, charging admission to his attraction.

By the mid-1970s, the Michigan Department of Natural Resources had begun hassling divers about taking artifacts off shipwrecks. State laws that had previously covered land-based archaeological sites were expanded to cover shipwrecks. Still seeing the *Clark* as a treasure, Hoffmann began legal proceedings to claim ownership of the vessel. In 1979, he got his wish. Under admiralty law a federal court awarded Hoffmann title to the *Alvin Clark*. In hindsight, this was the worst thing Hoffmann could have done, because he became financially responsible for the ship. However, at the time, he still thought it had value as an historical site. He even outfitted it with new sails and took it from port to port to try to generate increased support for his museum ship.

However, in the decade after the *Clark* had been exposed to the hot sun in summer and the snow in winter, it began to expand, contract, and decay. It had stabilized in the cold water, but exposure to the air would be its undoing. Unfortunately, Hoffmann had not anticipated this when he raised it. On a number of occasions he had been known to say, "We thought that once we brought it up someone else would take care of it." Proceeds from the museum came nowhere near paying off Hoffmann's incurred debt, much less providing maintenance and restoration funds. Conserving an entire ship is prohibitively expensive. The Swedish people had spent millions annually to maintain the King's warship *Vasa*. Conversely, Frank Hoffmann, a bartender, laborer, and scuba diver, had little experience with bureaucracy or grant writing.

Gate receipts at the Mystery Ship Seaport soon dropped off and by the

**To be able to walk the deck like the crew of the *Alvin Clark* had once done was an incredible experience.** *Courtesy of Dave Stevens*

early 1980s, the ship began showing more rapid signs of decay. Hoffmann desperately labored over applications for private or government grants, only to receive rejection upon rejection. Although he knew this was a mess of his own making, Hoffman found it incredulous that several organizations, like the Mackinac Island State Park Commission, had spent hundreds of thousands to build replica ships and yet no one was interested in saving the real thing. Then the Michigan Tax Tribunal began discussing whether Hoffmann would have to pay taxes on the ship. In 1984, the City of Menominee hired an appraiser to affix a tax value. The appraiser determined that although it had significant historical value it had no market value. Nonetheless, in September 1984, Menominee ruled that the ship was a private tourist attraction and subject to taxation. The frustrations of this and the last decade made Hoffmann bitter and depressed. He turned to drinking to drown his sorrows. Then his wife left him. During a drunken rage in June 1985, in which he blamed the *Alvin Clark* for his troubles, he doused the deck of the wreck with gasoline and set it on fire. He used his rifle to fend off the firemen who soon showed up, shouting, "I'm burning it down this time!" The blaze never took off and merely singed the ship. The police carted Hoffmann off to jail but eventually released him on a $5000 bond.

Realizing he was in no condition to care for the *Clark*, Hoffmann once again sought a buyer for the vessel, knowing he would not get his asking price. In 1987, Diversified Investors Group, the developer of a nearby marina, purchased it for $92,000. Diversified took it out of the water, setting it on a bed

**Fabricated stairs allowed visitors to access the cargo hold.** *Courtesy of Dave Stevens*

of pea gravel in an attempt to better preserve it and continue to keep it open as an attraction. Hoffmann, broken and bankrupt, left and settled in Florida.

Despite attempts by Diversified to save the ship, it continued to deteriorate. Eventually a storm would once again bring about the demise of this schooner. Winds blew the mast down upon the deck, tearing a hole in its side. As if following a parallel course, Hoffmann's health also declined. After years of alcohol abuse, in 1994 he suffered a stroke. He was in no condition to fight when he heard that the developer planned to construct a parking lot at the site of the *Alvin Clark*. Diversified made some attempts to find museums to acquire the artifacts and, although it is unclear how an eventual transfer occurred, the Detroit Historical Society was given more than one hundred artifacts from the ship. However, no one would take responsibility for the vessel.

Diversified ultimately decided that the cost to relocate the *Clark* outweighed its value. In May 1994, the company arranged to have the oldest merchant ship in existence bulldozed and carted off to a landfill. Frank Hoffmann followed his beloved ship to the grave just three years later.

In considering the sad saga of the *Alvin Clark*, there are many lessons to be learned—not the least of which is what can happen when an interest becomes an obsession. The fate of this schooner generated much discussion about whether shipwrecks and their associated artifacts should be recovered. The raising of this shipwreck allowed it to be studied in much greater detail than it could have been while underwater. However, had the *Alvin Clark* been

Several years after being raised, the *Alvin Clark* began to show signs of decay. After prolonged exposure to the heat of summer and the snow of winter, it began to fall apart as this view of the wheel near the stern indicates. *Courtesy of Dave Stevens*

The remains of the *Alvin Clark* are pictured in 1994 after a bulldozer knocked down the vessel and before it was carted off to a landfill. Had Hoffman left it on the bottom it would still exist. However, researchers and historians were able to study it with greater accuracy and detail when it was out of the water. *Courtesy of Joyce Hayward*

left on the bottom, divers would still be able to descend to it today. Ultimately, the fate of the *Alvin Clark* served as the partial impetus for tighter government controls over shipwrecks in the Great Lakes. Regardless, a debt is owed Hoffmann and his team for offering the rare and thrilling opportunity—if only for twenty-five short years—to see a century-old vessel rise up and out of the water and sail proudly once again.

The erect A-frame of the *Material Service* on July 30, 1936, at the site where it foundered just outside of the Calumet Harbor breakwall. *William Lafferty Collection*

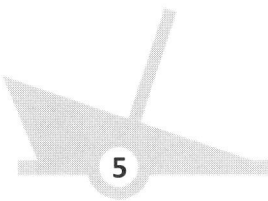

# 5

# DISASTER AND DETONATION

The long sleek shape and revolutionary design of the steel-hulled, self-unloading, sand-sucker *Material Service* generated tremendous favorable attention when it was launched, but its sinking in 1936 and the death of many crewmembers so close to shore in southern Lake Michigan spawned just the opposite attention. Four decades later, divers made the shipwreck legendary when their explosive actions once again called attention to this unique vessel.

The year after the *Carl D. Bradley's* launch as the Queen of the Lakes, another smaller, but technologically remarkable, Great Lakes self-unloader entered service. The *Material Service* would become a flagship and namesake for the Crown Brothers of Chicago, owners of the large construction supply firm Material Service Corporation. The design was credited to entrepreneur and shipbuilder Leathem D. Smith of the Leathem D. Smith Dock Company and his partner Rufus Putnam, engineer and former head of the Army Corps of Engineers' Chicago District. They conceived of a canal-sized motor vessel to operate efficiently on the Chicago area's unique waterway system. Smith and Putnam convinced the Crowns to allow their shipbuilding yard to design, construct, and then operate under their Leathem Smith-Putnam Navigation Company, a truly innovative vessel. It was intended to service the new, state-of-the-art gravel plant at Lockport on the Chicago Sanitary and Ship Canal carrying that plant's output to its various supply yards on the North and South Branches of the Chicago River, the Sanitary and Ship Canal, and Calumet River.

During World War I Smith had expanded the Leathem & Smith Towing & Wrecking Company in Sturgeon Bay, Wisconsin, by building a number of harbor tugs for the government. After the war, he turned his attention to the family's nearby stone quarry, launching a massive expansion that turned the plant, the Leathem D. Smith Stone Company, into one of the region's largest and most technically advanced stone producers. While immersed in building the stone

The *Material Service* operating as it was designed to do: passing under Chicago's bridges, this one at Monroe Street, as it heads to the North Halsted Street yard of Material Service Corporation. *William Lafferty Collection*

company, Smith devised his innovative "Leathem D. Smith Patented Tunnel Scraper System," a less costly self-unloading system using dragline scrapers as opposed to the conventional belt conveyors then in use on self-unloading lake vessels. By the time Smith and Putnam formed their partnership, Smith's shipyard, then called the Leathem D. Smith Dock Company, had converted six freighters to self-unloaders using his system and had embarked upon steel vessel construction, later earning Smith the moniker "the Frank Lloyd Wright of shipbuilding."

The proposed 240-foot by forty-foot self-unloading vessel appeared ideal for hauling Construction Material Company's product and a solution to problems that arose from the high volume of shipping in Chicago. A movement had existed in Chicago since the late 1890s to legislate regulations governing the daily and disruptive passage of vessels on the Chicago River and the Calumet River that necessitated the opening of drawbridges, causing delays to street traffic. In addition, there was another movement to curtail the sooty smoke these vessels spewed. The *Material Service*'s shallow draft, exceedingly low profile, and collapsible unloading A-frame would allow it to navigate the shallow inland waterways without requiring the opening of any bridges and its diesel engines would eliminate the smoke problem. The vessel also would carry an eighteen-inch sand dredging pump and flue, enabling it to siphon sand off the Indiana shoals, which the company had previously done by hiring out chartered sandsuckers.

The vessel's unloading operation involved raising the A-frame, which would then hoist the ninety-foot-long conveyor off the deck. The entire deck assembly consisting of A-frame, hopper, and conveyor sat on a huge swivel that could be set to almost any angle to discharge cargo. Below deck, the sand or gravel would be stored in a massive W-shaped cargo hold, then, as unloading began, hoppers would discharge it below to two tunnels that ran the length of the ship. Crescent-shaped scrapers would drag the cargo through the tunnels, up an incline, to another hopper, which would transfer it onto the deck conveyor. In this fashion, the ship's capacity of 2400 tons of cargo could be unloaded at 800 tons per hour, in other words, in just three hours.

For the seven years following its placement into service, the *Material Service* fulfilled the expectations of Smith, Putnam, and the Crowns. However, when another vessel retrofitted with Smith's tunnel scraper system, the *Andaste*, sank with all hands in September 1929, fingers pointed to the inherent dangers of his vessels. It also reminded everyone that another Smith-built self-unloader, the *Clifton,* had sunk in similar circumstances in 1924. However, the *Material Service* was of such a low profile, no one thought it could ever founder as the others had.

A typical trip for the *Material Service* would begin at the Lockport dock of the Paul Ales plant, where 1800 tons of gravel from the Material Service Corporation's quarry would be loaded on the vessel. The loaded draft was well within the controlling depth of both the Sanitary and Ship Canal and Cal-Sag Channel, so it could load a bit more above its hatch coamings, provided its destination was inland on the Sanitary and Ship Canal, Chicago River, or Calumet River, since its hatches need not be closed and secured on these voyages. However, if the *Material Service* were to venture into Lake Michigan, its coasting license required that the hatches be secured and covered with tarpaulins. Clearly, its most efficient and cost-effective operation would

**The *Material Service* unloading in 1929 at the Material Service Corporation's 92nd Street yard, about a mile from the mouth of the Calumet River.** *William Lafferty Collection*

be inland to the Material Service Corporation's four docks, but severe use restrictions on the Cal-Sag Channel often forced the vessel to instead take a route along the Sanitary and Ship Canal to the Chicago River, then into Lake Michigan for the trip south to the Calumet River.

## LOST

While the *Material Service* had been Smith's shining success, another tragedy would cause Smith concern over whether he could continue to build and operate ships. Late in the afternoon of Tuesday, July 28, 1936, the *Material Service* completed the loading of 1890 tons of gravel at the Paul Ales plant. It left Lockport under the command of Captain Brown with a crew of twenty-two, at 5:30 p.m., trip number 114 of the season, drawing twelve feet, nine inches, its maximum allowable draft for operating within ten miles of shore on the lake, and with a freeboard of two feet, six inches. Although its destination would be the Material Service yard near the mouth of the Calumet River, its master, Charles Brown, decided that the vessel would take the route along the Sanitary and Ship Canal to the Chicago River, then south down the lakeshore to the Calumet River, seeking to avoid oncoming traffic at night along the constricted Cal-Sag Channel. Anticipating no problems with rough water on the lake, Brown did not direct his crew to undertake the time-consuming process of securing the tarpaulins over the vessel's hatch covers. He had, perhaps, no indication that the weather would change.

While off the Hyde Park water crib, the wind grew fresh and the water became choppy. Second Engineer Joseph Weber of Sturgeon Bay, was surprised to discover at least two feet of water, and rising, in the vessel's engine room bilge. At first Weber started a three-inch bilge pump, and soon after, seeing it was making no headway with the rising water, he employed a six-inch pump, which also appeared to have no effect. Weber decided to ask First Mate John Johnson for permission to use the vessel's sand dredging pump to evacuate the bilge; his permission was needed since that pump was connected to the vessel's starboard propulsion engine. However, Johnson denied permission, indicating that "she was weathering it all right," and saying there was no need since the *Material Service* would be secured to the wall at the dock shortly. In fact, someone then ordered that the unloading A-frame be raised before docking, to effect a speedy unloading. However, shortly thereafter, at 1:20 a.m., the *Material Service* took on a sudden forty-five-degree list to port. "I was on deck duty with Joe Weber," related Johnson. "Suddenly, I felt the boat swerve. It listed to port. Then all hell broke loose."

Torrents of water cascaded down the main hatchway in its stern, making escape for those below deck nearly impossible, while those above found themselves buffeted by debris and water as Lake Michigan began to quickly consume the vessel. Wheelsman Joseph Melby later recalled, "I was asleep when I felt my roommate, Herbert Larson, shaking me. He said there was something wrong on deck. I jumped up and grabbed a life preserver and ran on deck."

Struggling into the vest, Melby and six other sailors managed to race up the ladder leading to the deck. Melby was caught up as a big sea swept him overboard. "I saw [my father [the other wheelsman] go down with one hand in the air."

Twenty-six-year-old Joseph Change also managed to get on deck, but recalled, "I didn't get off the boat until there was about twelve feet of water in her."

Herbert Larson managed to grab hold of a floating hatch cover.

In the pilothouse, Johnson grabbed the captain's arm to help steady him,

**The low profile of the *Material Service* is apparent when viewed from the perspective of this rare photograph.** *William Lafferty Collection*

but lost his hold when the vessel continued to lean more drastically on its side. The men were thrown down as the vessel tipped even more precariously toward its starboard side. For a moment the crew thought the ship might make it when it righted itself, but then it rapidly settled upright on the bottom of the lake just outside the Calumet Harbor breakwall.

Melby was pulled under by the suction of the sinking ship. "I could feel the cold lake water swallow me," he recalled. "Everything was black. I clung to the life preserver with both hands and I felt it lifting me to the surface. As I came to the surface I heard voices crying, 'Swim to shore!' Near him, two or three men were clinging to a piece of wreckage. "I shook the water from my eyes," he continued, "and turned around several times trying to sight some lights on the shore so I would know which direction to swim. Finally I got my bearings and started out." Elton Washburn, a handyman, was one of the other men Melby encountered. He found himself in the water where he grabbed hold of a plank to keep him afloat.

Several of the crewmembers had escaped to the main deck, but at least four men were trapped inside when the *Material Service* sank. Seven men had made it into the water, including the captain. They flailed about in the choppy seas between the northerly arm of the Calumet breakwall and the submerged vessel, clinging to pieces of the pilothouse's wooden interior and the cover of the vessel's one lifeboat that no one had had time to properly launch. From his plank, Elton Washburn attempted to keep a struggling Captain Brown above water. As the captain thrashed about, Washburn heard him exclaim something that would later be considered quite correct, "It was those damn hatch covers!"

Newspaper reports conflict on what happened next: Either a flare set off from the deck of the *Material Service* just before its fatal plunge or the cries of crewmen in the water attracted the attention of A. E. Pierce, keeper of the Calumet Harbor light, who immediately summoned surfboats from both the Jackson Park and South Chicago Coast Guard stations. They found the site easily in the dark. Searchlights illuminated the still upright A-frame and bow light staff visible above the surface.

Within twenty minutes of the sinking, the life-savers pulled Melby, Washburn, Webber, and Change into the surfboats, while the tug *New Jersey* of the Great Lakes Towing Company, which had been sitting with steam up at its owner's dock just a few blocks from *the Material Service*'s intended destination, rescued Halgert Hansen and Larson. The last survivor, Joe Johnson, swam to within a few yards of the Calumet Harbor light, where Pierce threw him a life preserver and hauled him onto the breakwall.

Captain Brown, the Chief Engineer, and thirteen others perished in the tragic accident. Many were trapped in their berths, drowned in the water, or were pulled under by suction. Several weeks later, on June 24, a waterlogged lifebelt from the *Material Service* washed ashore in Sturgeon Bay, Wisconsin, just one mile from the site of the *Material Service's* launching, a trip of over 250 miles.

The survivors were taken to a hospital in South Chicago. The only one hurt was Washburn, whose left leg and right shoulder were cut. The rest suffered from exhaustion and shock. Melby was despondent because his father, John Melby, the forty-nine-year-old wheelsman, was among the missing.

Once Leathem Smith heard about the tragedy, he found himself in the uncomfortable position of having to speculate as to why yet another vessel that incorporated his self-unloading equipment had foundered with heavy loss of life. He reasoned that, given the suddenness of the loss of the *Material Service*, it must have hit the Calumet Shoal and opened its hull plates. However, when it was pointed out that there existed at least twenty feet of water over that bar, and the *Material Service* drew less than thirteen feet, Smith countered with the hypothesis that it had hit the shoal in the trough between two heavy seas.

Meanwhile, the local Bureau of Marine Inspection and Navigation office convened an inquiry for the evening of July 29, 1936, seeking testimony from crewmembers and rescuers. This would be the first such inquiry under a new law that allowed the Bureau, Justice Department, and Coast Guard to conduct speedy inquiries and to wield broader powers in affixing blame. From the testimony of the surviving crewmembers, several theories emerged as to what caused the disaster. The least credible centered on the possibility that the vessel had become unduly top-heavy in the seas with the raising of its self-unloading boom's A-frame, which had been elevated before the *Material Service* had gained the protection of the breakwater, despite a navigation rule that it should not be raised in moderate or heavier seas. Another posed that the vessel had somehow, perhaps by striking a submerged object, shipped water throughout the lengths of its self-unloading tunnels. A third, matching Smith's explanation, conjectured that the vessel had found the bottom between two waves. However, a consistency among the testimony of every surviving member of the *Material Service's* crew was that tarpaulins had not been fastened over the vessel's hatch covers. Moreover, testimony from Coast Guardsmen who had participated in the survivors' rescues indicated that several had said that not even the hatch covers had been secured, let alone the tarps.

The hastily convened inquiry swiftly reached a conclusion: Captain William Nicholas of the Bureau of Marine Inspection and Navigation, conducting the inquiry, told the *Chicago Daily News* that the disaster resulted from Captain Brown's "failure to order the hatches battened down." While answers were sought on land as to the causes of the tragedy, the Great Lakes Dredge & Dock Company dispatched a diving crew aboard Walt Bruzser's wooden gas tug *Mayflower* to search the wreckage for bodies. News footage of that gruesome task showed divers hauling a naked body aboard the tug. It and other bodies were sent to Emmerlings, a Hammond, Indiana, funeral home to await an inquest there, since the *Material Service* had foundered in Indiana waters. Within two weeks of the sinking, Great Lakes Dredge & Dock employees removed the vessel's light staff and A-frame, and placed a spar buoy above the hull. Meanwhile, to keep operational, the Material Service Corporation contracted with towboat operator R. V. Warner of Memphis to shuttle barges among its yards and the Paul Ales plant to augment the firm's steam tug *Sol R. Crown*.

Two months after the loss of the *Material Service*, Smith signed a $75,000 contract with Sincennes-McNaughton Lines Ltd. (Sin-Mac), of Montreal, a well-known lake towing and salvage firm that boasted among its employees the famous Captain Tom Reid, son of the successful wrecker James Reid, who had attempted to raise the *Cayuga* decades earlier (as described in Chapter One). Reid's first order of business was to try to locate the bodies of three crewmen who had died in the wreck. He selected his diver Dave Seagrave (whose name seemed ironically suitable for the work to which he was assigned). The half-crazed wife of the engineer, one of those missing, stood vigil on the work boat as Seagrave went down. He scouted around inside the below-deck cabins, but had no success. Before surfacing, he closed the portholes in preparation for the effort to pump the hull with water to raise it. He found one porthole resistant and as he struggled with it, he felt a nudging against his back. Turning to investigate, he saw before him a dead body, and though accustomed to this work, this grim incident unnerved him. He managed to ease the body through a small opening, but it was so bloated that as he brought it up, it got away from him and bobbed up and nearly out of the water. The body turned out to be the engineer, whose widow had, unfortunately, witnessed it surfacing. Eventually, the other bodies were recovered as well.

Salvage operations commenced. The workers were able to recover most of the gravel cargo and seal up the vessel by early December, when Sin-Mac abandoned the job for the winter. Work continued in late summer of 1937, but air pumped into the vessel's hull in hope of raising it instead blew out parts of its deck and after section. Reid had studied the blueprints carefully and had expected the structure to withstand the pressure, but he later learned that substantial changes had been made that had not been disclosed. This led Reed and Sin-Mac to abandon the contract for good.

The liability charges against Captain Brown would normally have made the recovery of insurance against the *Material Service* by the Leathem Smith-Putnam Navigation Company a straightforward process: An insured can collect if the negligence of a vessel's officers or crew was a contributing factor in this loss. However, attorneys for the insurance company did not accept the captain's negligence as cause. Digging into the vessel's records, they found that during April and May of 1936, the *Material Service* received a modification of its sandsucking equipment that "consisted in cutting, by acetylene torch, 48 eight-inch holes in twelve hatch covers, and installing heavy flumes which emptied into the holes." In that method, as the sand accumulated in the hoppers, water would be removed from the hoppers by gravity before the sand passed through the screens and into the vessel's hold. Apparently, this proved a much more efficient means of dewatering and stowing the sand than afforded by the system previously in use on the *Material Service*. It is not in the least clear, from newspaper accounts or court testimony, if the entire system had been put in place by the time of the vessel's loss, although it is likely only the holes to accommodate the spouts from the hoppers had been completed by July 1936. This may also be the reason the salvage effort failed. The insurance companies covering the *Material Service* refused to pay claims amounting to over $200,000, including fees for the unsuccessful salvage by Sin-Mac. Smith instituted suit in the Federal District Court in Milwaukee in January 1937, forcing payment, but in May the presiding judge dismissed Smith's claim. Smith appealed, but the appellate court upheld the original dismissal. Both courts found that, on the morning of July 29, 1936, the *Material Service* was in an "unseaworthy condition" because of those holes, and so the insurers were not bound to pay the claims. With its only paying asset sitting in twenty-five feet of water off the Calumet breakwall, the Leathem Smith-Putnam Navigation Company defaulted on its mortgages, and as a result, the official enrollment document of the *Material Service* could not be surrendered. It remained a documented vessel, despite it being underwater.

The loss of the *Material Service* would be a great financial blow to Smith's shipbuilding firm, but just as war helped build the company in the late 1910s, war would again save the company in the 1940s. In 1943 Smith sold the remains of the *Material Service* to Captain William Nicholson of River Rouge, Michigan, a well-known lake vessel operator, who, in the midst of the World War II demand for tonnage, intended to raise and refurbish it, or at least reclaim what he could for scrap. However, his efforts, begun in August 1945, came to naught. Additionally, between 1941 and 1945, Smith would build nearly one hundred vessels for the government, but he would not live to see the fruits of his labor. He died, coincidently, in much the same manner as those on board his three cursed self-unloaders, the *Clifton, Andaste,* and *Material Service* (incidentally, not far from where the wreck of the *Alvin Clark* waited patiently to be found). In June 1946, his sailing sloop *Half Moon* foundered in a sudden squall in the Lake Michigan waters of Green Bay in Wisconsin. Smith and three others, including shipyard supervisor Elton Washburn, who had a decade earlier survived the sinking of the *Material Service*, perished. Only Smith's daughter survived.

**FOUND**

Little more than two decades after the *Material Service* sank, a very active shipwreck diving community developed on Lake Michigan and in the other Great Lakes as well. Divers began discovering shipwrecks by various means. Initially, they focused on ships that sank in shallow water and for which good historical information existed to pinpoint the site. Some divers searched by dragging grappling hooks behind a boat, not unlike the wreckers of a century past. Others were towed on underwater sled-like devices, hoping to run into a shipwreck (literally). When divers did find a wreck, however, they often had difficulty relocating it because the technology to record a location did not exist. All they could do was triangulate the position by referencing features on land. The advent of fathometers and Loran-C positioning devices in the late 1960s provided those who could afford them the tools to search for, find, and relocate shipwrecks. This period marked the heyday for shipwreck hunters, among them, John Steele of northern Illinois and Gene Turner of Indiana (who are mentioned in Chapter One in connection with the discovery of the *Cayuga*) and who are credited with many early discoveries in Lake Michigan. Other early and successful Lake Michigan shipwreck hunters included Dick Race, Kent Bellrichard, Chuck and Jeri Feltner, Steve Radovan, Fred Leete, Paul Ehorn, Dan Johnson, and Jerry Guyer, some of whom are still actively searching today. These early explorers were collectively responsible for making Lake Michigan a rich playground of historic attractions that enticed many people into the sport of scuba diving.

Although exactly who initially found the wreck of the *Material Service* has been lost to time, it would not have been too difficult to locate. Photographs of its A-frame still protruding above the water, taken in the days after its sinking, showed the wreck's relationship to the breakwall off the Calumet Harbor. A boat ride out to the general vicinity with photograph in hand, and a few passes back and forth when the shoreline appeared similar to the picture, may have resulted in a telltale bump on a bottom finder.

A *Chicago Sun Times* photograph published on August 15, 1960, shows two divers, Frank Lockwood and John Kostvol, posing by the recovered telegraph of the *Material Service*. This image depicts the early motivation for locating shipwrecks: the opportunity to be among the first to recover artifacts. Some sought out artifacts as a souvenir of their accomplishment, others for personal collections, still others offered the artifacts for sale to collectors or museums. It was generally accepted that whoever spent the money on a boat and scuba gear, and the time and effort to find a wreck, deserved a piece of it. A telegraph, ship's wheel, or an anchor were among the most coveted of artifacts. Steam whistles, portholes, binnacles, deadeyes, and dishes were other sought-after items. Great Lakes ships rarely carried traditional treasure of gold or silver, but

**Divers Frank Lockwood (left) and John Kostval are pictured proudly displaying the recently recovered telegraph from the *Material Service* in an August 1960 *Chicago Sun Times* news article.** *Courtesy of Allan Petrulus*

to Midwestern divers these artifacts were the treasure.

At the time of the *Material Service*'s discovery, statutes within admiralty law, a distinct body of law which governs maritime questions and offenses, regulated the salvage of sunken property from shipwrecks long ago abandoned by their owners or insurance companies. This was often referred to as the "finders-keepers" law: Those who found a shipwreck could claim ownership of the vessel and its artifacts through specific legal procedures. Early Great Lakes' divers operated under this finders-keepers law, but rarely followed legal protocol. Since there existed no enforcement for such oversights, small-scale pilfering became common and acceptable.

First dives on the wreck of the *Material Service* revealed the presence of salvage cables still strung under the keel and hogging in the hull caused by the 1936-1937 salvage attempt. Other than that, the steel ship was virtually intact and among the few that had been found off Chicago offering any opportunities for exploration inside a ship. The lure of such a challenging dive in only thirty-five feet of water and the potential of finding artifacts inside the wreck made the *Material Service* one of the premier diving sites in lower Lake Michigan, especially a draw to new divers. Chicagoan Larry Czachor, a member of the SeaDucers Dive Club, made his checkout dive on the *Material Service* in

**A view taken from inside the cargo hold on the wreck of the _Material Service_.**
_Photograph by Cris Kohl_

the early 1970s. By then, divers had stripped any salvageable artifacts off the deck and outer hull. To find any other artifacts, Czachor would have to try to locate a way into the ship. However, sand and silt had made their way into the many passages that once allowed the crew access below deck. Czachor recalled that he found a passage into the engine room, but sand restricted his access so much so that he had to remove his tank and fins, push the tank through the narrow opening, and follow behind it. One such entry netted him a brass electrical panel from a switchboard. Only those daring enough to go to those lengths could claim that kind of "treasure."

Allan Petrulus, a diver, harbor master at Monroe Harbor, and an all-around handyman on the water, also took great interest in the _Material Service_. He began diving the wreck with a charter operator in the late 1960s soon after it became a popular site. Like those before him, he intended to score an artifact. However, there was stiff competition between divers. One time Petrulus spent an entire dive unfastening a porthole and only had time to secure it to a line that he had rigged to a floating buoy. By the time he surfaced to haul up his prize, another diver had already hauled it up and claimed it for himself. To avoid this in the future, Petrulus bought his own boat and only took divers out who would play by his rules. In 1973 when scrap metal value was high, Petrulus developed a plan to salvage the _Material Service_ piece by piece. In mid-January 1974, he contacted the Material Service Corporation seeking the legal standing of the wreck. Within one month, Howard Turner of the legal department at Material

Service asserted his company's ownership of the shipwreck and through a quitclaim agreement (which by its nature admits that ownership is not certain) offered to transfer any and all of the company's interest to Petrulus. The proposed agreement also would transfer all liability for the wreck from the company to Petrulus. Unwilling to accept the liability, Petrulus never signed the agreement. In time, though, he abandoned his plans to scrap out the wreck when he realized the effort would cost more than the return.

His next goal involved raising one of the propellers from the vessel for a memorial at the Burnham Harbor Yacht Club. He contacted club officials to make a case for the memorial to honor the fifteen men lost and to heed a mindful warning to all who travel on Lake Michigan that disaster can strike even a massive steel ship. The club, however, did not accept his offer. All that was left for Petrulus to do was recover any artifacts or personal possessions that other divers had not yet found. He knew many items still remained buried deep inside the silted-in hull.

Petrulus' method to reach those artifacts would have made Leathem D. Smith, the designer and builder of this revolutionary vessel, cringe had he been alive. One summer afternoon, Petrulus headed his boat *Grubber*, named in recognition of his own talents, out of Monroe Harbor and south to the wreck. He took several dive buddies along including a newly sworn-in police officer and diver, who hesitated to get in the boat when he saw the specialized equipment Petrulus had brought with him that day: two small thirty-eight-cubic-foot tanks filled with gunpowder, each with a long cord extending out of the neck.

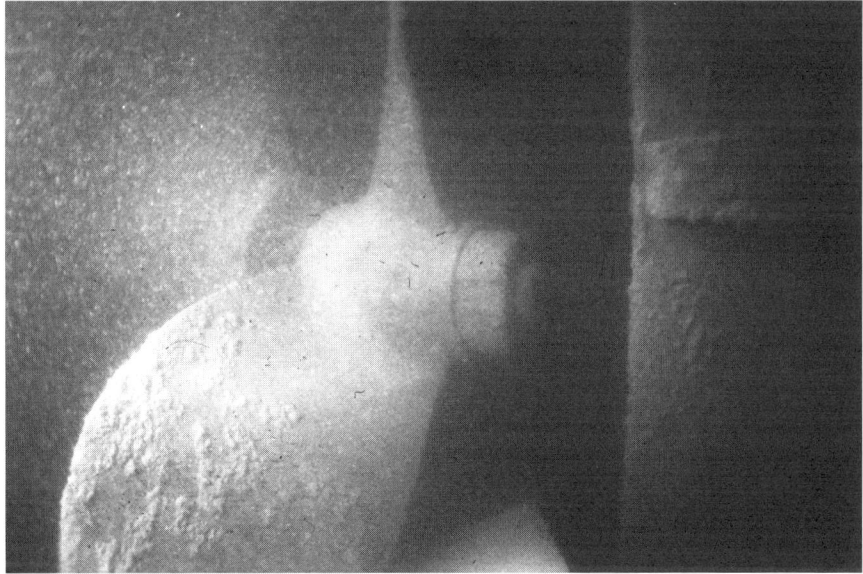

**The propeller that Allan Petrulus hoped to salvage remains on the *Material Service*.**
*Photograph by Larry Czachor circa 1984*

**(Upper) An access hatch to the forward engine room is invitingly open. Inside (lower) is a generator that would have supplied power to the unloading equipment.** *Photograph by Larry Czachor circa 1984*

After anchoring on the wreck, Petrulus geared up, clutched the two small tanks under his arm, jumped in, and headed down. He carefully positioned the explosive devices strategically near the stern where he had calculated the detonation would create openings large enough to both access the interior and wash away sand blocking the passageway. After he and the other divers surfaced and retrieved their anchor and line, he turned on his movie camera, lit the fuses, and waited with anticipation. About thirty seconds later he heard a muffled boom, saw through his camera lens a huge air bubble breaking the surface, and felt his boat rise on the crest of an aftershock wave. However, the explosion did not seem as big as he expected. Petrulus and his divers headed back to Monroe Harbor, intending to return another day after the silt had settled and the water cleared to see what his homemade bombs had accomplished. Incidentally, for fun, he would eventually set his movie footage to Wagner's classical score "Flight of the Valkyries," though that footage has long been lost.

As it turns out, Larry Czachor made a dive on the wreck before Petrulus returned. He was surprised to see that everything in the stern had changed, and knew immediately that the damage was not natural. When Czackor found a tank with a length of fuse coming out of its neck, he realized what had been done, and also realized the job had not been completed. He hightailed it out of the water, unsure if the other tank might still explode. Word traveled quickly after that, and news of Petrulus' handiwork spread. Someone quickly retrieved the dud tank. Then the dive community got back to exploring the wreck once again with new areas opened up for their inspection. A side effect of Petrulus' deed was that he did make the wreck safer by opening up tight areas that may have trapped other divers intent on getting inside. This "incident" became legendary among Chicago divers, but the details have not been published until now.

These were "the glory years" of diving, according to the first generation of divers. However, change was afoot in the mid-1970s. Divers began to realize that they were ruining their own dive sites. In 1977 in Wisconsin, a group of divers realized how information could be lost if shipwreck artifacts were recovered without proper documentation and scattered out among many divers. Led by LaMonte Florentz, this group set out to conduct an archaeological examination of the newly discovered schooner *Lucerne* in the Apostle Island area of Lake Superior. They recovered over 200 artifacts in collaboration with the Canal Park Maritime Museum, and began conservation efforts intending the artifacts to reside in perpetuity at that institution rather than in the basements of the divers. Unfortunately, Florentz died before the work could be completed, but to this day the artifacts remain on display at the museum, now called the Lake Superior Marine Museum.

Activities like the raising of the *Alvin Clark*, the explosive damage on the *Material Service,* and myriad other cases of shipwreck stripping gave rise to a government movement to regulate diving activities on shipwrecks, something that John Cronin and Ralph Erickson, the founders of PADI (as mentioned in the introduction), had tried so hard to avoid.

The damage done to the *Material Service* and pilfering from it and other wrecks in Indiana waters infuriated Gary Ellis, who at the time served as Indiana's state archaeologist. He realized that shipwrecks are nonrenewable resources and became incensed that divers were decimating these historical vessels for their own pleasure or profit. Although a terrestrial archaeologist, Ellis took it upon himself to become certified in scuba diving and then, in addition to his responsibilities for managing Indiana's land-based historical sites, organized a shipwreck program in Indiana to locate, identify, and evaluate the shipwrecks in Indiana water of Lake Michigan. Although Indiana claims the smallest portion of Lake Michigan bottomlands and the fewest number of shipwrecks of any of the Great Lakes states, Ellis' Submerged Artifact and Vessel Evaluation Program (SAVE) became one of the first such shipwreck preservation programs in the Great Lakes. Ellis trained conservation officers in underwater archaeological techniques to help conduct the surveys and made presentations to charter boat owners, dive store owners, and clubs soliciting the assistance of divers to survey the wrecks, essentially encouraging them to give up their crowbars and gunpowder and take up pencils and cameras instead.

The *Material Service* would be among the first wrecks surveyed by Ellis and one he would remember not only for being a unique vessel, but also because it could have cost him his life. While measuring one of the deck winch spools, part of the unloading system, the wire shifted and slid over his wrist, pinning his hand to the winch. His dive partner alerted members of the dive crew, who worked to free his hand using a pry bar. Ellis would breath down several additional tanks of air, brought down to him by his team, before they could free him. This incident served as an example to other divers that shipwrecks can be unstable and caution should be taken on any dive to avoid interacting with the wrecks.

A number of divers jumped at the new opportunities to get involved in surveying shipwrecks with Ellis, but others chose to continue doing as they pleased. Over several years, Ellis and a small group of dedicated volunteer divers documented fourteen shipwrecks including passenger boats, freighters, and car ferries, as well as the *Material Service*. The program would serve as a model that would help lead to a shift in diver attitudes toward historic shipwrecks.

**A side view of the wreck, completed during Indiana's survey of the wreck, shows the low profile of the *Material Service* and the deck plan, prepared some years later, shows the damage from explosives to the stern.** *Side view by Gary Ellis and deck plan by the author*

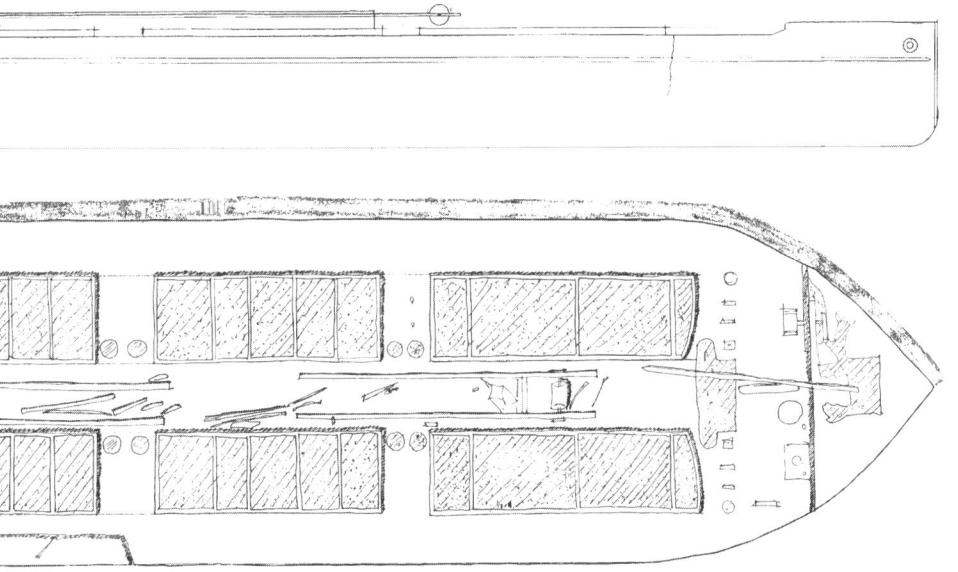

The wheel of the *Rockaway* moments after it was recovered from the lake bottom during an archaeological survey in the early 1980s. *Courtesy of Kenneth Pott*

# 6

# LOSS AND GAIN

The scow-schooner *Rockaway*, lost in a storm in 1891, became legendary after its discovery in 1983 in the waters off South Haven, Michigan, when the wreck became the subject of the first complete archaeological excavation on the American side of the Great Lakes. The seeds that led to that project began in the late 1970s when Michigan divers had a collective revelation.

"We finally saw the irony that we were actually degrading our own dive sites by stripping them of everything of aesthetic and historic interest," recalled Pete Lindquist of Munising, Michigan. Lindquist and other Michigan divers banded together and lobbied Michigan state government to designate certain areas with a high concentration of shipwrecks as underwater "museums" where the removal of artifacts would be illegal. The state legislators listened and acted, taking a lead over other states perhaps because Michigan claims more bottomlands, and proportionately more shipwrecks, than any other Great Lakes state. In 1980, Michigan passed Public Act 184 which afforded protection for shipwrecks determined to have cultural and recreational value. The Act authorized the establishment of bottomland preserves limited to no more than 400 square miles each, and no more than five percent of all Michigan bottomlands. The next year, Michigan designated both the Alger and Thunder Bay Underwater Preserves. Successful experiences in those initial preserves led to the establishment of preserves in the Straits of Mackinac and the Thumb Area in Lake Huron. The state established stiff penalties for salvaging anything from shipwrecks within preserve boundaries. Those caught removing anything from a shipwreck could have their boat, car, and equipment confiscated and could face up to two years imprisonment and large fines.

Although Public Act 184 took a step in the direction of institutional management of shipwrecks, it did not authorize any funds for the preserves or related law enforcement. However, volunteer organizations and special interest groups sprang up largely to champion documentation and preservation of shipwrecks and to act as watchdogs to protect the wrecks. Some divers who had previously collected artifacts gave that up and took up underwater photography instead. This new movement in Michigan generated the attention of underwater archaeologists, who started to become interested in Great Lakes shipwrecks. As with all other branches of archaeology, underwater archaeology evolved from its roots in pre-history, but could not develop until the technology to work underwater became readily available. Because it emerged not only from the technology of land-based archaeology, but also from the skills and tools developed by shipwreck salvagers, it took awhile to be considered as a bona fide branch of the profession. When universities began teaching maritime archaeology in the late 1970s, it became broadly accepted as the study of human life, behaviors, and cultures in, on, and around the water. The active diving community, the new laws, and the new profession of underwater archaeology would all unite upon the discovery of the *Rockaway*.

## FOUND

On September 29, 1983, the *Captain Nichols*, a charter fishing boat based in South Haven, snagged its anchor on something about three miles northwest of South Haven's channel in sixty-five feet of water. Despite attempts to retrieve it, the anchor seemed hopelessly stuck. Captain Don Nichols affixed a buoy to the end of his anchor line, and took the vessel in to get the assistance of his brother Robert, a diver. Robert made it out to the site of the anchor later that day and discovered an interesting irony: The *Captain Nichols'* anchor had become entwined in the anchor chain of a shipwreck. During his dive, Nichols noted that the ship's hull structure was broken up. The deck was gone and the sides had fallen outward, exposing the main keelson and floor of the vessel. The highest feature was a centerboard trunk that stood about eight feet off the bottom. This convinced him the ship had been a sailing vessel.

After recovering his brother's anchor, he shared the news with Kenneth Pott, an anthropologist, maritime archaeologist, the curator of the Michigan Maritime Museum in South Haven, and a diver. Pott took interest in the new find and made a trip out to dive the wreck. In addition to significant sections of the vessel's hull, Pott noted a wide range of artifacts, including a pile of chain, hand tools, fastenings, rigging gear, and other nautical items, including the ship's wheel. The presence of these portable and coveted artifacts indicated that the wreck had not previously been found. Pott knew that the untouched wreck could reveal some important information. He also knew that recent state regulations would mandate the proper way to conduct an investigation. He turned to John Halsey, then Michigan's state archaeologist, who had been involved in the development of Michigan Public Act 184, to discuss the discovery. Although the *Rockaway* was not within a preserve, they decided to approach it as if it were and conduct a preliminary survey to attempt to identify the wreck and determine if it could yield important archaeological information.

During subsequent dives that fall, Pott and a group of volunteer divers were able to measure, videotape, and photograph the wreck. Combing through records, Pott and other researchers developed a list of sailing vessels that had been lost within a ten-mile radius of the port of South Haven. Only one matched the dimensions and location of the wreck: the scow schooner *Rockaway*.

Launched on November 13, 1866, at the Chandler, Alvord & Company shipyard at Oswego, New York, the *Rockaway* began what would be a long career hauling a multitude of cargoes on four of the five Great Lakes. With a length of 111 feet, a width of 24 feet, and two masts, it was considered large at the time of its build, ranking in gross tonnage among the top ten percent of the scow schooners ever to sail the Great Lakes. The *Oswego Commercial Advertiser and Times* described it as "staunch and trim, sliding gracefully down the ways and out into her native element." The scows were a variation of the typical Great Lakes schooner, having flat bottoms and hard bilges. Some had the traditional "V bow" and bowsprit seen on schooners, others had a "barrel bow" design, and still others, like the *Rockaway*, had a semi-rounded "spoon bow." One of the main differences was the shape of the bilge. The scow was more angular than a schooner, which allowed it to carry more cargo. Considered first-class at the time of its build, the *Rockaway* had only a seven-

During Kenneth Pott's first dive on the wreck that he later identified as the *Rockaway*, he became convinced it had not previously been found because of the large number of artifacts scattered over the site. An encrusted plate is visible in the center of this image. *Courtesy of Kenneth Pott*

**No photographs have been found of the *Rockaway*; however, this image of the scow schooner *Augustus* shows the spoon bow and boxy shape indicative of a scow.** *C. Patrick Labadie Collection - Alpena County Public Library*

foot depth of hold, which indicated that the builders intended to use it in the shallowest harbors. The vessel had a centerboard, an innovation developed several decades earlier, that could be dropped when in deep water to provide stability and maneuverability.

The *Rockaway* was originally assessed at a value of $8000, a significant sum at the time. Chandler and Alvord built it for their own use to ship raw materials to their yard, as well as to carry consigned cargoes for other businesses. Although built for the lumber trade, the *Rockaway* was adaptively used to distribute a wide range of other materials. It carried cargoes ranging from salt, produce, and packaged goods, to the more common coarse bulk freights of lumber, coal, and iron ore. It even carried grain, a commodity which most scow schooners were restricted from carrying per their supposed "unseaworthy" condition. In its first two years, the *Rockaway* carried cargoes from U.S. ports on Lakes Ontario and Erie across the lakes to Canada. On a few occasions, it hauled salt west into Lakes Erie, Huron, and Michigan and brought grain east on return trips. Over the next twelve years, the *Rockaway* changed hands six times, but continued to operate mainly on Lakes Ontario and Erie, maintaining Oswego as its home port. Its career spanned both good and bad economic times. The tragic fire in Chicago in 1871 created the need for a great deal of raw material throughout the Midwest to help rebuild and resupply the city. This put the *Rockaway*, along with every other operational craft, in great demand. However, the stock market crash of 1873 and the five-year depression following it resulted in the *Rockaway* being frequently laid up. By the time the financial climate brightened, the *Rockaway* had been downgraded to a B-2 rating, which meant it should carry only nonperishable cargoes like lumber and iron ore.

A rebuild in 1877 prepared the *Rockaway* for the resurgence of the economy and the shipment of lumber. No place on the Great Lakes was quite as rife with timber as western Michigan. In 1880, Muskegon lumberman Winfield Scott Gerrish purchased the *Rockaway*. Gerrish was among the leading lumber producers in Muskegon. His mill's position on Lake Muskegon and its connection to the Muskegon River, one of the longest tributaries in the state, gave him access to the rich inland forests. In 1880 alone, Muskegon's numerous lumber producers shipped a record 590 million board feet of lumber and the *Rockaway* carried its fair share that year. The next year, a partnership between Muskegon lumbermen William Brinen and Thomas Munroe purchased the *Rockaway* and gave a one-quarter interest to Captain Ole Thompson, who would take command of the scow.

Thompson lived in Chicago with his wife and children and kept up a regular schedule back and forth from that city to ports along the shores of western Michigan to pick up lumber, frequently spending time with his family during the unloading process. The owners also decided to lay up the *Rockaway* in Chicago each winter where Thompson could keep an eye on it. The *Rockaway* had not experienced, up to this time, any major calamities. However, the violent storm of November 1883 that claimed dozens of ships nearly sank the *Rockaway*.

Thompson left Muskegon for Chicago on November 10, with a full load of lumber and with a crew of five. Just a few hours out of port, a fierce north wind blew in, snow began falling, and the waves battered the craft and its crew. Ice built up on every surface of the scow, including its masts, equipment, and the deck cargo. Soon, the frozen vessel became unmanageable. At the mercy of the winds, it was blown west for two days and its crew had no time to sleep or eat as they struggled to keep it afloat. Finally, they saw shore and managed to raise a flag of distress, which caught the attention of the Kenosha Life-Saving crew. When the life-savers managed to reach the struggling scow some hours later, they found the crew near death with frostbite and hunger, helpless to do anything to save themselves. The Life-Saving crew caught the attention of a local tug and secured the *Rockaway* for the tow into the harbor. It is certainly a testament to Thompson and his crew that after they had come so close to dying, they managed to carry on with their journey after just a few hours rest and several hours chipping ice off their ship. Thompson later offered profuse thanks to the crew at Kenosha for saving the men and his ship.

The next eight years saw ups and downs in the lumber business including labor strikes, economic struggles, competition, and an industry resurgence in 1887 when Muskegon broke its own record and shipped an all-time high of 700 million board feet of lumber out of its home port. At almost a quarter-century old, an age when some sailing vessels were converted to barges, the

*Rockaway* was overhauled to continue in the trade. In July and August of 1891, its owners had the Muskegon Booming Company rebuild the hull, add new frames and new keelsons, and recaulk the entire ship. However, the *Rockaway* would see little more than two months of service before a storm, like the devastating one in 1883, would claim it for good.

## LOST

On November 16, 1891, the *Rockaway* left Ludington, Michigan, bound for Benton Harbor, Michigan, about 130 miles south, carrying 200,000 board feet of freshly milled lumber. Captain Ole Thompson commanded the vessel and looked forward to the winter layup scheduled after this last trip of the season. His son, A. Thompson, sailed as first mate, along with seamen Andrew Larson and James Swanson, carpenter Martin Oleson, and machinist Louis Rees. As part-owner, Thompson would have had a choice in deciding whether to make this voyage. He knew the trip could be risky considering the notorious gales of November. However, unlike the trip in 1883, which nearly killed him, he would not need to cross the treacherous lake. Perhaps this, plus the high fee he would receive for a November trip, persuaded him to make the run. That trip alone would yield a tidy sum to get him through the long winter.

By the next afternoon, the *Rockaway* had reached a point just south of Saugatuck, Michigan, but the weather that Thompson risked defying instead defied him. What had been fresh winds, soon turned to near gale force straight out of the west. Even if he had considered turning into the Saugatuck harbor, the huge surf along shore would have made it impossible to navigate safely into the small channel. Instead, Thompson tried to take shelter in the lee of the land, but as he turned a few points more east than south, the scow's mainsail was blown to shreds and the foreboom and gaff sails were ripped from the ship. The high winds and freezing temperatures, like those he had experienced in the November gale eight years earlier, did not allow him to navigate the ship. Once again he found the *Rockaway* adrift at the mercy of the winds. The waves crested over the deck and leaking seams between the planking filled the hold, forcing the crew to start operating the pumps. Within just a few hours of constant use and in the freezing temperatures, the pumps failed. As unstaunched water built up, the *Rockaway* rode dangerously low in the water, so the crew began hurling portions of the deck cargo overboard to lighten the load. However, the wind continued to blow them southeast.

By dusk, the ship had reached a point just a few miles northwest of South Haven. Thompson realized that if he did not take action, his ship would be dashed to pieces in the shallows. He gave the order to set anchor and hoped that it would hold against the powerful winds. Through the night, water continued to fill the scow, even washing into the aft cabin. The crewmen were forced to huddle on deck to keep from freezing. One of the men was able to locate an iron kettle from below and build a small fire in it, allowing the crew to warm their hands. It must have been the worst night any of them had ever experienced. Just as the first streaks of daylight appeared the next morning, the crew raised a flag of distress.

Fortunately for them, Surfman William Webster, on lookout duty at South Haven's Life-Saving station, spotted the schooner, its distress flag, and even noticed the glow of a small fire on deck. He alerted station captain John H. McKenzie, who sent one of his crew to request the services of the steam barge *Lorain L* to tow the schooner into South Haven. When the captain of that vessel refused to help because the seas posed too great a risk, McKenzie had no alternative but to launch the station's surfboat. By 6:30 a.m., the crew had the boat in the water, but it took them over an hour and a half to reach the stranded vessel, an amazing feat considering that a much bigger boat chose not to go out in that weather. The South Haven Life-Savers found the crew in a pitiful condition just as the Kenosha Life-Savers had found them eight years earlier. Only two of the six men could actually move independently and the Life-Saving crew had to assist the others. First mate Thompson's hands were frozen so badly that the crew was almost sure he would lose them. Somehow in the raging waters, they managed to transfer all of the men to the lifeboat, then secure a cork life jacket on each.

By 10:45 a.m., they reached the South Haven station, where both crews changed into dry clothing, downed gallons of warm coffee, and ate a hearty breakfast. Medical attention saved Mate Thompson's hands. Captain Thompson remained optimistic that once the weather calmed, the *Rockaway* could be towed in. The next day, he arranged for a tow, then caught the train north to Muskegon to report the accident to his partners. The tug *Paine*, the schooner *Daisy,* and the Life-Saving crew headed back out to the *Rockaway*. However, as they neared the spot, they realized they would not be towing the ship. Overnight, the *Rockaway* had sunk. All they could see were about fifteen feet of the foretopmast, and a portion of the main topmast sticking above the water. They returned to South Haven empty-handed.

Three days later, pieces of a schooner, some lumber, and lath washed ashore at Holland, Michigan. It was undoubtedly from the *Rockaway*, although two other schooners had gone down in the same storm farther north. The loss of the vessel and its cargo was a great misfortune for the owners since it was not insured. Several newspapers reported the hardship faced by Thompson, who despite holding only one-quarter interest in the vessel, had his life savings tied up in it. Fortunately for him, many friends within the predominantly Scandinavian communities that then occupied areas of the Chicago waterfront were sympathetic to his plight. They held a dinner dance benefit in his honor at the Aurora Turner Hall and about 200 couples attended. The funds raised were the equivalent of about three months' salary for the captain and so would help get his family through the winter. He would eventually sail again, taking command of the Muskegon-based lumber schooner *Lyman M. Davis*.

Over the winter of 1983-1984, Kenneth Pott developed a plan to conduct a full archaeological investigation on the wreck of the *Rockaway*. The project would also serve as a field school project for undergraduate students at Western Michigan University, Pott's Alma Mater, as well as other Michigan universities. Coming so soon on the heels of Public Law 184, this project would also provide an opportunity to teach divers the value of archaeological study. Among other goals, Pott wished to raise and study the artifacts to learn about shipboard life and document the structure to learn about the construction of scow schooners.

The State of Michigan approved the plan and advised that all recovered artifacts would remain the property of Michigan after conservation work was complete. Pott retained the services of professional wet site conservator Katherine Singley, who began setting up a laboratory on the grounds of the museum. Field work began in July of 1984 and spanned through September to take advantage of the best weather conditions and the schedules of students and volunteers. The divers set buoys to mark the site, developed a grid system to record the scatter of artifacts, and began the process of creating a photomosaic. They recorded the initial condition of the wreck before anything was recovered and before any dredging activity exposed subsurface structure and artifacts. Visibility at that time averaged only three to six feet and some

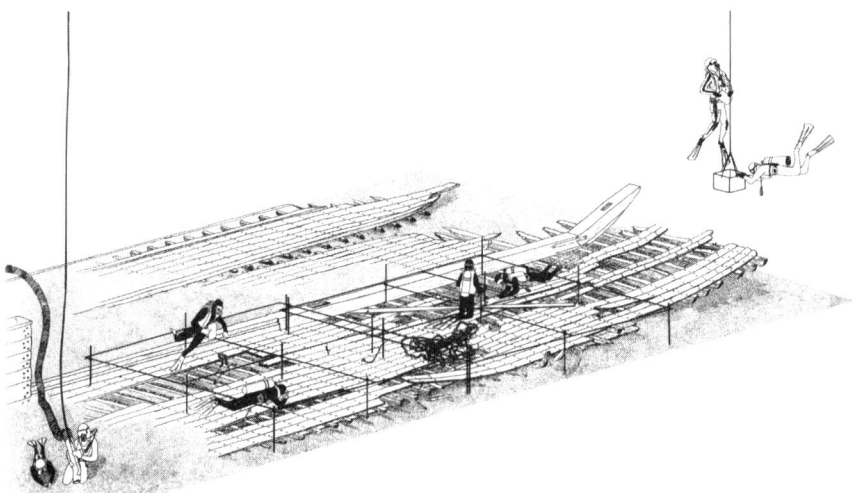

**An artist's illustration depicts the archaeological work on the wreck of the *Rockaway*.**
*Courtesy of Kenneth Pott*

**The documentation team affixed tags on each artifact and recorded its location before recovering it for conservation and later display.** *Courtesy of Kenneth Pott*

days the water became so stirred up it was like working in complete darkness. This lack of clarity meant that the work would be slow going, but the goal was accuracy, not speed.

Concurrent to the underwater work, Pott and museum intern Jay Martin began an historical study of the *Rockaway*'s career.

In 1985, the team began artifact recovery. A dive the preceding year had revealed that two objects had been removed by divers not associated with the project. Therefore, Pott opted to recover the wheel among the first items, concerned that it would have the greatest intrinsic or marketable value should those or other divers return. The team first affixed numerical tags to each artifact and mapped the position of each in relationship to the ship's structure. Then, over the next few weeks they began systematically recovering artifacts. After all the visible structure and artifacts had been recorded, they used a hydrolift to excavate buried sections of the ship and artifacts. That season, they recovered some 130 items including steering and rigging equipment, galley wares, tools, and personal items such as shoes. Pott had everything transported to the museum for storage in freshwater tanks in preparation for the conservation work.

Singley tackled the conservation of the artifacts with the help of students and volunteers. Field work continued in 1986 with more excavation, documentation, and the recovery of about sixty additional artifacts. In 1987, the team recovered eleven more artifacts, which seemed to be the extent of what they would find. Many artifacts recovered from the site were associated with the movement, loading, and unloading of cargoes, suggesting the crew was involved

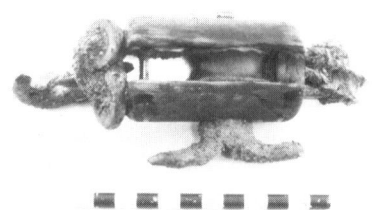

**Each artifact on the *Rockaway* was photographed in situ, then right after its recovery, and then again after conservators restored it to document the entire process.** *Courtesy of Kenneth Pott*

in this work. A number of tools also suggested the crew performed shipboard maintenance routines while either under way or dockside.

In 1988, Pott focused on studying the ship's hull. In 1989, project photographer Harley Seeley completed the photomosaic, divers documented the windlass in place, and selectively took wood samples from frames, planking, the keelson, stemson, and centerboard trunk to analyze the species and quality of woods employed in the vessel's construction and in areas of suggested repair. The hull proved to be planked mostly in white oak, with some chestnut frames and hemlock patches. This suggested that first-class materials were used in the manufacture of this scow rather than lesser-quality woods previously thought to have been used in the construction of scows. In 1991, Pott's team studied the hull curvature, learning that the *Rockaway's* hull was considerably more curved, and thus refined, than previously assumed of scow design.

The project resulted in an exhibit that debuted at the Michigan Maritime Museum, then toured five states in the Great Lakes region, eventually being viewed by over a half million people. Other results included the book *The Conservation of Archaeological Artifacts from Freshwater Environments* by Katherine Singley, which has become the guide for such work throughout the world; and scholarly papers by Pott and Jay Martin. In addition, the project formed the basis for a two-year exhibition at the State Historical Museum in Lansing, and a half-hour documentary produced in association with public television. A number of project students went on to professional careers in either archaeology or the museum field. To this day, Pott and the Michigan Maritime Museum continue to share the *Rockaway* in lectures and exhibits.

The wreck's loss is now the public's gain because so much valuable historical information was learned from the project. The State of Michigan, which now holds the *Rockaway* artifacts in storage, has loaned them out for related exhibits. The project has served as a model achievement in underwater archaeology. Despite these milestones, the *Rockaway* project also generated some uproar from several vocal members of the diving public. They argued that the State of Michigan operated on double standards regarding artifact recovery. It made the recovery of artifacts by sport divers illegal under the pretense of keeping the shipwrecks intact for divers' benefits, yet allowed the complete and total stripping of the *Rockaway* for the benefits of archaeology. Because of this, the project has also become a source of frustration for the state, which had to deal with a backlash from the diving community. This underscores the

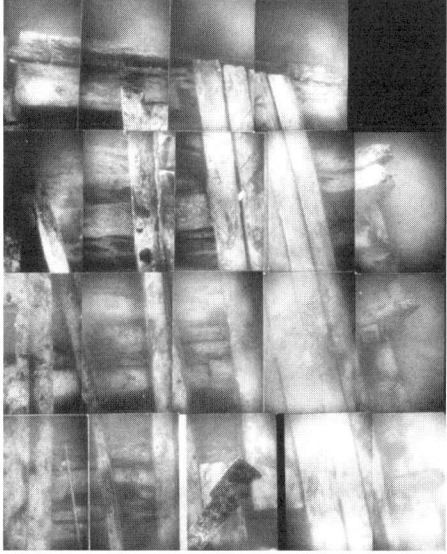

**In the days before digital photography and computer programs such as PhotoShop, photographer Harley Seeley created a photomosaic of the *Rockaway's* wreck site by combining individual photographs. This helped mark the location of each artifact.** *Courtesy of Kenneth Pott*

volatile disagreements that can arise when a shipwreck is newly discovered and how state governments must tread lightly when making decisions regarding the shipwrecks over which they claim ownership.

**All of the artifacts recovered from the *Rockaway* now reside in perpetuity with the State of Michigan. They may be viewed by appointment or loaned out to accredited institutions.** *Photograph by the author*

The author is pictured swimming under deck supports and a deck beam on the wreck of the *David Dows* in the early 1990s. *Photograph by Joseph Oliver*

# 7

# EVOLVING ETHICS

When launched in 1880, the massive, five-masted *David Dows* became famous throughout the Great Lakes as the largest and fastest sailing vessel then built, but its loss off Chicago in November 1889, when less than a decade old, ushered out the age of schooners and signaled the superiority of steamers. The survey of its wreckage in 1988, soon after the federal government enacted a new law to protect shipwrecks, made the *David Dows* legendary as one of the first volunteer-driven underwater archaeological surveys that would establish the techniques to document a wreck in-situ, without the controversial recovery of artifacts like from the *Rockaway,* detailed in the previous chapter.

In 1880, the Toledo firm of Carrington & Casey drew much attention in maritime circles when it decided to commission the largest sailing vessel ever to work on the Great Lakes, even bigger than its previous record-setting schooner *George W. Adams.* The *Adams* had worked well for the company and an even bigger schooner may have been a bold plan to dominate the Toledo grain trade and encroach upon the leadership of the monopoly of grain shipping out of Chicago. On April 21, 1881, with great fanfare, the Bailey Brothers Shipyard launched the schooner, described by the *Toledo Blade* as the "longest and finest sailing vessel in the world" and heralded by another reporter as a "leviathan." At 278 feet long, almost thirty-eight feet wide, and drawing eighteen feet in depth, it was more than twice as long as the *Alvin Clark* or *Rockaway*, built just three decades earlier. Its value at the time of its build was nearly $83,000. Carrington & Casey named it *David Dows.*

The "monster," as one reporter called the ship, was named for David Dows, head of one of the largest American commission firms with headquarters in New York. Dows was a friend and business acquaintance of M. D. Carrington, a clever marketer, who would have hoped that in so naming

**Artist James Clary painted this exquisite image of the *David Dows* as it existed soon after its construction. The *Dows* had a barkentine rig, as evidenced by the square sails on the foremast.** *Courtesy of James Clary*

the vessel, Dows would feel compelled to use his namesake for shipping his goods. The *Dows'* masts averaged ninety feet each and the top masts joined through the use of a mast-step added another forty feet, topping out at 130 feet. At about thirty-six-inch diameter at their bases, the masts were so big, a man could not wrap his arms fully around them. These massive "trees" were supported by wire rigging, an innovation developed a decade before the *David Dows* was built.

Merchant vessel owners always sought ways to save labor costs, and the *Dows* would not disappoint in that regard. Only seven crewmembers could handle the ship, counterintuitive because of its size, but in fact, more sails of smaller dimensions could be handled independently by a smaller number of men. The ship was designed with a steam donkey engine to assist in raising the 70,000 square yards of canvas. Even then, it took eight hours to set the sails.

The gross tonnage measured 1481, more than seven times the tonnage of the schooner *Alvin Clark,* which had been considered large when it sank in 1864. The ship could hold 140,00 bushels of grain. In fact, with a rating of A1, the vessel would first be employed in the grain and coal trades. The schooner could be loaded through all of its eight top hatches. To facilitate handling, the *Dows* had double retractable centerboards, operated by two huge manual winches. Two anchors weighing nearly 4000 pounds each and 540 feet of chain secured the massive schooner, which was used as a marketing tool by a saloon in Toledo serving draft beer in "*David Dows* glasses."

Crewmembers were quartered in the fo'c'sle and rear cabin. The fo'c'sle had eight berths and a sitting room for deckhands. The rear cabin had large private rooms for each officer, a dining room with ornate woodwork, and a kitchen and pantry with marble-topped wash basins. Amidships the *David Dows* had a storeroom that featured the novel presence of a refrigerator. The *Dows* sported a rather unique dragon figurehead at the bow and hand-carved scroll-work with the ship's name at the stern, very unusual ornaments for an ordinary bulk cargo schooner.

For all its grandeur, the *David Dows* seemed plagued with bad luck. Because of a flood on the Maumee River, it had to be scuttled by the builders while still on the blocks. Then shortly thereafter, the second mate assigned to the schooner died of a heart attack while supervising work on its construction. And, on its first trip while carrying coal to Chicago, it sat so low in the water due to the weight of the cargo that it could not make it into the harbor. Carrington & Casey realized that because of shallow harbor depths, it could not do what it intended: carry the largest cargoes of any ship in operation. It became a "white elephant," unable to generate the profits and superiority its owners had hoped for.

An oil painting by Thomas Chilvers, which resides in the collection of the Detroit Historical Society, depicts the steam tug *Winslow* towing the disabled *David Dows* in an 1880 storm. The canvas on the *Dows* has blown out and the topmast is down and floating in the foreground. This painting portends events that would play out almost a decade later when the tug *T. T Morford* rescued the crew of the *Dows*. *C. Patrick Labadie Collection - Alpena County Public Library*

The *David Dows* spent its first year and a half in the Carrington & Casey fleet, but its size continued to cause problems. In May 1880 it ran aground off Erie, Pennsylvania, while hauling 245 carloads of coal and remained aground at the wharf for two days. Tugs could not move the monster and its captain had to wait for a west wind to raise the water in the harbor. Although Carrington & Casey had intended the *Dows* to become the big sister of the *Adams*, the *Adams* held its rank as the largest hauler on the Lakes evidenced by a July 1881 run in which the *Dows* carried 81,065 bushels of corn and the *Adams* carried 81,738 bushels, fully 673 bushels more. In fact, the *Adams* remained the big sister.

The *Dows*' bad luck continued. On the night of September 10, 1881, a squall came up on Lake Erie and while the *David Dows* was taking down sail, another vessel, the *Charles K. Nims,* crossed its bow and collided with it just off Point Pelee. The *Dows*' foremast broke and hit the deck, nearly killing one crewman. In the spring of 1882, another vessel rammed the *Dows* and it spent a month being repaired. Things improved toward the end of the 1882 season: In the previous thirteen weeks, the schooner had made fourteen round trips between Buffalo and Toledo, with no mishaps, and averaged fourteen miles per hour, the speed it was intended to run.

Despite its minor success, Carrington & Casey decided to sell the *Dows* and in August 1882, Ohio Central Barge Company purchased it. However, its bad luck moved to its new owner. The *C. B. Benson* rammed it on May 25, 1882, while it unloaded grain at Buffalo. Then, in 1883, it was involved in a collision with the schooner *Richard Mott* on Lake Michigan and four crewmen died. This accident prompted the board of inquiry to deem the vessel "uncontrollable and dangerous," forcing it to be demoted from the rank of first-class merchant schooner to a schooner barge.

Even as a barge, the *Dows* was still plagued with accidents. In 1885, the Wilson fleet purchased the *Dows* and used it to carry coal from Lake Erie ports to Duluth, Minnesota, and return with iron ore from Two Harbors, Wisconsin. In that capacity, it ran aground at Lime Kiln Crossing in the Detroit River, near Bois Blanc Island, while under tow by the propeller *George Spencer,* causing an international incident because half of the ship lay on Canadian territory and a Canadian tug had to tow it off. In the process, it got loose, drifted off, and rammed and sunk the massive dredge *Wild Irishman,* moored nearby. Soon thereafter, it struck the *City of Montreal* moored in Sault Ste. Marie, causing considerable damage to the ship and wharf. It remains a mystery why after all the trouble the *Dows* had caused and experienced, John Corrigan of Cleveland purchased it in June 1887. He planned to use it as a tow barge behind the steamers of his fleet. In that capacity, the *David Dows* met its end.

## LOST

On November 16, 1889, the *David Dows* left Erie, Pennsylvania, for Chicago with a load of coal for delivery to W. L. Scott & Company. Captain Thomas Roche, a veteran lake captain who had taken over the *Dows* when the spring season commenced, commanded the vessel. Plans called for the *Dows* to sail up the lakes until it would be met by the steamer *Aurora* and taken under tow. Due to strong headwinds, the *Dows* made slow progress and did not make it into Lake Michigan until more than a week and a half later. It reached the area of the Manitou Islands in northern Lake Michigan by Wednesday, November 27. Captain Ed Kelley of the *Aurora* sighted it and took the *Dows* behind its big sister, the *George W. Adams*. The small convoy made little progress that day before it was caught in a fierce winter storm with gale-force winds that blew in during the early evening when the vessels had reached a point off Sa-

The barkentine rig was eliminated in favor of a fore-and-aft rig after the *David Dows'* owners and master realized how unmanageable it could be. Even so, the vessel would rarely sail on its own, but was instead towed as a barge. *Michigan City Lighthouse Museum Collection*

ble Point on the east side of the Lake. Mate E. J. Donohue later recalled never having seen such a rough sea as long as he had been sailing. The blizzard made it impossible for one vessel to see another and blinding sleet and temperatures well below freezing spread a glaze of ice over all three ships.

By 8 p.m. Wednesday, the *David Dows* began to take on water. The crew worked hard at the pumps throughout the night and into the next day with the assistance of the steam engine. They had no opportunity to eat during this time and rarely took a break from their task, becoming famished and finding their clothes frozen in a solid mass. However, try as they might, they could not keep pace with the inrush of water, and the holds kept filling at the rate of about three inches per hour. By Thursday in the dark of morning, the crew could no longer stanch the flow of water; three feet of water filled the lower hold saturating the cargo and it became clear they would lose the big barge. The crew lit torches to signal their distress to the *Aurora,* but besides taking note of their condition, Captain Ed Kelley could do little but continue on and hope time was in their favor.

Just after daylight, a tremendous wave swept over the deck of the *Dows*, leaving the cabin a wreck and clearing the decks of everything moveable, including one of the two lifeboats as well as Mate Donahue. By some miracle, the next wave washed him back on the deck and he scrambled to his feet. The next big wave swept off Captain Roche and Donkeyman Robert Keyes. Roche managed to grab hold of the rail and Keyes caught a floating rope.

At 3 p.m., the steam engine began to malfunction then stopped working all together. The crew labored with the hand pumps, but water poured in even faster. By then, the wind shifted to the northwest and the *Aurora* was pushed southeast away from Chicago. Kelley realized that he would never be able to make Chicago dragging the waterlogged *Dows* and *Adams*. The rolling waves were so bad, they lifted his propellers out of the water. He finally decided he had no choice but to cast off the towline and head to Chicago on his own.

From on board the *Dows*, Mate Donahue watched incredulously, not fathoming how the *Aurora* could abandon them to their fate. Captain Roche quickly commanded the crew to set the anchor so they would not be pushed sideways to the wind and surely capsized. Then, he tried to encourage them to keep at the pumps, but the exhausted, famished, and frozen crew become panic-stricken after the *Aurora* left. He tried to reason with them, assuring them that they were in only seven fathoms of water, so if the *Dows* sank, the masts would remain above water. The crew saw this as their lifeline and abandoned their posts, climbed the masts, and lashed themselves as high as they could safely stand it, hoping to survive the inevitable foundering. From there they watched the *Adams* drift a couple miles away before setting its anchor. Not as certain the sinking would happen soon, Captain Roche did his best to calm his crew; he was able to talk them down from their perches and convince them to make better preparations for survival. They gathered the bedclothes and blankets from their berths and carried them up into the masts; while they did that, Roche encouraged the cook, Michael Gallagher, to make coffee in what was left of the cabin, and one by one the crew joined them in the shelter. Before most could down a cup of the steaming liquid, a wave crashed over the ship, panicking the men once again. They hurried back to the masts and once again prepared for what they felt would be imminent doom. But still the *Dows* did not sink.

After several hours, the crew began shouting from mast to mast and making a plan to save themselves. Four of the men decided to launch the one remaining lifeboat and try for the *Adams*. Captain Roche and the other four members chose to remain aboard the *Dows* and take their chances in the masts. Roche may have regretted his decision when he watched, from high on his perch, the lifeboat reach the *Adams* safely with all on board, and especially when at 2:45 p.m. that Thursday, a series of massive waves swept over the *Dows*, pitching it precariously on its side. Roche and the other four crewmen held on for their lives, but as their ship sank lower in the water, the *Dows* righted itself and settled in the water up to its decks. Indeed, the masts provided the life support that Roche had expected, but the crew's plight was far from over. They had to spend the entire afternoon and all that night contorted in awkward positions in the masts trying to stay awake to keep from freezing.

As the dull, blustery Friday morning dawned gray, the crew were undoubtedly overjoyed to see the familiar silhouette of the tug *T. T. Morford* approaching them. Hoping that the *Dows* could be saved if the *Morford* could tow it to shore, the ever-responsible Roche overcame all that ailed him, and tried to convince the crew to heave anchor. However, they were simply too exhausted and famished to care. Giving in to his own pain, Roche struggled down from his mast and joined the others on the swamped deck of the *Dows* as the tug approached the side and maneuvered close enough to take them all on board. In the sturdy warm tug, they devoured whatever food they were given to satiate the gnawing pangs of hunger after not having eaten in forty hours. Little more than a couple hours later, they reached the dock in Chicago. The tug's crew arranged for them to be taken to the Marine Hospital in Chicago for frostbite treatment. Then the tug headed back out to tow in the *Adams*. Roche arranged for the tug *Chicago* to try to save the *Dows,* but just as they arrived on site at about 2:15 p.m., it rolled over on its side and sank.

After making it back to Chicago, Captain Roche immediately headed to the office of the tugboat's owner, James Dunham, where he coincidently found Captain Kelley of the *Aurora*. "She is gone," Rouche announced despondently, referring to the *Dows*. Kelley was caught off guard having just explained to Dunham that he had no idea the *Dows* was in trouble when he abandoned it to ride out the storm. Roche formally criticized Kelley, pointing out their use of the distress flames to warn him and admonishing him for not sending help sooner. Kelley backpedaled, defending himself by transferring responsibility for the delayed rescue. Upon reaching Chicago on Thursday evening, he had informed the Coast Guard of the approximate position of the two vessels. Dunham confirmed that the Coast Guard had alerted him. He had sent the *T. T. Morford* to the rescue that night, but the crew, fearing for their own lives, chose to wait until dawn. Soon thereafter, the *Dow's* owner, John Corrigan, who had heard of the ordeal, joined the men in Dunham's office. Upon learning of his ship's fate, he lamented as if he had lost a child, "No better boat ever sailed these lakes." Then he asked Dunham, "Can she be raised?"

"If she was my boat," he replied, "I should consider I would not see her again."

Dunham was correct in his statement, although Corrigan did try to raise the vessel. On December 1, C. A. McDonald, an underwriter, visited the wreck with wrecking master Captain J. J. Reardon. They found the masts protruding above the water and arranged for the tugs *Owen* and *Swain* and steam barge *Maxy Groh* to salvage the wreck. However, by the time they could reach the wreck, the wind and waves had already begun to break it up. The company eventually spent nearly $30,000 in an effort to raise the ship, but succeeded in recovering only about 1400 tons of the coal cargo and had significantly damaged the ship further in the process. Over the winter, the keel of the great schooner twisted and broke into pieces. When seen by diver Thomas Johnson in April 1890, the forward seventy-five feet of the hull had broken clear, the decks were gone, and what remained had broken amidships. He deemed any further salvage effort a waste of money. At the time of its sinking, the *David Dows* was insured for $60,000, about $15,000 less than its value.

The loss of the *Dows* signaled the end of the Great Lakes sailing era. Few new schooners were built after that and the number of steam vessels increased dramatically. Steam and diesel power permitted the building of larger vessels that could handle the shallow waters of the lake system. The concept of the *Dows* was faulty to begin with: Bigger was not better; mechanization would be the solution.

Even in death, the *Dows'* size proved a problem. Although the masts toppled and the last vestiges of the *Dows* were swallowed by the Lake, its massive hulk remained a hazard to navigation if a ship happened to unknowingly pass right over its remains. However, that never occurred and in time the wreck's location was forgotten. Eighteen years later, in August 1908, the United States survey steamer *Search* discovered it about seven miles from the South Chicago breakwater lighthouse, lying directly in the path of the heavy traffic for Chicago, Indiana Harbor, and Gary. Divers noted that when the water was at its lowest, only eighteen feet covered the wreck, not enough for the big steel freighters that had begun plying that busy route. The *Search* crew marked it with buoys, and the U.S. engineer in charge of the Chicago District used dynamite in order to further reduce the mass of wreckage to eliminate any hazard to freighter traffic.

## FOUND

Another half century would pass before anyone would lay eyes on the *David Dows* again. Although firsthand knowledge of its discovery is beginning to fade after more than a half century, most of the old-timers recall that diver Pat Delany found the wreck using a rudimentary bottom finder in the 1960s. The position had been accurately recorded by land sightings taken by the engineers who dynamited the wreck in the 1908, so once in the right vicinity, it would not have been too hard to find such a massive structure underwater.

As with the *Material Service* (discussed in Chapter Five), the *David Dows* immediately became a popular dive site on Lake Michigan. A 1966 article in *Skin Diver Magazine*, the major publication for wreck divers at the time, entitled "Wreck of the David Dows" by Teddy Remick, illustrates the climate in which divers freely operated at that time. Remick wrote, "Today, items from this particular wreck are in great demand by collectors of marine relics. We have received many such letters from collectors, asking if we knew where any items from the *David Dows* could be obtained. Our stock answer has been to send the writer the bearings of this wreck and tell him to take what he wanted! It would make good business sense, if some enterprising diver would locate the wreck and strip it of all removable items, and sell them to collectors. True, it is not as glamorous as hunting sunken treasure, though money is money, whether it is recovered treasure or money earned from the sale of recovered marine items and relics, and I doubt if anyone will argue."

And indeed the local divers agreed with Remick's statement. In short order, they recovered most every loose

The ship's wheel, recovered from the *David Dows* in the late 1960s, was originally purchased by artist James Clary. It now resides in the Collection of the Great Lakes Historical Society, which operates the National Museum of the Great Lakes in Ohio. *Courtesy Great Lakes Historical Society*

artifact and even affixed items that required tools and conveyances to haul them to the surface. In fact it must have taken quite an effort to cut loose the ship's wheel and bring it to the surface. Some years later, maritime artist and historian James Clary purchased the wheel from a diver and held it in his collection for years. It resides today at the Great Lakes Historical Museum in Vermilion, Ohio, for all to see. Clary had a fascination with the *Dows*, which he has painted and uses as his logo. In 1977, he mounted an effort to locate and recover the famed dragon figurehead from the *Dows*. However, David Groover, who dived the wreck on behalf of Clary, could never find it; most of the early divers presumed that the bow structure lies buried deep in the sand. Others fear that the entire bow was destroyed during the Army Corps' effort to clear the wreck. Instead, Groover recovered a five-foot-long oak plank for Clary, which was used by Harvey Neesley to construct a beautiful model of the *David Dows*, significant because it was made with a real piece from the ship.

However, as noted in the previous two chapters, in the late 1970s divers began to realize they were ruining their own dive sites by taking artifacts. By the early 1980s, archaeologists like Gary Ellis in Indiana and Ken Pott had already become involved in statewide movements to protect historic shipwrecks. In the mid-1980s, the plight of historic shipwrecks came up for discussion in Congress. The president of the National Trust for Historic Preservation, J. Jackson Walter, testified, "Historic shipwrecks are without a doubt the single most endangered resource in our nation today. They are irreplaceable time capsules containing unique data about human history." Walter noted that shipwrecks are endangered for two reasons. First, the trauma of the sinking and then the actions of the water and its organisms over years of being submerged degrade the structure and contents. Second, the hand of man can alter a shipwreck, either accidently, like hooking it with an anchor, or purposely by removing pieces of it. Like a crime scene, anything that gets moved or removed alters the ability to understand what occurred. After a ship becomes a shipwreck, it cannot be added to, only diminished, and therefore it is recognized as a nonrenewable resource.

The federal government decided to become more actively involved in trying to protect these nonrenewable resources with the writing of the Abandoned Shipwreck Act of 1987, a bill signed into law by President Ronald Reagan in the spring of 1988. Through the Act, the federal government claimed title to shipwrecks abandoned by their owners and expressly embedded in the bottom and/or eligible for inclusion in the National Register of Historic Places. The federal government then, in turn, transferred title and management responsibility to the states in whose submerged lands the shipwrecks lie, to be held in trust for the benefit of all people, not just divers. This law put the spotlight on shipwrecks and changed everything for sport divers engrained in the finders-keepers approach. Although divers in Michigan had already been impacted by Public Act 184 and the Underwater Preserve System, now all divers in any of the American waters of the Great Lakes were being compelled to change their behavior. In short order, each Great Lakes state wrote or rewrote its own archaeological laws. Although worded differently from state to state, each state's new laws made the recovery of artifacts from shipwrecks on their bottomlands a felony unless a special permit was issued. Although divers feared the government would soon make diving on wrecks illegal, the laws have not, to date, limited diver access.

As with any new law, and particularly one with limited budget for law enforcement, the Abandoned Shipwreck Act was not immediately embraced. Since the laws enacted by the State of Michigan in 1980 curtailing the activity of shipwreck artifact recovery, the state had already faced a backlash by divers who resented the government's infringement in their hobby. Now all the states faced similar objections by divers. Although newer divers were more inclined to accept the law as a way to protect and maintain the object of their recreational pursuits, some long-time divers—particularly those who had invested heavily in equipment to discover and salvage shipwrecks—felt that the federal and state governments had overstepped their authority. Their response to the law was somewhat like the general public's response to the federal Volstead Act—also known as the National Prohibition Act—that brought about state laws that made drinking illegal in 1920. Many divers continued to recover artifacts from shipwrecks after the law was enacted, just like many people continued to drink after prohibition. Suddenly these two groups of people became "criminals" in the eyes of the law, when previously they had been merely engaged in an enjoyable pastime.

Because of budget limitations within each state to attend to the new law, oversight fell mainly to various volunteer organizations that became watchdog groups, loosely comparable to the teetotalers in the 1920s. The Chicago Maritime Society (CMS) was one such organization. With a mission to preserve Chicago's maritime history, the society formed a committee of divers to work on behalf of the State of Illinois to help preserve these submerged maritime treasures. For its first project, the committee chose to document the *David Dows* because of its historical significance. The underwater archaeology committee of the Chicago Maritime Society, as it was called, organized by CMS board members David Truitt and Kurt Anderson, enlisted the aid of local professional archaeologist David Keene and historian and university professor John McManamon as volunteers.

The committee planned to gather the information necessary to nominate the site to the National Register of Historic Places. McManamon, a certified diver, led the efforts to research the history of the ship. Keene, although not a diver, developed some basic procedures that the dive team, under the direction of Anderson, would use to record the wreck. The Illinois Historic Preservation Agency, through its representatives, State Archaeologist Thomas Emerson and director William Wheeler, allocated $3000 for the training of volunteer divers to conduct site work on the *Dows*. Some of the funds were used to enlist the services of Kenneth Pott, who was at the time administering the archaeological work on the survey of the *Rockaway* off South Haven, Michigan. CMS divers traveled there to learn documentation techniques from him. The committee planned to develop a site map of the wreck, a necessity for the National Register submission. The team worked

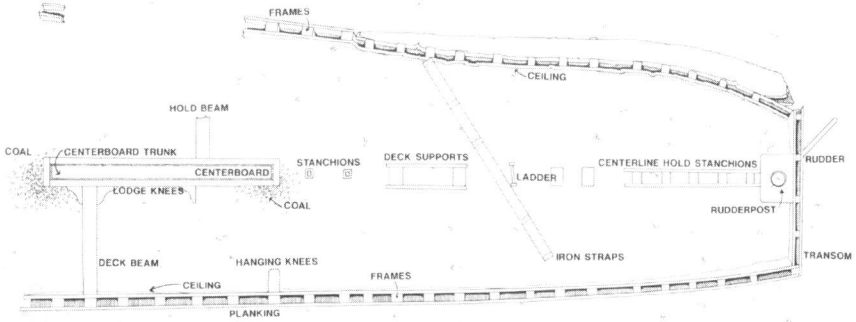

**A site plan of the *David Dows* as it looked in the summer of 1989, prepared by an artist with notes from the Chicago Maritime Society Underwater Archaeology team.**
*Author's collection*

out of Jackson Park Harbor using the forty-foot vessel *Intrigue* owned by Truitt, and made initial dives in the late summer of 1987. A seven-mile run brought them to the wreck of the *David Dows,* which lies in about forty feet of water near a shoal a few miles west of a highly polluted area of Lake Michigan that served for years as an industrial dumpsite.

At the time of the survey, water visibility never exceeded ten feet with less than five being the norm. Only the aft 120 feet of the massive vessel remains after it was dynamited in 1908. The absence of any artifacts or any loose portions of structure illustrated how completely the dive community had stripped the shipwreck. Like the divers in the 1970s, the team could find no evidence of the bow portion of the vessel. Only the lower sections of the port and starboard hull are present plus one of the two massive centerboard trunks lying in a roughly north/south axis with the stern at the southern end. That single trunk reflects the massiveness of the ship: At twenty-five feet long, two feet wide, and thirteen feet high, it is larger than most single centerboard trunks. None of the deck beams or decking remains, but the rudder exists, canted hard to the starboard side. The bulk of the survey work took place in 1988, at which time, this book's author became involved with the committee as a volunteer diver.

The team used a fifty-meter plastic surveyor's tape to measure and a twenty-four-inch diameter plywood disk with eight equidistant points plotted along the edge in the fashion of compass points, to establish direction of features they would measure, a clipboard with a plastic paper called Mylar, and a regular pencil to record their measurements. In recording conditions, the divers made the following observations: The entire transom and the rudder exists and rises out of the sand approximately eight feet off the lake bottom. From the rudder-post moving forward on the port side, the hull remains intact from the gunwale to the centerline and runs nearly 120 feet until what appears to be a break in the hull. Although the port hull is largely exposed, it gradually slopes downward into the sandy bottom. Along the port hull, several stanchions, which supported the decking, still remain.

From the rudder post forward on the starboard side, the hull has broken away; approximately one hundred feet of the starboard hull lies broken in large pieces, resting exposed on the bottom. The starboard side also slopes down into the sand and is gradually buried by sand and silt deposits. Moving from the rudder down the centerline of the ship, several structural features are visible and readily identifiable, including a ladder and the aft centerboard trunk. These dives provided the data to create the site plan.

The Chicago Maritime Society's project to document the *David Dows* represented the first collaboration between the State of Illinois and the sport diving community to embrace the new law and consider shipwrecks as both archaeological and recreational resources. However, the wreck of the *David Dows* could be likened to a "white elephant," just as the schooner had been during its career. It was never formally listed on the National Register of Historic Places, likely because after so much salvaging, there were insufficient remains to warrant its inclusion. However, the project to document the wreck received so much positive feedback from state officials and the diving community that it became a model for protocol for any other new shipwreck discoveries. Indeed, the Chicago Maritime Society's underwater archaeology committee was able to implement similar procedures in the fall of 1988, when, just a few weeks after the completion of site work on the *David Dows,* the discovery of the *Wells Burt,* an intact schooner off Evanston, Illinois, was called to its attention.

The forward capstan on the *Wells Burt* served to raise the anchors. *Photograph by Eric Brod*

# 8

# IMPETUS FOR CHANGE

In the late summer of 1988, just a few weeks after completing work on the *David Dows*, the Chicago Maritime Society's underwater archaeology committee learned about the discovery of an intact schooner in shallow water off Evanston, Illinois. This marked the first new shipwreck discovery in Illinois and among the first in Lake Michigan since the establishment of the Abandoned Shipwreck Act, a bill signed into law by President Ronald Reagan earlier that spring. The wreck was the *Wells Burt,* a schooner lost in 1883 in such tragic circumstances that the accident eventually brought about measures to better preserve sailors' lives. Ironically, the discovery of the wreck more than a century later would also serve as the impetus for change, bringing about measures to better preserve shipwrecks. For this reason, the *Wells Burt* has joined the ranks of legendary shipwrecks.

On July 13, 1873, the *Detroit Free Press* announced the launching of the three-masted schooner *Wells Burt,* the latest of twenty-six vessels built by the Detroit Dry Dock Company. Founded just one year earlier, the shipbuilder had grown out of preceding partnerships among entrepreneurs from the Campbell, Owen, and Kirby families. Experienced maritime men judged the schooner as being "a staunchly built vessel." George Hardison served as its architect and Frank Kirby, a Cooper Union-trained engineer, who had joined the family firm in 1870, also had a hand in its design. Kirby would go on to have a very prolific and successful career as a ship designer.

The year 1873 marked the pinnacle of schooner design, with the introduction of the largest number of sailing ships yet built. The *Wells Burt* was among the larger schooners of its day. At 201 feet long and 33 feet wide, it could carry over fifty thousand bushels of corn. Everything about the vessel was first class; one reporter indicated that "she is as strong as wood and iron can make her." The schooner's enrollment suggested the ordinary character of the design: one deck, three masts, plain head, and square stern. The *Wells Burt* carried the official number 80365. Hugh Coyne of Detroit, along with the man who would serve as the vessel's first master, Captain George W. Allen, had the schooner built for $70,000 and shared ownership on a three-quarter, one-quarter split.

They named the vessel after Wells Burt, the fourth son of William Austin Burt, a surveyor on Michigan's Upper Peninsula and the inventor of a solar compass in 1835. Following in their father's footsteps, Wells and his brother became surveyors and eventually ran a successful mining business in the Upper Peninsula. By 1873, Wells had settled in Detroit and established the Union Iron Company. Coyne and Allen undoubtedly hoped to acquire some of Burt's business shipping ore to his company on the *Wells Burt*. In fact, the schooner carried iron ore on its maiden voyage, but also moved grain and coal on return trips. However, they could not make a profit. The *Wells Burt* could carry an enormous amount of cargo, and was fast in heavy winds, but it became difficult to maneuver in light winds. It had a few mishaps in its first years of service, too, losing its centerboard on Lake Erie in May 1874 and grounding in the St. Mary's River in October 1874, both times incurring $300 in damages.

However, the panic of 1873 and the depression that followed affected business and the contracts did not come through to the extent that the owners hoped. Coyne was never able to recoup his investment in the schooner.

**A painting commissioned by the third owner of the *Wells Burt*, E. S. Stone of Milwaukee, Wisconsin, is now in the possession of Stone's great-grandson, C. T. Stone, Jr., of Oconomowoc, Wisconsin.** *Courtesy of C. T. Stone*

He was forced to sell the *Wells Burt* under foreclosure in 1876. John Owen, president of the board of the Detroit Dry Dock, purchased the schooner for only $23,000 when its value was $45,000. This was, perhaps, an insider's deal considering his firm built the vessel. He had made his millions in the banking business and the *Wells Burt* would serve as an investment. Owen operated the *Wells Burt* until 1878, when he sold it to E. S. Stone of Milwaukee. After six seasons on the lakes, the vessel's value had declined to $26,500, though it still carried an A-1 ranking, an indication of how well built it had been. Unlike its first owners, Stone was able to turn a profit of $50,000 in the three years that he operated the *Wells Burt*. He sold it in 1880 to J. Kelly from Milwaukee, who, in February 1882, had the Miller Brothers Boatyard at Chicago install a new stern and masts along with other general repairs at a cost of $2,500. Kelly then sold the boat in 1883 to James Dunham at Chicago.

Dunham had moved from New York to Chicago in 1854 to pursue a career in the maritime field. By 1883, he owned a good-sized tug boat fleet that he would soon incorporate into the Dunham Towing and Wrecking Company. The *Wells Burt* would prove his first foray into the cargo business, but it would not be long-lived.

## LOST

In mid-May 1883, Captain Thomas Fountain, in the employ of James Dunham, oversaw the loading of 1,540 tons of anthracite coal at Buffalo for Meeker, Hedstorm & Company, an iron manufacturer in Chicago run by Arthur B. Meeker. Meeker's partner, E. L. Hedstrom, resided in Buffalo and had consigned the shipment there. Dunham probably sent Fountain to Buffalo with a delivery of grain on its first run of the season, having left on May 1. The coal would not be a full load—the *Wells Burt* could have carried at least 150 tons more—but the fee would still generate a sizeable profit for Dunham. Dunham had employed the forty-eight-year-old Fountain for several years, giving him command of the *Wells Burt* as soon as he purchased it. Thomas Fountain had been born in England and trained on board the coastal trader *Sally* before coming to America to seek his fortune. Like most captains, Fountain had begun as an apprentice. He then served as mate with Captain Arthur Atkins on the bark *Northwest*, and afterwards commanded the sailing vessels *Marquette, William Crosthwaite, Board of Trade,* and *Pensaukee*, before coming to work for Dunham on the *Wells Burt*. He had been in command of the bark *Board of Trade* when it sank in 1874 twenty miles off Fairport, Ohio, carrying 30,000 bushels of corn. He and the crew made it off the wreck safely and Fountain was blamed for sinking it for the insurance payoff. However, investigators eventually exonerated him of wrongdoing. In fact, Captain Fountain was known as an excellent navigator and efficient sailor.

Despite long trips on the lakes away from home, he found time to father six children with his wife, Julia, seven years his junior: Daniel, 18, Margaret 15, Arthur 14, Mary 10, and the two youngest named for their parents, seven-year-old Julia and five-year-old Tommy. Fountain owned two houses, one on Church Street in Chicago in which the family lived, as well as another, plus two vacant lots, all together worth eight thousand dollars. With such a big family and a dangerous career, Fountain carried a sizeable life insurance policy, valued at about the same as his property. Desiring to bring his oldest son, Daniel, into the marine business, he took him along on this first trip of the 1883 season. This must have caused great anxiety for his wife, especially because he had recently expressed concern, telling her, "My steering gear ain't all right."

Fountain had experienced officers, including Captain William Cody as first mate, and Second Mate John White. Thomas George, T. Hickey, Jeff Powers, Wilkie McCarthy, and three others served as deckhands. After unloading his grain at Buffalo, the process of loading coal began. The seven sizeable hatches running down the vessel's deck would have allowed for an efficient filling operation, probably accomplished in just a few hours. Something must have occurred on the trip over or during the unloading to have caused Fountain to dismiss Deck Hand Jeff Powers, especially considering that he was the brother of Richard Powers, president of the Seaman's Union. Irishman Edward Hanlon took his place in Buffalo to complete the round trip.

The *Wells Burt* departed Buffalo under full sail in light conditions on Lake Erie, and Captain Fountain had no issues negotiating his way west past Fairport, Ohio. He could not have helped but think about the time almost a decade earlier when his schooner *Board of Trade* sank near there. The *Wells Burt* threaded its way nicely through the St. Clair Canal into Lake Huron, and spent at least two days running north until reaching the Straits of Mackinac, from which point Fountain took a bearing south-southwest toward Chicago.

Friday May 18 ushered in bright but cool with a fresh wind blowing from the southeast allowing the *Wells Burt* to sail steadily down Wisconsin's eastern coast. However, toward noon that day, the sky became overcast and by 4 p.m. lightning began dancing across the sky, but it brought little rain. Oddly, two hours later, the weather became oppressively warm. The arrival of hot and humid air from the south collided with the unseasonably cold air over the region and created a series of tornadoes that rolled across Illinois and southern Wisconsin. Residents of Chicago witnessed firsthand the destructive power of the storm: high winds, waves with crests thirty feet apart, and spray that reached heights of one hundred feet as the water crashed against barriers along the lakefront. A reporter from a Racine newspaper wrote ominously of the storm, "No ship that encountered this monster of air could by any possibility survive destruction." In fact, Racine landlubbers got hit the worst: 150 homes and barns were demolished and twenty people lost their lives in the storm. Yet many vessels sailed safely through the maelstrom.

The *Wells Burt* caught the worst of the weather when off Racine, but handled it well. Captain O'Conner of the schooner *American Union* saw the schooner several miles astern off Racine moving steadily with its mainsail, foresail, topsail, and jibs closely reefed. It had, so far, survived the onslaught of what Captain Smallman of the steamer *City of Milwaukee* said later was the severest squall he had seen on the Lake in years. At that point, Fountain would have had little choice but to proceed toward Chicago. There were no other significant shelters south of Racine and it would have been suicide to turn back in those high winds. Broaching had to be avoided at all costs. But Chicago was more than 100 miles distant. Hours later, as darkness began to fall, the *Wells Burt* reached Waukegan along the northern shores of Illinois. For a time, the crew sailed in the company of the schooner *Bailey* until the fury of the storm and the darkness caused the crew of each vessel to lose sight of the other.

Fountain's last hurdle was to pass Grosse Point, a spit of land off Evanston about thirty miles north of his destination where the shoal waters caused unpredictable currents and waves especially in a storm. The faithful light from the lighthouse, erected ten years earlier as a result of tragic accidents like *Lady Elgin*, would have given him a point of reference from which to navigate.

Sometime before midnight that Friday, at just about the time that the *Wells Burt* would have reached Grosse Point, the schooner *C. B. Jones* found itself in the vicinity as well. The waves piled up from all directions on the *Jones* and its captain must have struggled to give commands to his crew over the din of the storm. However, a distant voice caught his attention that would haunt him in the coming days. He could not even be sure his mind was not playing tricks on him, but scanned all around his boat to try to pinpoint the source of the voice. The inky blackness revealed nothing. But he did not forget the words he heard: "For God's sake send us a tug, we are sinking!" Even if he had believed his ears, he was powerless to do anything. To turn in those winds would have been the death of his ship and crew. He kept struggling south toward Chicago, with a nagging feeling of despair.

Saturday, May 19, dawned sunny in Chicago, but the surf remained furious. Morning's light revealed dozens of vessels, mostly schooners, including the *C. B. Jones,* anchored outside Chicago's harbor trying to ride out the storm. Watchers on shore saw the *Jenny Lind,* a two-masted schooner, break free from its mooring and get dashed on shore just south of Thirty-Third Street. Helpless, they watched as the seas swept four members of its crew to their deaths, one who became trapped between the ship and a piling, and whose body was pounded to and fro like a rag doll. The storm continued to blow all day until the winds began to die down as night fell. As the people of the lakefront com-

**James Sears Dunham owned the *Wells Burt* at the time of its loss.** *Courtesy of Thomas Lutz, author* Shaping Chicago

munities from Racine down to Chicago began dealing with the aftermath of the deadly and destructive storm, maritime people became anxious, none more so than James S. Dunham, who had heard nothing from the *Wells Burt*, which had been due in on Friday night.

On Sunday, May 20, the *Chicago Tribune* reported on "Friday's Furies," noting with surprise that there had been no maritime tragedies, "as it was feared that one or more vessels would have been lost or stranded on some treacherous shore." The reporter had spoken too soon. As the schooners that had been riding out the storm began coming in one-by-one, they brought news of a disaster. The *Onward* limped into Chicago on Sunday. Its captain reported he had passed a wreck approximately six miles east of Grosse Point. Likewise, the captain of the steamer *Ballentine* had seen two masts in the water off Grosse Point. This would have concerned Dunham, but nothing had yet connected the spars to his schooner. However, when Captain Smith of the *Rising Star* reported seeing two white masts rising out of the water east of Evanston, Dunham knew he had lost his boat: the masts of the *Wells Burt* were white.

Captain Fountain's wife, Julia, and her children had grown terribly worried for the head of their household. Julia had undoubtedly spent a sleepless couple of nights agonizing over her husband and son. On Sunday evening, she sent her fourteen-year-old son, Arthur, down to the dock to inquire of the *Wells Burt*. There, he found James Dunham, who happened to be at the time discussing the wreck with a number of other maritime men. They all became silent when they recognized the boy as Fountain's son. Arthur's anxious eyes scanned the crowd seeking some reassurance, but no one could offer him any, instead fidgeting and avoiding looking him in the eye. Dunham was overcome with emotion seeing the pitiful little boy and turned away so that Arthur would not see his tears. The other men became upset as well, though they said nothing. The boy inferred the truth from their reactions. Tears sprang to his eyes and coursed down his cheeks, but those present said he bore it like a man, and returned home without a word. He probably realized in that moment that he had become the man of the house, responsible for his mother and four siblings.

Dunham knew he would have to speak to Julia Fountain personally, but wished to wait until he had some solid proof, so he sent his tug *Mosher* out on

Monday morning to survey the wreck site. He waited too long. That morning, she came looking for him, seeking some reassurance that the talk of a wreck might not be the *Wells Burt*. Richard Powers also visited Dunham, worried for his brother Jeff, who had shipped out on the *Wells Burt*. Dunham did not have the heart to tell them he believed that the men were dead, refusing to give up hope that the crew had found some way to survive the ordeal. After they left, Dunham told reporters milling around his office that he expected his tugs to arrive about noon, "But I expect no news but bad news."

Indeed, the *Mosher* confirmed what everyone had feared: The *Wells Burt* had sunk. The spars still stood above the water and surrounding them were all manner of flotsam, smashed and splintered timber, and rigging swaying in the current. Evidence came drifting into shore as well. The upper portion of a schooner's cabin washed ashore at North Avenue and a large section of its roof came up at the foot of Chestnut Street. Just south of that point, a piece of the topmast reached shore with portions of rigging and canvas still attached. One vessel came into Chicago with an old and battered sea chest containing a compass and inscribed with the name *Wells Burt*. A pasteboard tag from an oil can was found with the name of the vessel written in pencil. Chocolate-colored window blinds, like those known to have been on the *Wells Burt,* washed ashore along with a red canvas cover that Dunham knew to be from his schooner. In fact, the sailmaker who had fabricated it just that spring confirmed it, recognizing the seams he had used. Subsequently, the ship's yawl washed ashore, but no one was in it.

Despite all the wreckage, no bodies were found. Dunham had printed in the *Tribune* a plea, "For humanities sake, if you discover any bodies in the lake, please take extra exertions to secure them and deliver at the lifesaving station at the south pier for identification." Only Richard Powers would find solace. His brother Jeff showed up in Chicago, very much alive, happy to report that he had been fired in Buffalo.

The sinking caused great consternation to the maritime community. Given the quality of the schooner, most knowledgeable maritime men were convinced that it could not have not foundered. A Mr. Harman of the Union Tug Line spoke to reporters, saying what everyone thought, "There was never wind or sea enough inside to sink the *Wells Burt*." Various alternative hypotheses were formulated: It may have struck Grosse Point and been holed, the coal may have shifted and split the ship amidships, or more likely, it may have been involved in a collision. In the ensuing days, however, some began suspecting that a structural flaw in the schooner's design caused the sinking. The *Wells Burt* had solid bulwarks which would not have allowed for the discharge of water if the ship had become swamped.

To solve the mystery, Dunham knew that he would have to examine the wreck. He first visited the site with a diver and a reporter from the *Daily Inter-Ocean* on May 23. However, the water was too muddy and choppy to permit the diver to descend. By May 25, the papers reported that Dunham had abandoned the vessel to the underwriters. Six different companies had policies on the *Wells Burt,* which totaled $25,700. The cargo carried a separate insurance policy of $7,500. On Sunday, May 27, conditions finally improved so that Dunham's diver, Captain Peter Falcon, could visit the wreck. He saw enough to draw a conclusion about why the ship sank. The vessel sat in forty feet of water and had worked its way deep into the clay, on its port bilge at an angle of approximately thirty degrees. The aft cabin and forecastle were gone, the mizzenmast torn loose, the hatches gone, portions of the deck gone, and much of the cargo washed out. The anchors were still in place on the bow and two axes lay on the deck. He found no bodies.

Based on this evidence, Falcon painted a picture of what happened that night. He reasoned that as the schooner headed south in the raging storm, its steering gear became disabled. Unable to be controlled, the vessel would have turned broadside to the waves. In that position, waves would have swept relentlessly over the deck, filling the hold and toppling the mizzenmast, which would have crashed through the cabin. To keep the mast from dragging the ship down, the crew likely used the axes to try to chop through the rigging that secured it to the vessel. The raging seas likely swept them all overboard before they could do so. Few of the crew could swim and even if they could, the icy water would have quickly ended their lives.

Based on the way the wreck had buried itself into the bottom, Falcon judged that it would be extremely difficult to pass chains under it, necessary to raise the schooner. Instead, he recovered part of the foremast and some booms, gaffs, and yards, but left the rudder where he found it, lying on the bottom of the lake. He also left behind the bowsprit and other portions of the rigging not worth raising. Falcon's explanation, however, did not satisfy all of those who wondered about the cause of the sinking. The reporter for the *Daily Inter-Ocean,* who accompanied Dunham and Falcon on the dive trip, continued to insist that the solid bulwarks probably contributed to the disaster. Even considering those other factors, all had to face the fact that the unimaginable had happened: The *Wells Burt* had foundered in the storm.

It would take until July for any further evidence of the wreck to be discovered. The bodies of Edward Hanlon and John White washed ashore and were buried by the Seaman's Union in Calvary Cemetery. The *Chicago Daily News* attempted to quantify the damage caused by the storm. It estimated $200,000 in property damage to ships and cargo, eighteen lives lost, and fifteen vessels destroyed or damaged, including the *Sea Gull* and the *Antaree* off Chicago. The *Wells Burt* was the worst casualty. Eleven people died, and the vessel and cargo were worth $40,000.

The 1883 season marked the worst for accidents and vessel losses in Great Lakes history. Another severe gale in November lasted two full weeks and losses exceeded those for the two previous seasons combined. Caught in that gale was the scow schooner *Rockaway* (detailed in Chapter Four), which was blown, ice-encrusted, for two days west across Lake Michigan where it and its crew were finally rescued from near sinking, among the more lucky of the vessels sailing that week. One hundred other ships were lost that year, with an estimated total value of three million dollars, and two hundred people were killed.

The loss of the *Wells Burt* touched off a flurry of controversy over the safety of ships and the adequacy of inspections. The *Daily Inter-Ocean* urged that lake ships no longer be built with solid bulwarks and encouraged closer inspection of steering gears. The *Chicago Tribune* pressed for better lighting and more protection at the Port of Chicago, and encouraged the many sailors who could not swim to learn so that they could help save themselves. In June, both the *Chicago Times* and *Cleveland Herald* ran a story that likened many lake vessels to "floating coffins," suggesting that builders were using inferior materials to construct them. The article further noted that improper maintenance, rotten timbers, and insufficient salting and caulking contributed to accidents. It accused ship owners of avoiding inspections by locking up their boats, bribing inspectors, or just paying a higher rate of insurance instead. Moreover, it pointed out that the six men who held jobs as inspectors could not possibly cover the entire fleet. All these issues, it noted, placed the lives of the sailors at excessive risk. The article singled out the case of the *Wells Burt* as the most dramatic evidence for a widespread scandal, which resulted in a movement to make shipping safer.

## FOUND

The discovery of the *Wells Burt* 105 years after it sank resulted in a movement of a much different nature. In the fall of 1988, A&T Recovery, a commercial salvage firm, approached the Chicago Maritime Society's underwater archaeology committee with an announcement and a challenge. The company had found the wreck of the *Wells Burt* in the

**Captain Thomas Fountain and his son Daniel were buried at Rosehill Cemetery on the north side of Chicago, marked by this distinctive monument displaying an anchor.** *Author's Collection*

133

course of its normal work, and would share the location with the society if it could develop a plan to protect the virgin wreck from looting, which had been the fate of several other shipwrecks that A&T had found.

Since the mid-1980s, A&T Recovery has been the United States Navy's primary contractor for the recovery of World War II airplanes lost in Lake Michigan. In 1942, the Navy began qualifying pilots for aircraft carrier landings and takeoffs from two former passenger liners, the *Sea and Bee* and the *Greater Buffalo*, converted to the aircraft carriers USS *Wolverine* and USS *Sable*. The Navy trained over 15,000 pilots between 1942 and 1945, during which time several aircraft were lost. Decades later, those lost planes have become historical treasures. The advent of commercial side scan sonar equipment in the 1980s provided A&T and other Lake Michigan-based salvors like Richard Race of the Hydrographic Survey Company and Harry Zych of American Diving and Salvage the tools to find shipwrecks. In fact, anyone who could afford the expensive equipment and time to mount an expedition, could more effectively search for shipwrecks. Side scan sonar sends out acoustical signals that bounce off anything that sits above the lake bottom and provides a printed image (or, in more recent times, a digital image) of the anomaly. Using side scan, A&T would go on to locate over thirty airplanes, most of which would be raised and sent to the National Museum of Naval Aviation in Pensacola, Florida, for restoration and display.

A&T realized immediately that this wreck was unique. The lake bottom is generally shallow at the southern end of the lake, and shipwrecks tend to take a beating from the waves and action of the winter ice, leaving little but a scattering of planks and machinery. However, the entire lower hull and deck of the wreck were intact, protected to a great degree because it had settled into the silty lake bottom up to its waterline. In addition, dozens of artifacts lay scattered on the

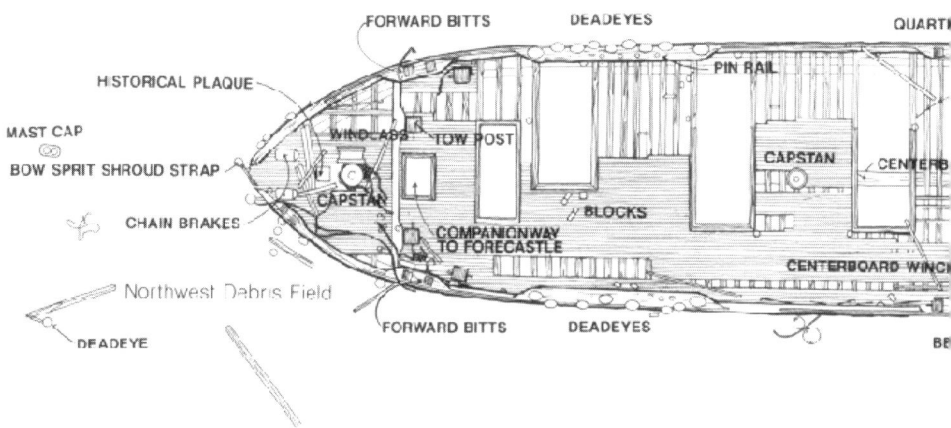

deck and in the debris field. Clearly, the vessel had never been dived upon, and to a firm keenly aware of the condition of sunken vessels, it represented the most intact schooner yet found in the southern third of Lake Michigan.

Previous to this discovery, the firm had located the remains of the schooner *Wings of the Wind*, lost off Chicago in 1866. The partners shared the location with diving friends, the coordinates leaked to other divers, and within a few weeks the site had been stripped of all its artifacts. Recognizing that the *Wells Burt* represented an archaeological time capsule and understanding the lure that a virgin wreck poses, A&T sought the involvement of the Chicago Maritime Society, based on its recent work on the *David Dows*. The organization stood ready to take on the *Wells Burt* as a test project, one of the first to document a virgin shipwreck, which unlike the *David Dows* had not yet been disturbed by the hand of man. To profess its desire to see the wreck preserved, A&T would not provide the precise location of the shipwreck until the group proved that it could raise the funding and gather the proper expertise and manpower to properly survey the vessel. Over the winter of 1988-1989, the underwater archaeology committee of the Chicago Maritime Society reorganized as an independent nonprofit under the name Underwater Archaeological Society of Society (UASC). The UASC met with the officials of the Illinois Historical Preservation Agency (IHPA), with whom it had collaborated to survey *David Dows*.

With input from the IHPA, the UASC began to develop a three-pronged plan to study and preserve the wreck. First, society members prepared a brochure explaining the benefits of shipwreck preservation to divers and began delivering a series of educational programs aimed at the sport diving community to champion the importance of the new laws. In the process, the UASC recruited new members to work on the project and promote preservation ethics. Next, the group conceived of and hosted a benefit event entitled "An Evening

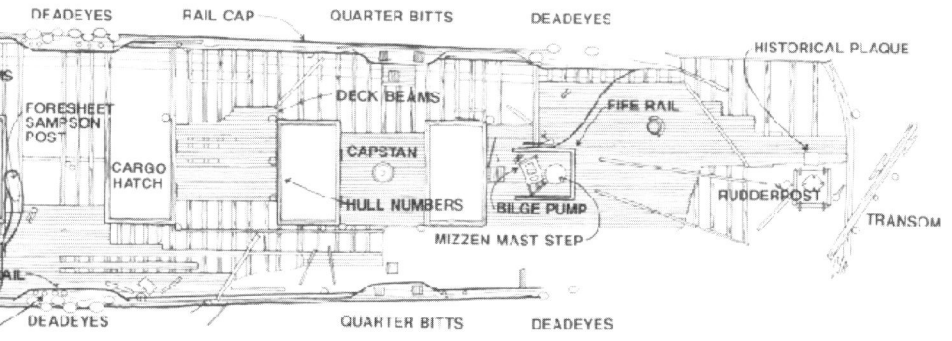

**A drawing of the wreck of the *Wells Burt* was the result of one summer of documentation efforts by over two dozen volunteer divers.** *Drawing by the author*

**The author documents a row of deadeyes along the rail on the *Wells Burt*. A regular No. 2 pencil was used on Mylar, a plasticized writing surface, to make notes and sketches.**
*Photograph by Eric Brod*

with Great Lakes Divers." The film festival, the first of many annual events, raised several thousand dollars as well as in-kind commitments for the project, including a boat and captain and the services of researchers, photographers, and videographers. Lastly, the group drew up detailed plans for implementing an archaeological survey, similar to the survey on the *Rockaway*, although the UASC planned to leave all the artifacts on the wreck. Team members met with Kenneth Pott during the last year of his work on the *Rockaway* to learn techniques that could be applied to the *Wells Burt* survey. Pott reminded the team that certain *Rockaway* artifacts had been tampered with before he could properly document them and warned the UASC of a similar possibility. The *Wells Burt* rests as close to shore as the *Rockaway*, and the UASC's presence on site could disclose the wreck's location. The UASC conceived of a plan to attempt to protect the artifacts: They would affix a small, numbered plastic tag to each artifact. This would help catalogue the artifacts as well as serve as a warning to other divers that the item had been recorded and would be noticed if it disappeared. Convinced that the UASC had developed a suitable preservation plan, A&T Recovery provided the location in the spring of 1989. On a clear day in May, 106 years after the *Wells Burt* sank, UASC divers made their first visit to the wreck under the direction of this book's author. The site was nearly identical to the way salvage diver Thomas Falcon described it a week after it sank.

The bow faces northwest, the vessel lists about twenty degrees to its port side, and the cabin, steering gear, anchors, and masts are gone. The hull, with its three-foot-high solid bulwarks, remains intact, but about forty percent of the deck planking is missing mostly on the starboard side, exposing the horizontal deck frames and hatch coamings. Deck equipment remains, including a capstan used to raise and lower the anchors, a winch used to raise the centerboard, and three sets of deadeyes and chainplates that once secured the masts. A variety of rigging rests off the port side of the vessel in a field of debris. It appears that sand and silt have made their way into the hold, coming within a few feet of the underside of the deck frames.

Although fairly certain of the wreck's identity from circumstantial evidence, the team found positive proof. Divers spotted the ship's registration number, 80365, carved into a main beam and the capstan's 1855 patent date and number, 13506, engraved on the unit. Both matched the historical data about the *Wells Burt*.

The team's first task involved the placement of two mooring buoys on the wreck, one at the bow secured to the sturdy capstan, and one at the stern secured to the top of the rudder post. These would mark the location of the shipwreck and eliminate the need to drop anchors to position the boat, an act that could do damage to the wreck. Next, the team installed four interpretive plaques at the bow, stern, and on both sides of the hull, reminding divers that removing artifacts is a felony. Then, using zip ties, the team systematically affixed over two hundred plastic tags to all the artifacts. Once that was accomplished, photographers swam from artifact to artifact and captured images of each item.

Since visibility averaged only three to ten feet during the summer of 1989, the team divided the wreck into a series of twenty sections that would allow them to focus on the recording of the wreck in smaller, more manageable pieces. This was accomplished by stringing a 200-foot line from bow to stern, then lines from side to side every twenty feet down the length. During each dive, team members were assigned a section where they would sketch the deck arrangement using a regular lead pencil on plasticized paper called Mylar affixed to a rigid slate board. Then they recorded the location of tagged artifacts. After each dive, the project director would collect the sketches and transpose the data onto one large draw-

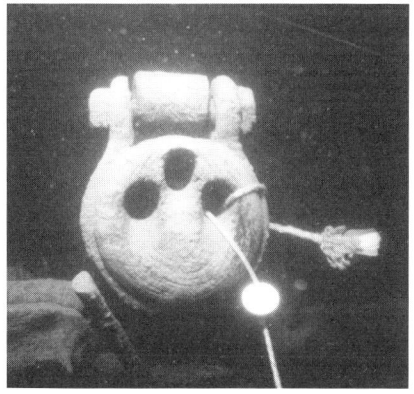

**Each artifact, like this deadeye, was given a numbered tag, photographed, and inventoried so that it would be documented in case of theft.** *Photograph by Clare Gadbois*

**UASC diver Mike Hoffner recovers artifacts from the *Wells Burt* under an emergency permit from the State of Illinois after a number of items had been removed from the wreck.** *Photograph by Joseph Oliver*

ing. By the end of the season, over seventy-five divers had participated in the project. Not only did they learn the techniques of conservation archaeology, but they produced a site plan, wrote an historic profile, created an artifact database, shot hours of video, and took hundreds of photographs that would be used in public presentations.

The next season, divers began regularly visiting the wreck and it became the busiest dive site in Illinois waters. The sport diving community seemed to embrace the concept of protecting its own historic attraction. However, on a follow-up survey dive in 1991, the UASC discovered that ten deadeyes had been wrenched off the wreck and were missing, along with ten other loose artifacts. In addition, one of the four interpretive plaques had been pried off the wreck, suggesting that these actions were done in contempt of the law. The IHPA and UASC had hoped that the diving community would protect its own recreational site, but it seemed that the finders-keepers mentality was too engrained to expect change overnight.

Fearing the loss of the other artifacts, the IHPA issued an emergency permit to the UASC for the recovery of all the remaining loose artifacts on the wreck. They left anything that would have required the use of tools to remove, including the twenty-six remaining deadeyes. To discourage any future theft of those, the UASC strung chains through them. Although the chains would not deter anyone with a bolt cutter, they would send a strong message.

Following the instructions outlined in *The Conservation of Archaeological Ar-*

*tifacts from Freshwater Environments* by Katherine Singley, published as a result of the *Rockaway* project, UASC members conserved the wood and iron objects. The IHPA offered a $2000 reward to anyone with information leading to the arrest and conviction of the persons responsible for removing the artifacts. This prompted the producers of the television show *Missing/Reward*, hosted by actor Stacy Keach, to produce an episode publicizing the theft. Despite all these efforts, the perpetrators were never found and the artifacts were never recovered. However, because of the survey, the information about these lost items has been forever preserved.

The *Wells Burt* project served to call attention to the new laws, as well as developing techniques that would quickly became a model throughout the Great Lakes for an efficient and accurate recognizance-level archaeological survey. Because of the actions of a few divers, other divers had to suffer the loss of the artifacts from the site. However, the *Wells Burt* served an important role in spreading a conservation ethic: The offense received so much negative attention that it may have precluded others from doing the same thing. More than two decades after its discovery, the *Wells Burt* still sports its remaining deadeyes and continues to be one of the main underwater attractions in Illinois waters.

Another television program even featured the *Wells Burt* eighteen years after its Hollywood debut: The History Channel's series, *Cities of the Underworld*, ran an episode about the mysterious sinking of the *Wells Burt*, eliciting the participation of this book's author. Observations made during that dive, in visibility that allowed the entire wreck to be seen in one glance, supported earlier theories about the cause of the sinking. The solid bulwarks make the ship appear to look like a giant bathtub. Water from crashing waves certainly would have filled the vessel and could easily have weighed it down until it foundered. Those same solid bulwarks have, ironically, helped maintain the shipwreck intact after more than 125 years underwater.

**Two hooks, probably part of an anchor snubber assembly used to take strain off the anchor chain, were among the small number of artifacts recovered from the *Wells Burt*, and photographed before conservation work began.** *Photograph by Mike Hoffner*

The author swims through the port sidewheel of the steamer *Sea Bird* during the 1990 survey.
Photograph by Joseph Oliver

## 9

# FIERY FIGHTS

The *Sea Bird* is a legendary story of loss and survival against a raging conflagration on a cold April morning in 1868. The fire—if the resulting death toll of 100 victims is correct—resulted in the tenth worst disaster on the Great Lakes, and the fourth worst on Lake Michigan, behind the capsizing of the *Eastland* in 1915, the sinking of the *Lady Elgin* in 1860, and the fire that consumed the *Phoenix* in 1847. The story of its discovery in 1989 and subsequent "fiery" legal battle over ownership of its charred and waterlogged remains ranks as the first case to challenge the constitutionality of the Abandoned Shipwreck Act, elevating it to one of Lake Michigan's legendary shipwrecks.

In 1859, Eber Brock Ward commissioned the building of a new steamer for use on Lake Erie that he would call the *Sea Bird* (presented as two words throughout its career). Until 1857, Lake Erie had been the home of several large "palace" steamers, but, the financial panic of the mid-1850s had resulted in a number of these vessels being laid up, too expensive to operate in those hard times. Ward saw an opportunity for a smaller and less expensive steamer to serve the dwindling, but still existing, transportation market. At 191 feet long and 28 feet wide, the *Sea Bird* had two decks, the lower for freight and the upper, called the hurricane deck, for passengers. On the hurricane deck, a cabin near the stern housed ladies and families and a cabin near the bow housed gentlemen. Each contained fifty two-bunk staterooms, affording ample accommodations for about two hundred passengers. The engine had been salvaged from an older steamer, the *Sam Ward*. Eber Ward initially operated it under the Buffalo and Lake Erie Steamboat Company, boasting rates of $2.50 for a cabin and $1.50 for steerage, half the railroad fare. In October, Ward transferred the *Sea Bird* to the Cleveland, Detroit, and Lake Superior route.

**This may be the only photograph of the *Sea Bird*. When the sidewheeler burned in 1868, photography was still in its infancy.** *C. Patrick Labadie Collection - Alpena County Public Library*

During the 1860 season, the *Sea Bird* had the first of many accidents. Serious damage to its engine nearly ruined it, and Ward had to install new machinery. In the following year it caught fire on the port side, just forward of the wheelhouse. The captain acted quickly and saved the vessel from destruction by stopping the engine and trimming the boat so that the flaming side dragged in the water. By this means, he managed to extinguish the fire without the passengers ever discovering the peril they had been in.

In 1863, Ward's business declined due to the expansion of the railroads and he decided to consolidate in the Detroit region. He sold the *Sea Bird* to Captain Albert E. Goodrich, who had just started his own steamboat line on Lake Michigan. Goodrich, who would later go on to become one of the most notable steam boat operators of Lake Michigan, paid $36,000 for the vessel that April. He intended to use it between Chicago and Lake Superior with stops along many of Wisconsin's lake ports.

During its first season on Lake Michigan, the *Sea Bird* ran aground at Whitefish Bay, Wisconsin, in a terrible snowstorm and remained grounded there for an entire year, until a salvor raised it and towed it to Chicago for repairs. In December 1864, it was involved in a collision in Green Bay and almost sank. During the spring of 1866, the *Sea Bird* became trapped in the ice near Sheboygan; during that summer it had an accident in Port Washington; and in the winter it was damaged by ice. All these travails plus normal wear and tear in 1867 and 1868 left the *Sea Bird* in bad shape when laid up for the 1868 winter at Manitowoc, so Goodrich arranged for it to be completely overhauled. A number of improvements were added for passenger comfort, up-to-date fire extinguishing equipment was installed, and the vessel received a fresh coat of paint inside and out, all for a cost of between $7000 and $8000.

The 1868 shipping season began in April with Captain John Morris assigned to the *Sea Bird* to run passenger and cargo trips from Chicago up to Two Rivers, Wisconsin. He had worked for Goodrich for more than a decade, beginning as a helmsman and working his way up to competent and trustworthy captain. By 1863, he commanded the *Sea Bird* and its crew, which usually numbered between seventeen and twenty-five men. By early April 7, the *Sea Bird* had already made three round trips. On April 7, Captain Morris began loading the vessel in Two Rivers for what would be his fourth trip that season.

The vessel took on board a variety of freight, including a number of newly made wooden pails that were all that remained from the Joseph Mann factory after a terrible fire the prior week. They were only part of the order placed by a Chicago retailer. The engineer fired up the *Sea Bird's* boiler, raising the steam pressure. The crew cast off the lines, Morris sounded the whistle, and the sidewheels began to turn. The familiar chugging sound and the rocking back-and-forth of the walking beam signaled the steamboat was under way. The lake was relatively calm.

*The Sea Bird* left Two Rivers at 6 a.m. on April 8, arriving at its first stop in Manitowoc by mid-morning. There, the vessel took on board 200 barrels of flour, 51 packages of tobacco, 30 hides, 25 sacks of turnips, 22 packages of furniture, 30 bags of peas, and 370 packages of hardware, which filled the vessel to near capacity. About thirty-five passengers, including nine children, boarded the *Sea Bird* before it sailed at noon that Wednesday.

As Morris headed south for the second leg of the trip, the winds began to pick up and soon a squall formed. The lake became rough. The *Sea Bird* did not reach Sheboygan until 3 p.m., much later than usual. The high winds even

A newspaper advertisement lists the regular sailing times of the Goodrich Transportation Company steamers, of which the *Sea Bird* was one. *Author's collection*

**A woodcut by W. B. Baird that appeared in *Harpers Illustrated Weekly* following the accident depicts how the movement of the boat spread the conflagration faster than if the vessel had been stopped immediately.** *C. Patrick Labadie Collection - Alpena County Public Library*

affected the vessel while it was at the dock in the harbor. The crew could not manage to keep the gangplank in position and had to receive the cargo tossed across the water by dockworkers. Even the passengers had to jump from the dock to the lower deck of the *Sea Bird*. Worried that the pounding against the wharf might damage the boat, Morris encouraged the passengers to hurry up, several times. Among the reported ten to twenty people who boarded at Sheboygan were two men, strangers to each other, whose paths would later cross. Furniture dealer Albert C. Chamberlain from nearby Sheboygan Falls intended to purchase some stock in Chicago for his store. Edmund Hennebury, a twenty-two-year-old sailor, planned to find work for the season on a vessel operating out of Chicago.

From Sheboygan, the *Sea Bird* proceeded south slowly, fighting the rough seas. The galley crew served dinner, and because of the number of passengers had to accommodate them in three different seatings. The food did not sit well with some because of the rocking of the boat. Many became seasick. The steamer finally made port in Milwaukee at the foot of Main Street by 9:30 p.m., over two and a half hours past its scheduled arrival. After spending an afternoon and evening jostled around on the Lake, several passengers decided to depart and finish the journey by train. They would be the fortunate ones.

## LOST

Twenty-nine-year-old Manitowoc store clerk James H. Leonard boarded the *Sea Bird* at Milwaukee. He had left for Chicago three days earlier, stopping in Milwaukee two nights before catching the *Sea Bird*. In Chicago he and his wife of one year, Martha, intended to purchase their own grocery store, which he had been saving up for while employed at George S. Glover's store in Manitowoc. Prior to that, Leonard had worked as a school teacher, and then enlisted in the Fifth Wisconsin Volunteers to fight in the Civil War. He saw action at Antietam, Fredericksburg, Gettysburg, and Rappahannock Station, among other places. He had been badly wounded at Rappahannock Station, but healed and rejoined his company. In 1864 he had returned to civilian life and began working for Glover, finding the grocery business more lucrative than teaching.

A number of other passengers boarded at Milwaukee, and the crew took on board more freight, including a prized horse, until the lower decks were at near capacity. Just before 11 p.m., the *Sea Bird* departed Milwaukee. By that time the winds had moderated, and the waves subsided, but it remained very cold. Most of the passengers including Hennebury, Leonard, and Chamberlain settled into cabins for the night, glad that the porters kept the cabin stoves stoked to provide heat inside the cabins. At 12:30 a.m., on April 9, 1868, the *Sea Bird* stopped at Racine to take on a small load of freight, continuing the journey south after just thirty minutes. According to later accounts, some eighty passengers in addition to the crew were on board when the *Sea Bird* left Racine.

At about 5 a.m. Thursday morning, Edmond Hennebury awoke. By his calculations, he went out on deck to get some fresh air about an hour and a half hour later. James H. Leonard, likewise, went outside at 6:30 a.m. There, Leonard met the first mate who informed him they were between Lake Forest and Waukegan, about twenty-five miles north of Chicago. "If nothing happens," he told Leonard, "we will reach Chicago about 10 o'clock." Leonard wondered what could possibly happen to delay them. He returned to his stateroom, where his wife still lay in bed, but a few moments later he heard an alarm bell. Rushing onto the deck, he discovered the aft end of the boat in flames. Before he could return for his wife, the cabin erupted in fire, and he was caught up in a rush of people running toward the bow.

At the same time, Edmond Hennebury saw the flames, heard the bell, and saw a rush of people coming toward him. Looking over the port side near the stern, he saw flames spring up from a pile of tubs and straw on the open lower deck. "I at once cried out 'Fire! Fire!,'" he later recalled. He could see several of the crew hurry to where the fire erupted. Retreating to the shelter of the forward cabin, he saw passengers begin tumbling out of their staterooms.

Albert Chamberlain was among those passengers. From his berth in the forward gentlemen's cabin, Chamberlain had been awakened by a loud cry at about 6:30 a.m. At first he thought it was the crew fighting below. He got up and looked out the stateroom door and saw a number of crewmembers and passengers running forward through the cabin. He could see that the tables had been set for breakfast. Then he heard the emergency bells. He dressed and rushed out, but until he heard the watchman rushing around the cabin rousing sleepers and crying, "Fire! Fire!" he had no idea what was happening.

Women stood paralyzed, screaming and crying, some with children clinging to them. The men rushed around frantically, looking for some means to save themselves and the women. Some ladies fell on their knees and prayed to God to save them. In their haste to escape from their staterooms, some people had forgotten to dress themselves and were running around in their nightclothes. The confusion of so many interfered with the few people who had sufficient presence of mind to attempt to stop the progress of the flames. Above the screams, Chamberlain heard someone yell, "Head her ashore," and he realized the boat was still moving quite quickly, pounding up and down on the churning waters. He noticed that the wind seemed to be increasing.

Standing among the crowd near the bow, Chamberlain spotted the captain in his shirt sleeves and bareheaded, apparently dumbstruck. "He issued no orders that I heard," he recalled, "so utterly was he taken aback." He just stood there staring at the crowd. Among those gathered, Chamberlain heard several people mention that they had seen a porter dump a bucket of live coals overboard from the upper deck on the windward side, and saw them blow back onto the lower deck where a number of pails had been packed in straw.

While the *Sea Bird* burned, several early risers walking along shore in Waukegan took notice of a flaming steamer, about five to eight miles from shore. One man reported, "It seemed to be on fire from stem to stern in a few moments." They stood there watching, unable to see anything except that the steamer had changed course and was running against the wind, and then began going in a near circle. Soon the beach was lined with people using opera glasses and telescopes to try to see the pillar of fire and smoke. No one could tell what kind of vessel it was. There was a government lifeboat on the beach, but because of the wind and the waves, no one volunteered to man it.

Someone in Waukegan must have suspected the burning boat was a Goodrich steamer, because a telegraph was sent to Goodrich's office between 6:30 and 7:00 that morning describing the catastrophe. Captain Goodrich feared it was the *Sea Bird,* and he immediately outfitted one of the ships in his fleet, the propeller *G. J. Truesdell*, to head up toward the area and search for any survivors. Goodrich himself boarded the 9 a.m. train north to Waukegan to investigate the situation.

On board the *Sea Bird* the fire spread into the ladies' cabin so rapidly that Hennebury assumed that many of the women had been trapped and burned. Everybody who had made it out of the cabins rushed forward. Hennebury noticed some of the crew banded together trying to reach the lifeboats near the stern, but they did not get beyond amidships by the smokestack before the fire forced them back. Hennebury knew the steamer was doomed but somehow remained calm, feeling confident he would survive. He watched a number of people jump overboard into the frigid waters. Most never surfaced.

James Leonard was among those who jumped soon after the flames erupted. He had donned a life jacket, which kept him afloat long enough to secure a hold on a plank. The waves pushed him toward a larger piece of wood, which he recognized as a portion of the paddlewheel box about eight or nine feet square. He managed to get on top of it, which kept him out of the water. He used his knife to stab two holes through the wood, binding his legs to it with the ropes of the life preserver. His extremities quickly became numb, so he resourcefully cut some cotton wadding from the lining of his overcoat and wrapped it around his head and hands. From the makeshift raft, he watched the pandemonium on board the flaming steamer, wondering how long he could sustain himself, and what had become of his wife.

As soon as Chamberlain realized the ship was doomed, he went to his stateroom for a life preserver, and found two, taking them both with him. Instead of going back out on deck, he went to the lower deck to see if any means of escape presented itself. The crew must have thought the same thing, because he found many of them trying to herd the horse overboard, which he presumed might save the men if they clung to it. Finding no other means for survival down there, he went back to the hurricane deck and for a time worked with the Second Mate Leander Packard to break away any loose wooden pieces that would add fuel to the flames. However, the intense heat forced them back. At that point, Chamberlain took off his overcoat, put on one life jacket, and then put his coat back on. He was in the process of donning the other life jacket over his coat, when another man requested it, so he gave it up. About this time, the engine ceased operating and the wheels stopped turning.

With great interest, Chamberlain watched a group of five or six men— among them Edmund Hennebury, he would later learn—wrestle a gangplank overboard just forward of the paddle boxes. One by one, the men followed it into the water. Fearful that the cold water would kill him, Chamberlain decided not to do likewise. Edmund Hennebury waited until the gangplank floated near the wheel, and then jumped toward it. The icy water must have pierced him like knives, but he hurriedly swam to the gangplank and clambered aboard. Some ten or fifteen other men followed his example, swamping its surface. "So many of us on the plank caused it to sink," Hennebury later recalled. He and the others struggled in the water, to try to get back onto the plank. Hennebury had just grabbed the edge of the plank and prepared to climb back on, when three or four others climbed onto his back. "I shook them all off, except a colored boy, the cook's helper. He put both arms about my neck, and I could not shake him off." Hennebury helped calm the boy, then managed to get him on the plank. Another man, already on the plank, caught hold of Hennebury's wrist and pulled him up. Then, Hennebury assisted a passenger, Johnnie O'Brien, but each time he dragged the man on board, the waves washed him off.

"We all struggled hard, but there wasn't a man said a word," Hennebury remembered. As soon as he felt somewhat secure on the plank, Hennebury found himself in the water again when a wave flipped it over.

"The water was almost at freezing," he later told reporters. "I was able to climb on to the gangplank because I knew that if I stayed in the water I could not live long."

Alone on the plank now, he stood up and steadied himself with the attached ropes. His clothes soon became frozen and stiff, but the same sense of calm that he had felt on the *Sea Bird* overwhelmed him again. "I had no thought of death," he recalled.

Meanwhile, Chamberlain laid out his own plan for survival. He moved through the crowd to the bow, intending to lash himself to the forwardmost stempost. He figured that as long as the vessel remained above water, the post would as well. With his knife he cut the halyards to use as ropes, and then spotted two men below him hanging onto the rails on the ship's side. However, they dropped off, probably when their fingers become numb. Just as Chamberlain was ready to climb over the bow, the second mate approached asking him to help him loosen the flagpole upon which he intended to float. Chamberlain helped him wrestle it down and throw it overboard. He watched as the mate jumped, but he never saw him surface.

Looking around in the water, Chamberlain could see planks, doors, benches, chairs, stools, and other things floating around. He also saw a number of ghastly looking bodies, burned and scalded, and some with no clothing. The sight made him sick thinking he might soon be in their position. By then, there were few people left on board. He watched as two of the last men shook hands and bid each other farewell, then jumped overboard. Like the others, they did not surface. Chamberlain hoisted himself up and over the bow and secured himself to the stempost with the rope. Soon, the heat from the flames became unbearable. "When the fire became too hot," he recalled, "I lowered myself down a little, and was protected by the bow of the boat."

From his new position, he spotted another man about thirty feet away, standing on a rail just forward of the gangway, clinging to the ship's side. The fire had burned the hull out on both sides of him, and he hollered to Chamberlain to throw the rope and haul him over. "It's not long enough," Chamberlain told him. Instead, the man jumped into the water, swam over toward Chamberlain, and caught hold of a rope hanging over the side, but in just a few minutes, he let go and sank into the water.

Concerned that the upper end of the rope that held him had started to burn,

Chamberlain clawed his way over to the anchor chain hanging nearby, coiled the rope around his body, and reached up to cut the flaming end loose. Although he burned his hand, he managed to grab the rope and tie it to the anchor chain. Once he felt secure in this new position, he surveyed the waters around him and took notice of a man standing atop a floating slab of wood some distance away.

From his vantage point on the floating gangplank, Hennebury could see the lake's surface dotted with debris and two men clinging to a bag of wool. One of them, not more than ten feet away, called over to him, "You're going pretty fast." Indeed, Hennebury's body served as a sort of sail, moving his little raft in the direction the wind blew.

Looking toward the steamer, he saw that it had burned almost to the water's edge. He could see no one alive on board. He watched as the walking beam engine, all but the diamond-shaped rocker once hidden deep within the ship, toppled over. "I was chilled through, and felt myself freezing. I did not dare let go of the rope, for if I did I would be washed away," he later recalled.

At about 9 a.m. as the *Sea Bird* smoldered, Captain Yates of the 359-ton schooner *Cornelia* sailed south toward Chicago. (Several accounts list the schooner inaccurately as *Cordelia*, but in all likelihood it was the 1857 Bidwell and Banta-built, Chicago-owned *Cornelia*.) Yates spotted smoke coming from a vessel that he reckoned to be about three miles southeast of Waukegan and a mile from him. Yates ordered his helmsman to make for the spot. The crew raised full sail and in short order reached the steamer and circled around it, but found no one alive in the water. Then, Yates spotted a man flailing his cap from a precarious position under the bow and immediately ordered the yawl boat launched to retrieve him.

From more than a mile away, Hennebury watched the actions taking place near the steamer and hoped that the schooner would head toward him soon. He could see the yawl boat approach the *Sea Bird* and hover there, but he could not see exactly what the crew was doing from that distance away.

When Chamberlain realized he had been seen by the schooner crew, he almost fainted, but managed to keep his composure. He kept his eyes riveted on the four crewmen in the small boat. It took them almost twenty minutes to reach him, which, he recalled, "seemed about twenty hours to me, so anxious was I to be rescued from my dangerous position." Because the swell was very heavy, they had to approach with caution, making two ineffectual attempts to reach Chamberlain. When they got near a third time, Chamberlain hollered for a knife. The swell carried the boat away some distance, but after hard pulling they got near enough that the mate caught hold of Chamberlain's coattail and passed him a knife. With hands so numb they felt like stones, Chamberlain managed to sever the ropes. He fell like a dead man into the bottom of the boat. While pulling toward the schooner, the mate asked Chamberlain if he knew of anyone else alive. "No one on the boat, I'm sure, but I saw one man standing atop a plank awhile ago," he said pointing toward a speck in the distance. The crew rowed as fast as possible back toward the *Cornelia*, but it took twenty-five minutes to get there. After getting Chamberlain aboard, and securing the yawl, they set sail toward the other man.

Meanwhile, Chamberlain, who had not eaten in more than fourteen hours, went below to get out of his frozen clothes, devour some food, and drink the spirits offered him. Then he passed out in the cabin.

Just when Hennebury thought he could not hold out any longer, he saw the schooner bearing down on him. By the time the crew had again launched the yawl and reached him, Hennebury had been on the raft for almost four hours. Once safe on board the *Cornelia*, he learned that only one other man had been rescued, and after struggling out of his wet, frozen clothing joined him in the cabin to sleep.

During the day, increasing numbers of people gathered along the beach in the vicinity of the burning wreck. Many came from Waukegan, but others arrived by train and horse from distant parts. The number grew to thousands. Some were fearful relatives and friends of the passengers, some were curiosity seekers, and some were pillagers there to pick up a relic or two from among the debris washing ashore. They found charred clothespins, broken stools, piles of cordwood, boxes of cargo, and flour barrels, but they saw no sign of people alive or dead. Those with spyglasses kept a lookout. They watched a schooner tacking around the burning steamer for an hour or more, then watched the burning hulk drift further south and closer to shore.

After a diligent search around the hulk, Captain Yates of the *Cornelia* determined that there was no one else alive, and so he set sail for Chicago. Though almost delirious from his perch on the paddle box about one mile away, James Leonard attempted to signal the sailing vessel, but realized he was too far away to be seen. He watched despondently as it sailed south away from him.

Back in Chicago, there was little to do but wait. Captain Goodrich had returned on the train at about noon with little information. The propeller *Truesdell* was still out, and there was no new information from telegraph or eyewitness reports. The one remaining hope was that a schooner seen in the vicinity would arrive in Chicago with news. Anxious people, including friends of the passengers and crew, merchants who had goods on board, newspaper reporters, and curiosity-seekers crowded the Goodrich offices on the south bank of the Chicago River just east of the Rush Street Bridge. Captain Goodrich and his clerks tried to reassure them, but as the time wore on, their doubts and fears increased.

Just before noon, the hulk had drifted nearly three miles south of Waukegan and a mile from shore. From the bluffs people could recognize projectiles, like paddle boxes, on either side, confirming that it was a steamboat. They watched it remain stationary for a long time, not moving out or in, as though stranded on a sandbar. Suddenly one end of it raised about ten feet in the air, remained poised for an instant, then plunged beneath the waves. Only a small piece of the vessel remained above the surface. Soon thereafter at about 1 p.m., a section of a paddle box washed ashore. A group of people turned it over. There, on its bottom side, they saw the large painted letters SEA BIRD. Word spread quickly. Local newspapers issued special editions reporting the tragedy.

The *Truesdell* arrived on site in the early afternoon. Captain Perritt spent three hours traversing the waters in every direction. He and the crew could see remnants of the wreck everywhere, including gang planks, doors, boxes, barrels, and other items, including fifteen or twenty floating hats, but they did not find anybody dead or alive. Finally, the captain and crew gave up and headed back to Chicago.

The *Cornelia* reached Chicago just after 4:00 that afternoon, entering the Chicago River with a flag of stars fluttering at its mast, under tow by a steam tug. The pair headed toward a mooring opposite the Lumber Exchange between Wells and Franklin Street. A throng of people on both sides of the river anxiously awaited word from the schooner. One of Captain Goodrich's employees hailed the crew: "Where do you come from?"

"The foot of the lake."

"See anything of the *Sea Bird*?"

"Got two of them here."

"Where are the rest?"

"That's all, these two."

Chamberlain and Hennebury stood motionless on the afterdeck. Crowds of unbelieving people chased after the boats asking repeatedly about the *Sea Bird* and receiving similar answers: "She is burned and all her passengers and crew are lost, saving the two men you see before me." The *Cornelia* hadn't even finished mooring before people swarmed the deck. Captain Goodrich made it aboard, too, and promptly started questioning the survivors.

A few hours before the schooner arrived in Chicago, James Leonard on his paddle box raft had neared shore. He cut the rope that bound his legs and even had to cut away some of his frozen coat to gain enough movement to tumble into the churning breakers. He found that he could touch the bottom with his feet, and soon reached dry land. With one leg partially frozen, he clambered up the bank, and wandered south along the shore in search of a human habitation. At about 4 p.m., he came upon the Evanston House, a boarding establishment. Its proprietor, E. Adams, heard the voice of a man pleading to be let in. Upon opening the door, Adams beheld a man encased with ice in pitiful condition. Leonard introduced himself as a survivor on the ill-fated steamer *Sea Bird*. Adams immediately ordered supper for his guest, to which Leonard replied with tears rolling down his cheeks, "But I have no money, sir. I had some, but it was to the keeping of my wife, and she is gone." Adams kindly cared for him, providing him with food, lodging, and a suit of clothes.

It would be days before Leonard talked to reporters. The accounts of his ordeal were so confused that some did not believe him. In explanation, Leonard described his utter exhaustion, his grief over his wife, and the suffering he had endured with little hope of rescue.

Ironically, a schooner also named *Sea Bird* sank off Kelley's Island in Lake Erie the same day the side-wheeler *Sea Bird* sank. In that accident everyone lived, confusing some newspaper readers.

Months later, on August 4, the propeller *Truesdell* traveled to the wreck site three miles south of Waukegan. A diver went down and reported the hull had been broken in two about amidships. He salvaged an anchor and the safe, which bore evidence of having been exposed to great heat. Upon being opened, the contents were found to have been reduced to ashes.

Two days later, a body was found, only the fourth of the many missing victims. The gruesome details were described by the *Chicago Tribune*: "The remains of a woman, supposed to have been one of the victims of the terrible *Sea Bird* catastrophe, was found at 7 o'clock yesterday morning, outside the breakwater, at the foot of Randolph Street. A boy while bathing in the lake, first discovered the corpse floating in the water, and notified Officer Clark, who secured it by a rope. The coroner afterwards had the body removed to the dead-house, where he minutely examined it. It was almost entirely nude, the remnants of a chemise and a figured alpaca dress only clinging to the shoulders and waist. From appearance it seemed to have been in the water for some months, which gives rise to the belief that the deceased was on board the ill-fated vessel, and met her death at the time of the calamity. The feet and hands were nearly gone, having been food for fishes, and the hair, of a dark brown tinge, was also partly gone. The body was greatly swollen and the features were so blackened and otherwise disfigured as to render identification impossible."

Goodrich retained salvage diver Peter Falcon to raise the hulk, but when he arrived weeks later, he found it was not worth the effort. He retrieved a few pieces of the machinery, but left the bulk of the wreck untouched.

Captain Goodrich was devastated by the loss, particularly because the company carried no insurance on the *Sea Bird*. Business dipped, presumably because people, frightened by vivid accounts like described above, became scared to sail on a Goodrich boat. To try to maintain his share of the passenger business, Goodrich issued a statement to the press announcing that because of the porter's criminal carelessness, he would remove the stoves from his vessels and install steam pipes instead. He also blamed the captain for negligence in not immediately stopping the engines to reduce the spread of fire.

Of course, neither the porter nor Captain Morris survived to recount their versions of the accident. Evidence later surfaced that could exonerate both men of any wrongdoing and clarify the origins of the fire. On April 25, more than two weeks after the accident, two teachers from the Academy of L. M. Johnson, Esquire, found a jacket swirling in the surf off Lake Forest. They waded out, dragged it to shore, went through the pockets, and found a wad of soaked papers, which they spread out to dry. They were all letters and receipts written in the same hand. A hastily scrawled note caught their attention:

> *"On board the Sea Bird. Whoever picks this up, will please have it published in some paper or carry it to the owner of the boat. The fire caught in the engine room and then spread to some pails on the deck. The captain give orders to stop the boat, but the flames would not permit anybody to go into the room. Everything was done by the captain that he could and the mate too. They are brave men, lots jumped into the water and are drowning, and some are burning to death. The captain gave orders to stop the boat by throwing anchor, but it still moves. I shall try to swim on a board to shore. I can't write much more the fire burns so fast. The captain has put all the money and some watches with a cask and thrown it over. Everything is marked. (signed) Carl Bostwick."*

Although the teachers did bring it to the attention of the *Chicago Tribune*, which printed the contents of that note and other documents in the pocket, there is no evidence that Alfred Guthrie, the supervising inspector of the 8th District, considered this statement when he wrote his official report. He, like Goodrich, blamed the blaze on the porter's carelessness and found Captain Morris at fault because in steaming for shore, he fanned the flames and spread the inferno. Guthrie urged Congress to set a law requiring that engineers immediately stop the engine in the event of fire.

## FOUND

In the late fall of 1988, Harry Zych of American Diving and Salvage found the *Sea Bird* while under hire to locate and raise a recently sunken pleasure boat off Waukegan, Illinois. Zych had installed his side scan sonar on an associate's boat and according to Bud Brain, a diver who worked with Zych that day (incidentally, one of the divers who participated in the raising of the *Alvin Clark*), Zych oversaw the cable and Brain kept an eye on the sonar. Suddenly Brain noticed an unusual splotch print out on the sonar paper and immediately threw a jug, with a line and weight, overboard to mark the spot, while hollering to Zych that they had found a shipwreck. Zych, a consummate diver with a great interest in historic shipwrecks, took one look at the image and agreed with Brain that it did represent a shipwreck, but immedi-

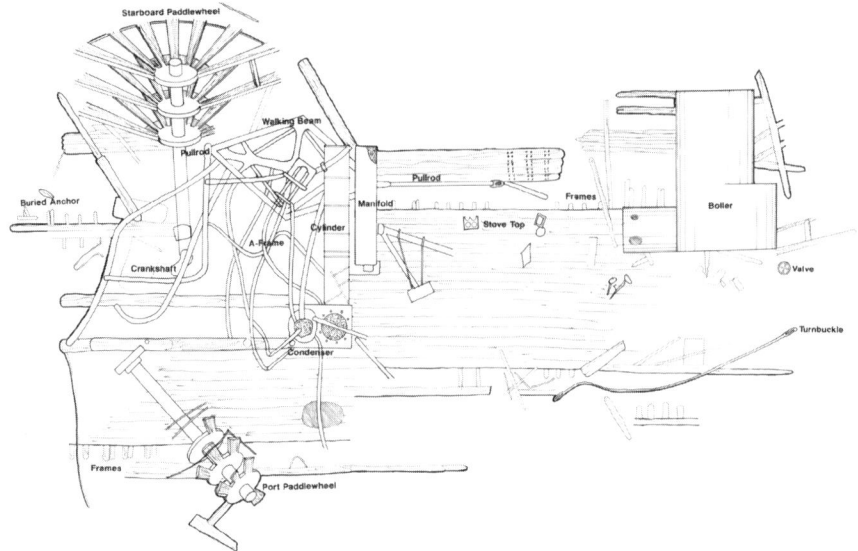

**The *Sea Bird* as it existed in 1992 when surveyed by the Underwater Archaeological Society of Chicago.** *Drawing by the Author*

ately assessed that it was too big to be the vessel they were searching for. He circled around to retrieve the jug, so they could proceed with their work, but not before he jotted down the coordinates of the wreck. Not long thereafter, the sonar plotted out a target that appeared to look more like the small boat for which they hunted, but a dive revealed a much older tug. With the end of the day nearing and the object of their goal undiscovered, Zych returned to the first target to take a look. He and Brain suited up and dived in.

They immediately realized the ship had been significantly damaged in a fire. Only about 100 feet of the charred, broken, and twisted wreckage remained sunk partially into the mucky bottom. Two massive paddle wheels, one still intact, dominated the site, and a large boiler and distinct walking beam engine made it obvious that the vessel had once been a sidewheel steamer. It did not take them long to realize they had found the *Sea Bird*, the only sidewheel steamer known to have burned in that general vicinity. The divers were thrilled since the *Sea Bird* represented such a significant accident. Brain managed to bring up two cast iron pots from that first dive.

The public learned about the discovery when on August 29, 1989, Zych filed an admiralty claim in federal court, presenting artifacts he had recovered from the *Sea Bird* and seeking title to the *Sea Bird* under the "law of finds" or a salvage award under the "laws of salvage." He probably did not realize that the lawsuit would mark the beginning of a legal battle that would last five years.

The State of Illinois intervened in the case, claiming title to the shipwreck under the Abandoned Shipwreck Act. Under the act, a state can claim ownership of a shipwreck if it has been abandoned by its owner, and it must also be either embedded in state lands or eligible for the National Register of Historic Places. Coming so soon on the heels of the 1988 establishment of the Abandoned Shipwreck Act, it is probable that Zych was using this wreck to test the strength of the law and challenge its constitutionality. In fact, one of his lawyers, Peter Hess, indicated that he had partial legal and financial backing from a consortium of insurance companies also interested in testing the law and potentially setting a precedent that might have application when other, perhaps more valuable, shipwrecks are found. However, the Eleventh Amendment, which prevents a federal court from rendering a decision that would bind a state, would pose a significant obstacle for this case. In September 1990, the federal judge dismissed Zych's suit, indicating that because the *Sea Bird* had been abandoned, Illinois had a justifiable claim to the shipwreck *if* it was embedded.

Since "if" was the significant word in the ruling, Zych filed an appeal in April 1991, arguing that Illinois had no claim to the wreck because the court never actually found the *Sea Bird* to be embedded. In August that year, the appellate court agreed with Zych and sent the case back to the federal court to determine whether the *Sea Bird* was in fact embedded.

Legal strategizing, filing, deposing witnesses, and scheduling hearing dates delayed movement in the case. Over one year later, after hearing testimony, the federal judge determined that in fact the *Sea Bird* was embedded, and so again dismissed Zych's case in December 1992. Zych appealed once again, this time changing strategy. To test the law using a different approach, in December 1993 Zych argued that *since* the wreck was embedded in Illinois, the State of Illinois owed him a salvage award for finding it and recovering the lost property. This new strategy could never be fully explored again because of the Eleventh Amendment. The federal appellate judge ruled that he could not make a decision that would bind Illinois. In fact, the judge used some tongue-and-cheek language in his final decision, noting that "Zych's case is sunk, and the decision of the federal court is upheld." After five years of legal wrangling, the outcome of this case found the Abandoned Shipwreck Act to be constitutional, and substantiated that if a diver or salvor wished to seek ownership of a shipwreck, he would have to do so in state court *not* federal court. Zych's battle did not end with the dismissal of the *Sea Bird* case. He would use his discovery of the shipwreck *Lady Elgin* to take the fight into Illinois state court.

A drawing by artist Robert McGreevy provides a unique perspective from behind the lumber schooner *Augusta* just moments before it hit the port side of the *Lady Elgin*. *Drawing by Robert McGreevy*

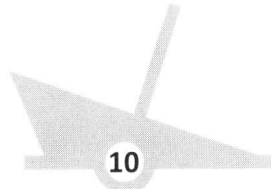

# 10

# TRAGEDY AND TRIALS

Everything about the sidewheel *Lady Elgin* is legendary. Many superlatives describe it: The *Lady Elgin* was a most luxurious passenger steamer, its sinking ranks as the deadliest disaster on the open waters of the Great Lakes, its remains represent the most scattered shipwreck in the Great Lakes, and the discovery of its wreckage led to the longest series of legal trials over shipwreck ownership in the Great Lakes.

The circumstances leading up to this tragic accident and eventual battle over its remains began during the tumultuous decade of the 1850s. At the time, the southern states were fully entrenched in a slave-supported agricultural economy, and the northern states were involved in industrial growth. The new Bessemer steel manufacturing process spurred large-scale construction. Newspaper presses could print 10,000 papers per hour. The country's first oil corporation drilled in Pennsylvania. Isaac Singer patented the first commercially successful sewing machine. Elisha Otis installed the first elevator. The first transatlantic cable linked North America to Europe. The growing railroad system increased westward expansion. The introduction of percussion and rifling systems revolutionized weaponry allowing for rapid fire in all weather. The Gold Rush that began in California in 1848 spurred a strong economy in the early half of the decade. The large quantities of gold that began pouring into Philadelphia prompted the U.S. Mint to create a $20 gold coin. As strong as the economy was at that time, the issues of slavery, particularly the Fugitive Slave Act of 1850, divided the county. The act, which allowed southern slave owners to venture into the free states of the north to retrieve their escaped human property, caused great uproar in the north.

In Wisconsin, radical abolitionist Sherman M. Booth, editor of Milwaukee's *Free Democrat*, took a stance against the act when he led a posse to break loose a recently captured escaped slave, Joshua Glover. For his role in doing what he believed to be morally correct, Booth was jailed, fined, and subjected to a lengthy court trial. As these issues festered the country sought solutions through the upcoming presidential election of 1860. Democrat Stephen Douglas supported states' rights to determine whether to allow the expansion of slavery. Republican Abraham Lincoln made his policies known through his 1858 speech in which he said, "A house divided against itself cannot stand. I believe this government cannot endure permanently half slave and half free." This was the turbulent period into which the *Lady Elgin* sailed.

Built in 1851, the *Lady Elgin* became one of more than 400 sidewheel steamers to operate on the Great Lakes. Bidwell and Banta of Buffalo, the most acclaimed shipyard on the Great Lakes and builder of some of the most famous passenger steamers of the period, constructed the *Lady Elgin*. At 256 feet, the *Lady Elgin* was among the larger of the lavishly appointed sidewheelers called palace steamers. It was powered by a walking-beam engine with two boilers just forward of amidships. The thirty-two-foot paddlewheels featured the ship's name in elegant letters. Cargo was carried in the hold and on the main deck. Passengers traveled on the promenade deck that ran almost the entire length of the ship. Sixty-six staterooms surrounded an open saloon with a grand staircase illuminated by clerestory windows. Aaron D. Patchin and Captain Gilman Appleby of Buffalo, New York, commissioned the building of the *Lady Elgin* to replace their recently wrecked *A.D. Patchin*, used in the immigrant trade. Although they salvaged a number of items from the wreck for the *Lady Elgin*, it still cost $96,000. The new steamer, named for Lady Mary Louisa Lambton, the wife of Canada's governor-general James Bruce, 8th Earl of Elgin, cleared Buffalo on its maiden voyage on November 7, bound for Chicago. It ran on the Michigan Southern Line, calling every fortnight at ports in Ohio, Michigan, and Wisconsin. In 1855, Albert Spencer, a Chicago merchant, acquired the *Lady Elgin* to serve the new Lake Superior trade and formed the Chicago, Milwaukee & Lake Superior Line. The vessel became a connecting link between isolated Lake Superior ports and the cities of the lower lakes. Watchers always greeted the beautiful steamer at the dock with enthusiasm.

Captain Jack Wilson took command of the *Lady Elgin* in 1858. Born at Ogdensburg, New York, just thirty-six years earlier, Jack, as he was known, began his sailing career as a deckhand on schooners and soon became one of the Great Lakes most respected shipmasters. On July 6, 1860, Gurdon Hubbard, a business entrepreneur and agent of Aetna Insurance who had been associated with Spencer for many years, purchased the vessel to serve the same route. He carried multiple insurance policies on the vessel totaling $24,000. The 1860 shipping season passed without incident—until the excursion that began on September 7, 1860.

Just after midnight that early Friday morning, hundreds of anxious people, most of them members, family, friends, or supporters of Wisconsin's independent Union Guards, boarded the *Lady Elgin* on the river in Milwaukee's Third Ward. They had planned a democratic rally in Chicago to coincide with Stephen Douglas' visit, but due to his delays on the campaign trail Douglas would not be there in time. The excursion went on despite that. Most of the passengers had never been to Chicago and looked forward to seeing the city.

The events that transpired to prompt the excursion began six months earlier at the hand of Wisconsin's Republican governor Alexander Randall. At the time, Sherman Booth's legal struggles over helping to free the escaped slave were ongoing and had created much turmoil in the state. Governor Randall believed the federal government had overstepped its boundaries in signing into law the Fugitive Slave Act. He began considering the possibility of having Wisconsin secede from the Union. Standing in his way was Garrett Barry, the leader of the Irish Union Guards, who had indicated he believed that secession would be treason and so would not support Randall's plan to secede. In a radical move, Randall had disbanded the Guards, and took away their weapons. In retaliation, Barry formed an independent unit and purchased from the St. Louis Armory eighty surplus flintlock muskets that had been altered with a new percussion cap system. They cost him $2.00 each. The excursion to Chicago at $1 per person would help repay the $160 debt.

The travelers' spirits must have lifted as they entered the Chicago River Friday morning accompanied by the fanfare of Milwaukee's brass band. The *Lady Elgin* docked at the south side of the river near LaSalle Street. Photographer Samuel Auschular must have been captivated by the gorgeous vessel and excited passengers. He captured the second photograph ever taken of the vessel. The excursionists had a wonderful day of marching through Chicago with their new weapons to show Democratic support for Douglas. Many had breakfast at the new Merchants Hotel. Some attended McVicker's Theater. Others saw the Irish Cyclorama, and still others attended an auction at the Tremont House. Many partook in good food and drink that evening before returning to the vessel at 10 p.m. In addition to the returning excursionists, the *Lady Elgin* also took on board many passengers destined to Lake Superior as well as a herd of cattle and a consignment of cast iron cook stoves. About 400 were on board for the trip north.

Although he knew a storm was brewing, Captain Wilson gave the command to steer the sidewheeler from the dock at about 11 p.m. at the encouragement of the passengers. As the *Lady Elgin* left the calm river and steamed north toward Milwaukee, fog rolled in, the action of the waves increased, and the boat started to rock. By midnight, the sky turned inky black, clouds rolled overhead, and the rain began. The wind built quickly to a gale. Those who had berths turned in for the night. Others took places on chairs or on the floor to

**The most famous of only two photographs known to exist of the *Lady Elgin*, this one by Samuel Auschular, shows the vessel at the dock at LaSalle Street on the morning of September 7, 1860, the day before it sank. Three-quarters of the passengers pictured would not live to see the light of the next day.** *Author's Collection*

get some rest. Still others remained awake and carried on with dancing and drinking in the shelter of ship's main cabin. At the same time, the 357-ton schooner *Augusta* sailed south heading toward Chicago. Captain Darius Nelson Malott commanded the vessel, which carried nearly 160,000 board feet of lumber piled deep in the hold and high on the deck.

## LOST

Three hours into the trip, Captain Wilson spotted a schooner closing in on his port side about a half-mile distant and immediately took action to try to avoid a collision. On board the *Augusta*, Captain Malott saw the same thing and hurried forward to get a better view. He called out to the wheelsman, "Hard up!" But the vessel did not respond quickly enough and the waves conspired to push it toward the steamer. Standing on deck near the bow of the *Lady Elgin* watching the storm, John Jarvis saw the schooner and realized it was on a collision course. He called out to warn his friends, "Get back, it's heading right toward us!" John Herbert jumped back just as the schooner pierced the *Lady Elgin*. It was so close he considered jumping aboard but thought the smaller schooner was more badly damaged than the steamer.

On board the *Augusta,* Captain Mallot also feared his schooner mortally wounded. While he was trying to assess his damage, the wind forced him away from the other vessel. Watching the schooner back away, passenger Tom Eviston raced to the port side. Looking down, he saw a hole big enough to drive a team of horses through and dashed off to tell his brother and their spouses to prepare for the worst. As he did, the vessel began filling with water: Anything loose in the lower decks spilled out onto the lake bottom. Captain Wilson knew his ship was mortally wounded as he felt the decks shift and sink lower toward the water. He ordered the crew to herd the cattle over the side to lessen the weight and eliminate the possibility that in their confusion they would further damage the ship. He also expected that their drowned carcasses might later support some survivors. Then, he ordered the crew to shift the cargo, especially the cast iron cook stoves. If he could raise the hole up and out of the water, he could launch a lifeboat and send the crew around to stuff mattresses into the hole. The crew anticipated his plan and launched one boat on the starboard side, but found only one oar in the small vessel, rendering them helpless to maneuver. The thirteen people in that boat, including a few lucky passengers, were among the more fortunate. The boat drifted toward shore and would safely land several hours later.

About fifteen minutes after the collision, passenger Frances Boyd braced as a monstrous wave struck the boat, weakening the structure. He could hear the groans of wood as the hull cracked and a wild rumble as the vessel leaned to the port side, then quickly bobbed back in the other direction. He assumed that some machinery in the lower hold had tumbled out of the ship. Hearing that same grinding, wrenching noise and feeling the ship topple, Captain Wilson ordered the crew to chop loose the upper hurricane deck in the hopes it would float and serve as a raft. Hundreds of people, most who could not swim, forced their way up the narrow ladder-like stairways grappling with the wooden life planks and pieces of furniture they hoped to use as flotation devices. While climbing up to the hurricane deck, sixteen-year-old Freddy Kuetemyer heard

This woodcut of the final moments before the *Lady Elgin* broke up appeared in the *New York Illustrated News*. *Author's Collection*

**Captain Jack Wilson was among the hundreds of victims, dying just a few yards from shore.** *Author's Collection*

a terrible noise and water swept him off his feet. As he tumbled, he realized he was caught up in a maze of machinery as the huge engine toppled. It ripped through the massive hogging arches, breaking the ship in two and sending the paddlewheels careening to the bottom.

With hundreds of people clinging to the upper deck, the stern drifted south on its own. As it sank lower in the water, the hurricane deck separated just as Captain Wilson expected, but within minutes the waves broke it into four or five smaller pieces. Hundreds of men, women, and children were washed into the churning water. Over the booms of thunder and the shouts of many, passenger John Eviston heard the pitiful scream of a little girl, "Mama, help! I'm afraid of the water."

For those in the water, their struggle was just beginning. The full force of the thunderstorm struck after the *Lady Elgin* went down. Flashes of lightning illuminated scores of terrified people unable to swim, clawing their way onto anything that floated. The lake was strewn with floating wreckage and the bodies of the dead and dying. The sounds of screams and prayers and curses echoed through the night. The waves pushed the survivors and debris southwest toward shore about ten miles distant. Those who made it through the night found their greatest challenge near shore, where the pounding surf beat upon the bluffs of Winnetka, Illinois. Most would die just a few yards from shore, including Captain Wilson, who perished in the breakers as he attempted to land his raft bearing twenty-five people, including one infant. Likewise, Union Guards' commander Garrett Barry, who had organized the excursion, survived most of the night, but died in the rough water near shore.

By noon the next day, only about one hundred people had been rescued from the still-violent waters. Some three hundred lost their lives that early morning, including the infant on the raft. On Saturday, the *Augusta* labored into Chicago to report the mid-lake collision at just about the same time as news of the tragedy reached the city from the northern shore. Newspapers announced the "Alarming Catastrophe" in special editions. No city bore the news with more sadness than Milwaukee. More than 200 of the 300 victims were Irish who hailed from the close-knit Third Ward. In the weeks that followed, bodies continued to wash ashore. Churches conducted funerals each day for weeks—sometimes months later—as bodies were found. A piece of the stern washed ashore and a section of the bow appeared to ride at anchor off Highland Park, Illinois, until it disappeared a few days after the accident.

The election of November 1860 overshadowed the worst disaster on the open waters of the Great Lakes. In the wake of Lincoln's ascension to the presidency,, the Civil War soon erupted. Although the country had more pressing matters to deal with, memories of the accident never faded. Newspapers ran anniversary stories nearly every September after the tragic accident.

## FOUND

Beginning in the late 1970s, several divers set out on a quest to find the wreck of the *Lady Elgin*, spurred on because of its significance as the Lakes' greatest marine disaster. The possibility of treasure intrigued other searchers. The 1981 book *Treasure Ships of the Great Lakes* indicated that the *Lady Elgin* supposedly went down with $5,000 to $10,000 in gold in its safe.

The Chicago area boasted a very active diving community. Many of them regularly dived the *David Dows,* the *Material Service,* and a handful of other wrecks that had been found off Chicago and the northern suburbs. With the advent in the 1970s of fathometers and Loran-C, divers finally had the tools to search for, find, and then return to shipwrecks, which led to several new discoveries. But the *Lady Elgin*, considered the "Holy Grail" of Lake Michigan shipwrecks, eluded them. Dozens of divers wanted to be the one to find it and salvage it. However, the Abandoned Shipwreck Act of 1987, and Illinois' resulting law making artifact recovery illegal, may have quashed their dreams. But it did not stop one particular man from pursuing the wreck.

On May 23, 1989, Chicago marine salvor and side scan operator Harry Zych detected a target on the bottom of the Lake in fifty-five feet of water. An exploratory dive revealed two very large boilers and a field of debris nearby, which he quickly recognized were from the *Lady Elgin*. According to the *Chicago Tribune*, "During a dive in May, he and his crew brought up a steamship whistle, which turned out to be part of that Holy Grail for which Zych had searched so long." *Chicago Magazine* published an article noting that "as proof of the discovery Zych displayed a rifle, sword, a chandelier, and spoon engraved with the ship's name," as well as the purser's stamp confirming the identity of the shipwreck. In fact, Zych removed about two hundred items from the wreck between June and August 1989. The flaunting of these recovered artifacts drew the State of Illinois into the mix and forced Zych's hand. The only way to avoid being charged with a felony was to seek ownership or a salvage award.

On August 29, 1989, Zych filed a joint claim in federal court seeking title or a salvage award under federal admiralty law to both the *Lady Elgin*, and the *Sea Bird* (as discussed in the prior chapter). Soon thereafter, the filing was split into two different cases. As with the *Sea Bird* case, the State of Illinois intervened to dismiss the case under the grounds of the Eleventh Amendment indicating that a federal court could not make a decision to bind a state.

For Zych, a move he made early in the legal proceedings would be significant: Shortly after locating the wreck, Zych notified CIGNA Insurance (successor to Aetna which insured the *Lady Elgin*). CIGNA agreed to transfer its interest in the wreckage to Zych for twenty percent of the gross proceeds from recovered artifacts. CIGNA had located a key piece of evidence in its files that indicated the insurance company had never abandoned the wreck. The handwritten letter noted in part, "Permit us to confirm Capt. Dorr's instructions NOT to accept an abandonment of the vessel."

In December 1990, the federal court awarded Zych ownership of the *Lady Elgin* on the grounds that it was not an abandoned wreck. However, in March 1991, Illinois appealed. A year later the appellate court upheld the earlier decision, but added one caveat: Zych owned the wreck over all the world with the exception of the State of Illinois. This decision forced Zych into state court to seek ownership over Illinois.

As litigation moved forward during the summer of 1992, Illinois initiated an effort to determine what remained of the *Lady Elgin,* over which it sought ownership. The state requested the pro-bono services of the Underwater Archaeological Society of Chicago (UASC), the organization with which it had previously worked on the surveys of the *David Dows* and *Wells Burt.* They also brought in Dr. Paul Johnston of the Smithsonian Institution to work with the UASC. By then, it had become known that the *Lady Elgin* was not in one piece like most shipwrecks—it was scattered in five different areas more than a mile apart. The location of one field of debris had become public knowledge and local side scan operator John Steele helped find other areas of wreckage. In the fall of 1992, the UASC documented these three distinct areas of wreckage, dubbed the debris field, the boilers, and the bow section, in about fifty feet of water off Highland Park, Illinois.

That year marked a time in Lake Michigan when the visibility underwater dramatically increased from a previous record of a few feet to as much as forty or fifty feet underwater. The increased visibility was attributed to the introduction into the Great Lakes of zebra mussels, indigenous to Russia, that were released accidently from the ballast tanks of foreign freighters. These small, filter-feeding, fingernail-sized mollusks consumed particles from the water, thereby increasing clarity. Despite improving visibility for divers, they became a nuisance because they attach to most anything, using string-like threads, and cover up the details on shipwrecks that divers wish to observe.

The debris field of the *Lady Elgin* lies about three miles offshore and covers an area roughly 300 by 150 feet. The UASC documented over one hundred artifacts, apparently left behind by Zych, including decorative grillwork, wash-

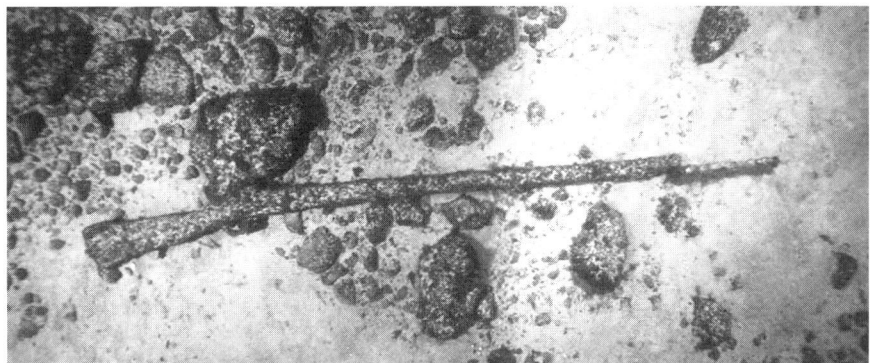

This musket is one of eleven documented in the debris field after the salvor had recovered nearly two hundred other artifacts including at least two muskets. It exhibited both a cut-off flint tray and a percussion cap, proving that these were the very refurbished muskets purchased by the Union Guards to rearm their unit. *Photograph circa 1992 by Joseph Oliver*

basins, a capstan, the pilothouse ladder, the compass, boiler room wrenches, four wooden hand trucks, commodes, a copper bedpost, a bucket, silverware, ceramic plate fragments, and four identical cast iron cook stoves, part of a cargo destined for Superior, Wisconsin. Several pieces of musical instruments were found, some of the only personal possessions remaining. The team also documented eleven muskets, seven of which lay side-by-side as if a wooden crate decayed around them. Upon closer inspection, the muskets revealed the presence of both a cut-off flint tray and a percussion cap, confirming that they were some of the eighty refurbished muskets purchased by Garrett Barry to rearm his unit. The Union Guards apparently transported them to Chicago to be used as the men marched through the city. Lying on the bottom 132 years after the sinking of the *Lady Elgin*, these muskets represented the very essence of the shipwreck. Raising the funds to pay the $160 debt for the purchase of these weapons

Rich Doose from the UASC examines a hand truck, one of several found in the debris field, which would have been used to load passenger luggage and other cargo. *Photograph circa 1992 by Joseph Oliver*

165

A large wrench from the boiler room landed atop one of four stoves found in the debris field that were being transported on the *Lady Elgin* by passenger John Newton for resale at his store in Superior, Wisconsin. *Photograph circa 1992 by Joseph Oliver*

was the main reason for the excursion on the *Lady Elgin*. The items in the debris field likely spilled through an opening that ruptured catastrophically soon after the *Augusta* impaled the *Lady Elgin*. As water rushed into the lower hold, the vessel would have sunk lower into the water and the pressure would have weakened the structure.

Approximately 1000 feet southwest of the debris field sit two large riveted-iron steam boilers on their sides about twenty feet apart. Their location undoubtedly marks the spot where survivors recall machinery falling through the bottom of the boat. One of the boilers is intact, while the second has a number of ruptured shell plates, perhaps a result of its fall to the bottom. There is no trace of any hull structure in the area. Survivors reported the *Augusta* piercing the *Lady Elgin* just forward of the port paddlebox. This would have

One of the paddlewheels of the *Lady Elgin* rests about 500 feet from the other and both are over a quarter mile from any other wreckage. Their locations probably mark the spot nearest to where the *Lady Elgin* broke in two and where hundreds of men, women, and children were washed into the violent waters. *Photograph by Tony Kiefer*

been near the boilers and the initial inflow of water at the hole would have quickly extinguished their fire. The weight of the in-rushing water would have stressed the hull, accounting for the boilers breaking through the floor. Based on the location of a third field of wreckage almost one mile south of the boilers, it can be surmised that even with the massive hole caused by the boilers, the *Lady Elgin*'s hull stayed together, perhaps through the support of the rigid hogging arches. The vessel remained somewhat buoyant for a little while longer, still supporting the majority of passengers.

Two more sites of wreckage are located about a half mile south of the boilers. This wreckage probably marks the place nearest to where the *Lady Elgin* broke up, and where passengers were forced into the water. At one site rests a paddlewheel, broken and lying on its side. Fully five hundred feet from there rests the other wheel. Each wheel consists of a huge triple iron hub with about one-third of the wooden paddle blades still attached, although twisted out of place. Considering that both wheels were once connected to the large walking-beam engine, the devastation must have been so traumatic as to have separated the paddlewheels from each other, breaking the ship in two.

The fifth area of wreckage, about one-quarter mile south of the wheels, contains the only portions of the hull yet found, representing the lower hull structure forward of the paddlewheels to the bow. The debris is spread over an area roughly 400 by 500 feet. A huge boulder sits at the southern end of the site. From the boulder, about 100 feet of chain lies fallen on the lake bottom forming a trail toward the hull sections. Four broken pieces of the steamer's

**Mark Shanabrough of the UASC works near the massive wood stock anchor of the *Lady Elgin* located in the bow section, the farthest wreckage south.** *Photograph circa 1992 by Joseph Oliver*

The hogging arch on the *Lady Elgin* lies broken and some distance from other wreckage at the site of the *Lady Elgin*'s bow structure. The exact portion of the arch could be determined when compared to a photograph of the *Lady Elgin*. Pieces of the wreck are spread out over more than a square mile of lake bottom, like a giant jigsaw puzzle.
*Photograph circa 1992 by Robert Gadbois*

structure, a large iron windlass, a massive wood-stock anchor, another smaller collapsible iron-stock anchor, a bilge pump, and a piece of one of the hogging arches are all that remain. The bow section provides evidence of what witnesses observed still afloat several miles offshore. Based on these remains, it

**Obtained through a Freedom of Information Act request, this photograph shows a variety of artifacts recovered by Harry Zych from the wreckage of the *Lady Elgin*, including swords, muskets, dishes, and other ship's fixtures. During legal proceedings, Zych allowed officials from the State of Illinois to photograph them. These artifacts all now belong to Zych.** *Courtesy of the Illinois Historic Preservation Agency*

seems likely that after the engine collapsed, the wheels separated and the vessel broke apart. The anchor chain spilled out and dragged along the bottom as the bow half drifted south until it got hung up on the enormous boulder. After that, the waves likely broke it up and the sections and pieces sank in a random heap. This traumatic sinking resulted in the remains of the *Lady Elgin* being spread over more than a square mile of lake bottom, making it the most scattered shipwreck in the Great Lakes. Only about ten percent of the vessel and cargo exists in the various sites as surveyed by the UASC.

Of course, Zych had recovered some 200 artifacts from the wreckage before the UASC began survey work. During the legal proceedings, the IHPA was given access to the items Zych recovered, most notably muskets, swords, lamps, and other ship accoutrements. Most intriguing were two pocket watches and seventy gold and silver coins, which in a deposition Zych indicated he had found in a safe in the debris field. According to the list submitted by Zych, the coins include $20, $10, $5, $2.50, $.50, and $.25 denominations, with dates ranging from 1834 to 1860. The face value of the coins seems rather insignificant totaling just over $300, however Zych testified that their value in 1992 was about $40,000-$50,000, certainly much more today. Despite the coins being openly discussed in court and included in legal filings and photographs, the media somehow never learned about their discovery. Consequently the public never learned about the only modern day recovery of "treasure" in the Great Lakes during the time of the legal action.

Once the UASC had completed its survey, members of the organization,

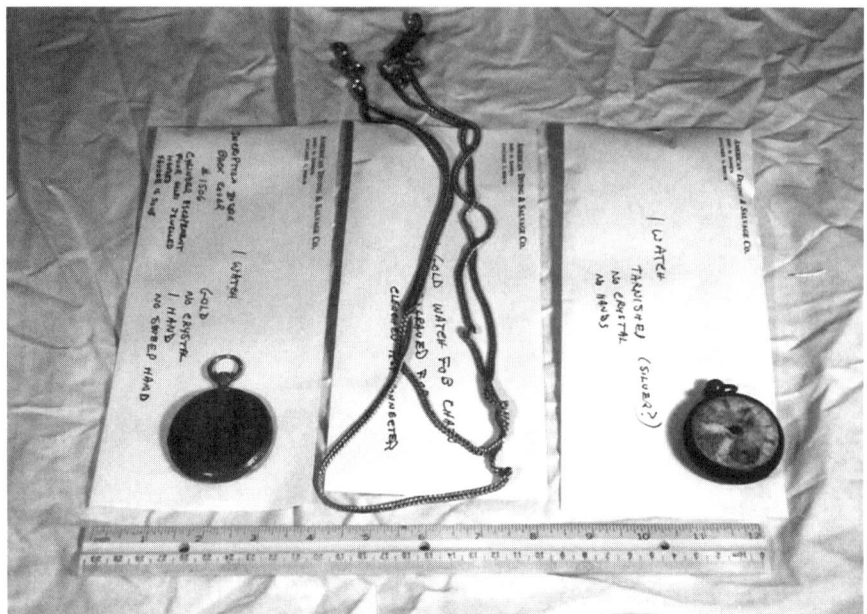

**Obtained through a Freedom of Information request, this photograph shows the watches and gold watch fob found in a safe by salvor Harry Zych. He retained these items along with all the gold and silver coins and other artifacts when he won ownership of the wreck of the *Lady Elgin*.** *Courtesy of the Illinois Historic Preservation Agency*

including this book's author, were made a third party to the case. Zych initiated a separate suit to file for rights to the organization's photographs and drawings so that he could be granted exclusive media rights to the materials. He later withdrew the suit because federal copyright law supported ownership of the images by the photographers and artists. The suit over ownership of the wreck continued. In May 1996, an Illinois judge ruled in favor of Zych, because the letter in CIGNA's file indicated that the *Lady Elgin* had not been abandoned. Illinois listed the *Lady Elgin* on the National Register of Historic Places and appealed the decision. Three years later, the appellate court reversed the decision, granting Illinois ownership. Zych took the case to the Illinois Supreme Court, which in April 1999 reversed the appellate court's decision. After a ten-year legal battle, Harry Zych finally won salvage rights and ownership of the *Lady Elgin*, a decision much different from the outcome of the *Sea Bird* case.

This decision set a precedent that if abandonment cannot be proven, then a state cannot claim ownership of a shipwreck. A permanent injunction issued by the district court in 1992 restricts divers from visiting this privately owned shipwreck without first obtaining permission from Zych. However, divers regularly visit the various sites of wreckage. Unfortunately, a number of artifacts that Zych left on the bottom have since been removed by other divers, including all eleven muskets from the debris field. Zych then asked that Illinois take his shipwreck off the National Register.

The wreck of the *Lady Elgin* has become legendary for what took place after its discovery as much as for the tragedy of its sinking. The contentious legal battle gives reasons to consider how this situation might be better handled in the future. However, none of the alternatives offers a significantly better outcome. *If* Zych had left the artifacts on the bottom, *then* a proper archaeological survey could have been conducted, *but* other divers would have undoubtedly pilfered the artifacts. *If* Illinois had not contested the original court ruling in favor of Zych's ownership, *then* the state could have teamed up with Zych to conduct an archaeological survey and develop a museum display, *but* this would have established a precedent for other divers that the state would certainly not desire. *If* Zych had just taken the gold and silver without announcing it publicly, *then* he could avoided ten years in court, *but* he would then have done something illegal. In hindsight, it seems that Zych did what he thought was best to protect the artifacts, follow proper legal procedure, and recover a financial reward for his efforts. Unfortunately, the cost of both time

Coins, like these, ranging from a twenty-dollar gold Double Eagle to a twenty-five-cent silver quarter, were recovered from a safe in a debris field of *Lady Elgin* wreckage.

and money to mount a ten-year legal battle may not have been worth Zych's ultimate reward.

The final tragedy is that although Zych has attempted to find an institution to display the *Lady Elgin* artifacts, no museum has been willing to acquire them because the policies of most museums preclude acquiring commercially salvaged artifacts. For now, all that remains is the story of this legendary shipwreck.

A detail from a postcard shows sailors aboard the *UC-97* while it was docked in Chicago.
*Author's Collection*

## 11

# TO THE VICTOR

There exists one shipwreck unique in Lake Michigan, in fact, unique in all the Great Lakes. *UC-97*, a German World War I submarine, among the many spoils of war, made history on several occasions: in 1918 when it was surrendered to America, in 1919 when it began a war bond drive, in 1921 when the United States Navy sank it in Lake Michigan, and in 1992 when the wreck was found. However, today the *UC-97* remains rather obscure, taking a backseat to its distant cousin, the *U-505*, another German submarine—from World War II—that now exists as a major exhibit at the Museum of Science and Industry in Chicago. In fact, the museum's web site makes a somewhat erroneous claim when it invites patrons "to step inside the real *U-505*—the only German submarine in the United States." The museum obviously overlooked the submerged *UC-97* that rests some fifty miles north of the museum and more than 200 feet below Lake Michigan as well as other sunken German subs in coastal waters.

The *UC-97* was launched by its builders Blohm & Voss at Hamburg, Germany, on March 17, 1918, as a mine-laying submarine of the UC-90 class for use by the German Imperial Navy during World War I. The 185-foot-long, 491-ton U-boat was to be operated by a crew of thirty two as a deadly warship, equipped with three twenty-inch torpedo tubes, one 3.4-inch gun, and six mine tubes. It could carry fourteen mines. The submarine had no time to lay its deadly mines because it was never commissioned in the Imperial German Navy. On November 11, 1918, a date later known as Armistice Day, Germany surrendered before the *UC-97* had been readied for sea. Just eleven days after that momentous occasion, Germany gave up the *UC-97* and various other vessels, under the terms of the cease-fire. Soon thereafter, the United States Navy sought to acquire several of the surrendered submarines to study their construction and equipment technology and to take on tour in the United States during a Victory Bond drive to raise funds to pay off the war debt.

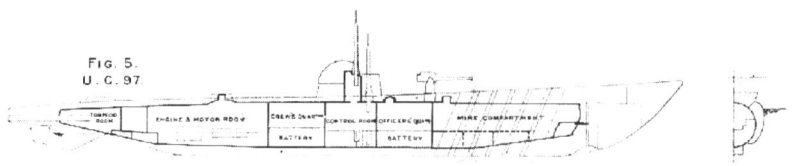

**A starboard side section view of the *UC-97*.** *Author's Collection*

The United States was allotted *UC-97* and five other U-boats *U-111, U-117, U-140, U-140, UB-88, UB-164,* for this purpose, with the understanding that they would be destroyed upon the conclusion of the bond campaign. Twelve American officers and 120 sailors, referred to as the Ex-German Submarine Expeditionary Force, went to Harwich, England, and took possession of the submarines on March 23, 1919, and readied them for the voyage across the Atlantic. Command of the *UC-97* was assigned to Lt. Commander Holbrook Gibson. He and his crew worked diligently to familiarize themselves with the German war machine; however, they had issues with the engine. When the time came to depart with the fleet, *U-111* and *U-140* travelled independently. *UC-97* had to be towed by the *Bushnell,* a submarine tender intended to lead it as well as *U-117, UB-88,* and *UB-148* to the United States. While underway the first day, the crew of *UC-97* were able to make the diesel engine operational, so once the submarine was under its own power, they tossed off the tow line.

The Ex-German Submarine Expeditionary Force sailed the submarines to the Azores, then Bermuda, then on to New York City, arriving on April 27, 1919, after what officers indicated was a rough twenty-four-day voyage. Upon reaching New York, the submarines became the center stage

***UC-97*** is pictured docked in Alexandria Bay in upstate New York along the shores of the St. Lawrence River at the start of the Victory Bond tour. Incidentally, the famous Cornwall Brothers store, now on the National Register of Historic Places, is pictured in the background. *Author's Collection*

***UC-97* while on tour in Toronto.**  *Author's Collection*

attraction for a horde of tourists, reporters, and photographers, as well as for technicians from the Navy Department. That spring, the *UC-97* participated in wreath-laying ceremonies outside New York harbor to honor the victims of submarine attacks during the war.

After several weeks in New York, orders arrived dispersing five of the six U-boats to different sections of the American coasts and waterways for Victory Bond visits in ports along the way. The *UC-97* was assigned to the

***UC-97* docked in Racine, Wisconsin, while on the Victory Bond tour.**  *Author's Collection*

**Lt. Commander Charles A. Lockwood commanded the *UC-97* while on the Victory Bond tour. He is pictured here in 1946 after promotion to vice admiral.** *Author's Collection*

Great Lakes region and put under the command of Lt. Commander Charles A. Lockwood. It left New York and headed north to enter the locks of the Canadian-controlled St. Lawrence Seaway. Lockwood caused quite a stir at Kingston, Ontario, when he flew only the U.S. and German flags aft and not the Union Jack at the fore, a Canadian tradition on man-of-wars. He later explained that U.S. man-of-wars only fly foreign flags under certain conditions, including surrender, which is why he flew the German flag, but Canada did not play a role in that vessel. His action was later supported by the Canadian naval officers. Lockwood would, in time, become the Commander of Submarines in the Pacific Fleet during World War II.

In the Great Lakes, the *UC-97* began a whirlwind series of visits to ports in Lakes Ontario, Erie, Huron, and Michigan; however wear to its engines prevented it from traveling to Lake Superior. By the last week in August 1919, the *UC-97* reached its final stop on the tour, tying up at Navy (then Municipal) Pier just shy of three weeks after the end of the Chicago race riots. Residents weary of the violence that had claimed thirty-eight lives suddenly had an interesting diversion. The *Chicago Daily News* boasted of America's win when it

**The USS *Hawk* casts off the line with the *UC-97* after towing the submarine about twenty miles into Lake Michigan.** *Reprinted from* Naval History *Winter 1989*

described the submarine as a disabled monster in an article entitled, "A German Sea Serpent with its Fangs Pulled." In fact, a photograph accompanying the story shows a little girl, Ruth Waterman, thumbing her nose at the German coat of arms on the sub, expressing a collective disrespect toward the former enemy.

The Chicago City Hall displayed an illuminated sign that proclaimed, "Welcome *UC-97*," and the U-boat received a post office address: Cherry Avenue and Weed Street on the north branch of the Chicago River. Hordes of visitors flocked to the lakefront to see what many considered the most advanced enemy weapon of the war. After all, Germany's campaign of unrestricted submarine warfare—where ships were torpedoed without warning—served as one of several reasons that the United States had entered the war in April 1917.

After the bond drive, Lockwood and most of his men moved on to other assignments, and the *UC-97* was turned over to the Ninth Naval District at Chicago for management. It was moved to the foot of Monroe Street at Chicago's lakefront at Grant Park and opened to tourists, but the Treaty of Versailles required it and all combat vessels held by the Allies to be destroyed by July 1, 1921. Rather than waste the submarine, the Navy decided to use it for target practice during the first week of June when all of the ships of the Great Lakes flotilla would participate in maneuvers. First, the Navy removed the equipment and machinery it considered valuable, including one of the two diesel engines and the periscope.

On June 7, 1921, the USS *Hawk* sailed south from Milwaukee to Chicago to take the *UC-97* under tow. The *Hawk* was the converted civilian yacht *Herm-*

*ione*, built in Scotland in 1891 for the U.S. Representative from Massachusetts Henry L. Pierce, purchased by the U.S. Navy in 1898, and renamed *Hawk*. The Naval vessel USS *Wilmette*, with its crew and deck guns ready for the operation, headed out at 8:17 that morning and within about two hours caught sight the *Hawk* and *UC-97* when they were reportedly twenty miles east of Fort Sheridan. Ironically, the *Wilmette* had begun life as the *Eastland*, the famous passenger vessel that overturned at the dock in the Chicago River in 1915, killing almost 850 people. The cursed ship could not be sold, so the Navy took it over for the value of its scrap and rebuilt it into a training vessel. Two men aboard the *Wilmette* had a special place in what would be a ceremonial training operation. Gunner's Mate J. O. Sabin, who had fired the first American shell in World War I, and Gunner's Mate A. F. Anderson, who had fired the first American torpedo of the conflict, would be on hand for the operation. In addition, about thirteen civilians were given the honor to be aboard. They pooled their money and gave the gun crews an honorarium of $100. Among them were Willard W. Jaques, president of the Jaques Manufacturing Company, and his nine-year-old son, Willard K., of Lake Forest, Illinois, who had been invited by the *Wilmette*'s captain, Edward Albert Evers.

The Jaques were quite excited when they spotted the submarine. They took a spot on the *Wilmette*'s foredeck about thirty feet from the port gun. "We stuffed our ears with all the cotton they'd given us," young Jaques later

**Civilian guests, including young Willard Jaques, watch the sinking of the *UC-97* as the port side 4-inch gun on the Wilmette opens fire.** *Reprinted from* Naval History *Winter 1989*

recalled, "and stood on a large coil of rope to cushion the guns' concussion." Once the *Hawk* cast off the tow line, the crew of the *Wilmette* prepared for the task at hand. At 11:45, J. O. Sabin had the honor of firing the first shot. Jaques remembered, "My father stood behind me and with each shot would lift me by the elbows. The heat was intense because we were so close to the firing." In all, the gunners fired eighteen rounds from its 4-inch guns at the submarine, of which ten found their mark. A. H. Anderson's final shot, fifteen minutes after they began, sent the sub to the bottom, some 200 feet below. Captain James E. Wise Jr., who later wrote about the sinking, noted that this was the first time that a U.S. Naval gun had fired an explosive shell on the Great Lakes since Oliver Hazard Perry defeated the British on Lake Erie in September 1813, more than a century earlier.

The concussion may have been felt as far north as Kenosha. Calls came into the police department from all parts of the city just before noon that day. Some people thought an earthquake had hit. Others worried that an explosion took place at the Pleasant Prairie Powder Plant. The police concluded that they had heard the noise from the sinking of *UC-97*. As the years passed, few remembered the incident.

Beginning in the 1960s, Waukegan businessman and naval historian David Myers, who was familiar with *UC-97* because his father often talked about it, became captivated with the idea of raising and restoring the submarine. He began researching the sub and thought he had pinpointed the area of its sinking. He was able to convince Captain Alban Weber, commodore of the Ninth Naval District division, the same division that sank the submarine four decades earlier, to attempt to locate the wreck. Weber thought that the project would be both an admirable undertaking as well as a good way to train his reserve crew. "Our men hadn't gone through sonar drills for about four years," Weber told a *Chicago Tribune* reporter in 1967, "and I thought looking for a real target rather than an imaginary one would offer them a great incentive." Weber located the log book from the *Wilmette*, which provided the coordinates 42.10 x 87.20, marking a position about twenty miles east of Highland Park, Illinois. They spent one weekend per month in October and November of 1967, hoping to locate it, send divers down to survey it, and if in good condition, raise it for possible display at the Great Lakes Center. Unfortunately, they could not locate the target that year or in further efforts the next one.

For some time David Weber became distracted by another submarine project. He and a group of individuals worked on restoring the World War II submarine USS *Silversides* for display as a museum vessel. Meanwhile, several divers in the Chicagoland area attempted to locate the *UC-97*. Rumors that valuable mercury worth more than one million dollars, used as ballast by the

Germans, might still be aboard may have fueled these divers, but eventually that was discounted by experts. Even so, no one was ever successful in finding it. Some had a theory for these failures: Perhaps the U-boat had not sunk completely and so moved with the lake currents. More likely, the location of the sinking was either accidently or purposely misrecorded.

In 1978 when the restoration of the USS *Silversides* was significantly complete and the submarine had been relocated to a permanent home in Muskegon, Michigan, David Myers, on behalf of the new USS *Silversides* Museum, resumed his effort to find the *UC-97*. This time he teamed with the Glenview Naval Air station and Navy Reserve commander Vincent Shanahan, a former diver with the authority to raise the submarine. Commercial salvor Richard Race of Chicago volunteered his side scan sonar services and his sixty-seven-foot work vessel *Neptune*. However, after multiple expeditions, the submarine remained elusive.

**FOUND**

Another fourteen years would pass before the *UC-97* was found. The victorious discovery announcement was made by A&T Recovery, the commercial salvage firm that had recovered a number of World War II airplanes and had found the *Wells Burt* (as described in Chapter Eight). The company indicated that on July 7, 1992, it had located the wreck in approximately 250 feet of water. Representatives of A&T told reporters that they had worked sporadically over four years using side scan sonar and had covered over 140 square miles before locating the submarine. The company used a remote-operated vehicle to videotape the wreck. Viewed by this book's author in 1992, that footage showed the submarine resting upright on the bottom. The designation *UC-97* was visible on the conning tower. The vessel seemed to be in one piece although it had several areas where the damage from the *Wilmette*'s guns was apparent.

A&T proposed that the sub be raised for permanent display. In fact, the company felt that it would be significantly easier to raise the submarine than the smaller and more delicate airplanes it had raised. However, it would still take considerable money for such an undertaking. Taras Lysenko, one of the firm's partners, provided an estimate for a *Chicago Tribune* reporter, indicating that it would require more than one million dollars for the salvage work alone. Much more would be needed for the conservation and long-term preservation of the vessel. Ownership of the submarine could also be an issue. Although the Abandoned Shipwreck Act and Illinois laws could suggest that the State of Illinois would own the vessel, the United States Navy would likely claim ownership of it as it had done with all the war birds that A&T had recovered. However, the Navy had only approved the recovery of the airplanes that A&T had salvaged once an institution agreed to accept them and fund the salvage and long-term preservation. Initially, the parties thought that perhaps the Museum of Science and Industry would want the vessel to sit beside the *U-505*. However, that institution was, at the time of the discovery announcement, in the midst of a campaign to raise almost twelve million dollars to enclose, restore, and fund an endowment for the U-boat already in its possession. Others thought that the submarine should be exhibited at the Wisconsin Maritime Museum in Manitowoc, Wisconsin, where a United States submarine, the USS *Cobia*, is on display. However, the *Cobia* was built in Manitowoc and its presence at the museum represents Manitowoc's shipbuilding contribution's during World War II. A German submarine would have little interpretive synergy in that city. Only one institution showed interest in the sub. The USS *Silversides* Submarine Museum in Muskegon, Michigan, which had previously attempted to locate the wreck, indicated it would be willing to help restore the U-boat and would like to have it on display beside the *Silversides* as another museum vessel. However, the costs were too exorbitant for the museum.

Now, two decades after the sub's discovery, the USS *Silversides* Museum is interested in sending a remote-operated vehicle down to film the sub, and in creating an interactive exhibit for visitors. However, A&T Recovery has never made public the precise location of the submarine. It remains the spoils of that company's hard-earned effort. Consequently, the museum has mounted yet another expedition, decades after its first, to attempt to find the wreck. Perhaps in the future, the museum or other explorers will find it on their own. This legendary shipwreck, should, indeed, take more prominence as one of the few remaining World War I German submarines in American waters, a reminder of how close our former enemy came to winning the "war to end all wars."

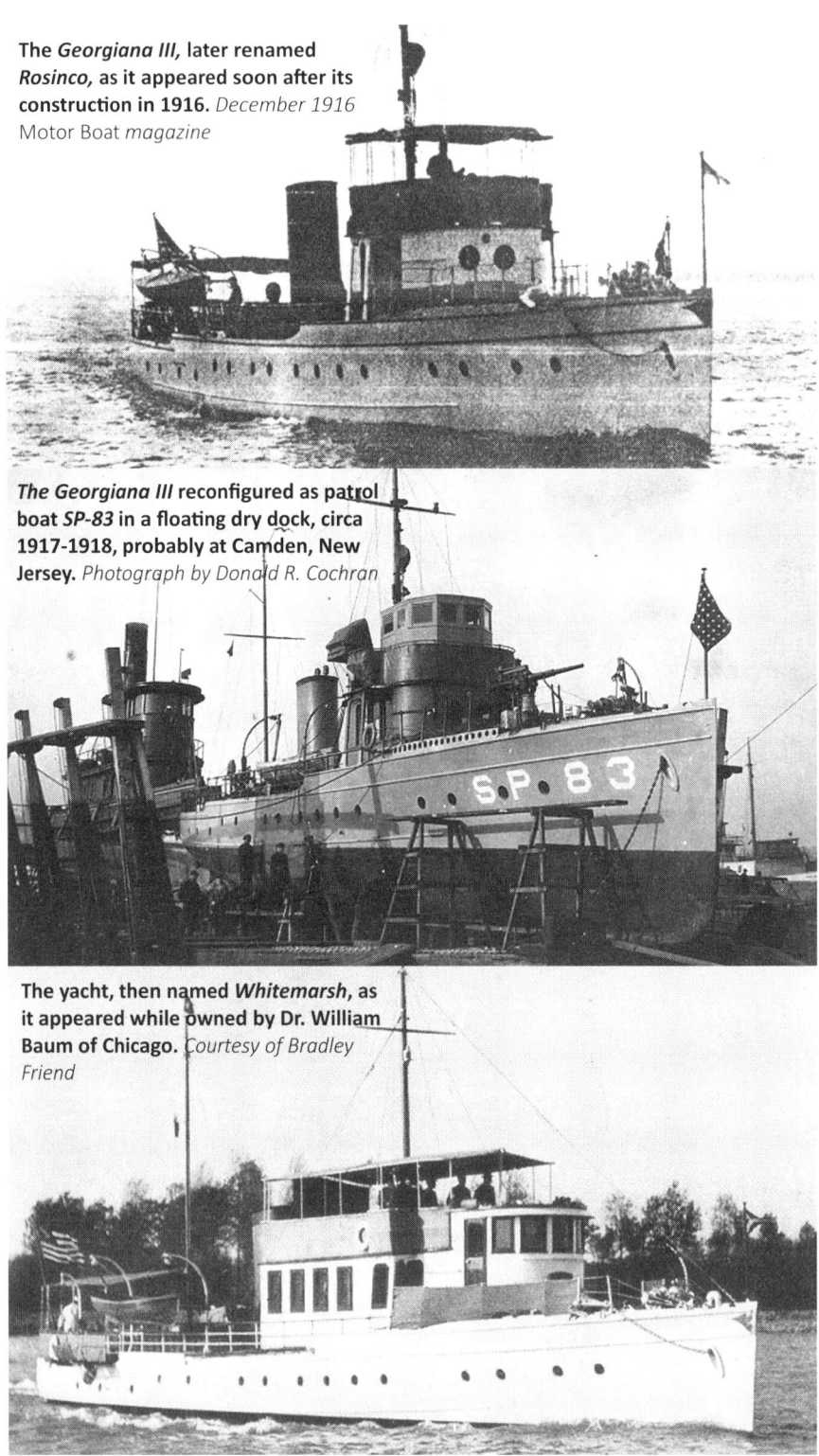

The *Georgiana III,* later renamed *Rosinco,* as it appeared soon after its construction in 1916. *December 1916* Motor Boat *magazine*

*The Georgiana III* reconfigured as patrol boat *SP-83* in a floating dry dock, circa 1917-1918, probably at Camden, New Jersey. *Photograph by Donald R. Cochran*

The yacht, then named *Whitemarsh,* as it appeared while owned by Dr. William Baum of Chicago. *Courtesy of Bradley Friend*

**12**

# UNFORTUNATE OCCURRENCES

The *Rosinco* takes its place among legendary shipwrecks not only for its rank as one of the Lakes' most palatial diesel yachts, the victim of an unfortunate accident, but also for the unfortunate consequences that resulted from the recovery of an artifact from the wreck in 1998. Eventually, the *Rosinco* would become one of the first shipwrecks to be listed on the National Register of Historic Places in Wisconsin's waters of Lake Michigan, and serve as the catalyst for many other such listings and an active underwater archaeology program in that state.

The ninety-five-foot steel yacht *Rosinco* would take many different shapes and change hands six times in its short career of only a dozen years. It was built in 1916 as the *Georgiana III*, a diesel-powered yacht, by Wilmington, Delaware, shipbuilders Harlan and Hollingsworth for forty-six-year-old William G. Coxe, president of the shipbuilding company. Harlan and Hollingsworth had grown out an early nineteenth-century relationship between a carpenter and a machinist who began manufacturing railroad cars in Wilmington. Business changes, the introduction of new partners, and experience with railcars and other ironwork, led the company to become one of the first iron shipyards in the United States. It built nine iron ships in the 1840s, including the *Ashland* and *Ocean*, two of the earliest iron steamboats to be constructed in the United States, as well as the *Bangor*, acknowledged as the first seagoing iron propeller steamship. By the time of the Civil War, Harlan, Hollingsworth & Company was the dominant iron shipbuilder in Wilmington, and the most prolific iron shipbuilder in the United States, having built by then seventy-five iron hulls. In 1886, the company built its first steel yacht, followed by several more. In the early 1900s, the Bethlehem Steel company took partial control of the firm, which by then principally built merchant vessels, and ferry boats, as well as torpedo boats and destroyers for the United States Navy. The *Geor-

Edward T. Stotesbury, a multi-millionaire from Pittsburgh, was the second of five owners of the yacht that would eventually be renamed *Rosinco*. It was in his possession when taken over by the Navy for use in harbor patrol during World War I. *Public Domain*

*giana III* would be built alongside other vessels destined for service in the war. Coxe would name the vessel after his and his wife, Helen's, eleven-year-old daughter, Georgiana.

Owner William Coxe collaborated with the company's chief naval architect, A. M. Main. Coxe desired impressive luxury and built his yacht with the finest materials, furnishings, finishes, and appointments. The main salon, with watertight doors at both ends, was paneled in quartered oak with brown oak deck beams and cream mahogany ceiling panels. Furniture and fabric wall panels were upholstered in English tapestry. The rich carpeting harmonized with the brown oak. Custom-built furniture included three built-in sofa beds, a Pullman bed, an eight-person dining table, and two sideboards all fashioned in quartered oak. Cabinet and sideboard doors were glazed with leaded glass. The owner's grand stateroom featured a built-in three-quarter bed, two dressing tables, and a cheval mirror. The master bath had a tub and washbowl, piped for hot and cold fresh or salt water, which were arranged to drain easily overboard. All rooms, including one for children, were well ventilated and lighted by both natural and electrical light. Paneled in mahogany, the roomy deckhouse contained a large davenport, card table, and movable chairs. Two fifteen-inch portholes and seven large plate glass windows provided ample lighting and panoramic views. Like the bathrooms, the galley sink could be supplied with freshwater or seawater, and featured a range and an ice-box. The *Georgiana III* ushered in the age of pleasure yachting, where successful industrialists could flaunt their wealth.

In addition to luxury, Coxe and Main also set out to design the yacht for strength, safety, speed, and stability. The use of lightweight steel for its hull made the vessel lighter and stronger than a wood or iron yacht. Heavier steel was used in areas that might encounter exceptional stress, particularly the garboard strake, a place where leaks often occurred at the juncture of hull and keel. The vessel had steel bulkheads dividing it into seven watertight compartments, an unusual feature for a yacht, but in keeping with the shipbuilder's designs for torpedo boats. The yacht had a double bottom, between which it carried freshwater both as ballast and for use on board.

*The Georgiana III* was powered with a two-stroke-cycle, 240 hp, Southwart-Harris fuel-efficient diesel engine, also known as a compression-ignition engine, a technology that had been invented by Rudolf Diesel in 1893. The internal combustion engine used the heat of compressed air to initiate ignition to burn the fuel injected into the combustion chamber. This is in contrast to spark-ignition gasoline engines which use a spark plug to ignite an air-fuel mixture. The diesel engine could be brought to full power from a cold start in just ten seconds, a considerable improvement over the time required to bring a steam engine to full power. The diesel engine was fuel efficient and required fewer crew to operate than a steam engine. *Georgiana III* con-

**Robert Morse owned the *Rosinco* at the time that the yacht sank. Ironically, his crew used the signaling code developed by his distant relative Samuel Morse, to be spotted offshore in the motor launch hours after the sinking.** *Public Domain*

sumed only eight gallons of fuel per hour and could carry over 1000 gallons, giving it a cruising range of 2000 miles, exceptional even by present-day standards. For shore access in harbors and for safety, the yacht carried a sixteen-foot Luders motor launch and a fourteen-foot tender.

Coxe incorporated these features so that his vessel could be handed over to the United States government for use in shoreline monitoring. Since the torpedoing of the *Lusitania* in the spring of 1915, Americans feared that the Atlantic Ocean offered the Germans a convenient path to the east coast. German submarines had been caught in American waters, some to lay mines as the *UC-97*, described in the previous chapter, had been designed to do. American yachtsmen sought out opportunities to serve as naval auxiliaries. At first the federal government did not embrace this idea, but as the war progressed, the Navy created a division to seek out and acquire appropriate vessels for public service. Most personal boats lacked the strength for gun mounts, but steel vessels like Coxe's yacht caught the attention of the Navy. In fact, the United States government did acquire the *Georgiana III* for use as a patrol boat on the east coast.

Government records indicate the yacht was purchased from Edward Townsend "Ned" Stotesbury a sixty-eight-year-old multi-millionaire, Philadelphia-based investment banker, and a partner in Drexel & Co. and its New York affiliate J. P. Morgan & Co., which suggests that Coxe had by then sold the *Georgiana* III to Stotesbury. Both Coxe and Stotesbury as well as their wives

**A rare side profile of the *Georgiana III* as it appeared as patrol boat *SP 83* during 1917 and 1918. Notice the large guns mounted on the forward and aft decks.** *Photograph by Donald R. Cochran; album of his naval service from 1917-1919. Donated to the Navy by Dr. Mark Kulikowski, 2010.*

were active in the war effort in Pennsylvania; in fact, Coxe served as the Delaware River District officer. Stotesbury served on several advisory boards. It would have been probable that the two men knew each other through business as well as through the war effort. In any case, the Navy took over the yacht on May 11, 1917, at Philadelphia and on the same day put Lt. J.H.R. Cromwell, USNRF, in command of it in the 4th Naval District. *Georgiana III* set off for Wilmington, Delaware, on May 26 for conversion to a section patrol boat by Harlan & Hollingsworth, its original builder.

On July 25, the Navy christened the new vessel USS *Georgiana III*. It sported a raised pilothouse, a gun on the front deck, another on the stern, and the big, white letters "SP-83," to indicate it as a section patrol vessel, painted on its port and starboard sides near the bow. The patrol boat immediately reported for duty at the harbor entrance at Cape May, New Jersey. During the balance of World War I, it was used to patrol the entrance to Delaware Bay, cruising between Cold Spring Harbor, New Jersey, and Lewes, Delaware. While on patrol duty on June 3, 1918, the *Georgiana III* received an SOS from the oil tanker *Herbert L. Pratt*, "Overfalls Lightship Delaware Breakwater have struck a mine or am torpedoed."

The *Pratt* had sailed from Mexico on May 26, 1918, commanded by H.H. Bennett, with a full cargo of crude oil and a crew of thirty-eight men and was just approaching the Delaware breakwall when a small concussion tore a hole in the hull. Although Bennett had no idea what happened, he ran his vessel full speed toward shore hoping to ground it. However, after fifteen minutes it became clear the tanker would sink. Bennett hailed the *Georgiana III* and another patrol vessel, the *Miramar*, informing them he was sinking and asking them rescue the crew. Both vessels hurried to the scene and between the two took aboard the captain and all the crew. Later, other boats swept the area for mines and sank two of them before they could be detonated. The Navy later came to understand that a German submarine, the *U-151*, which the prior day had sunk six U.S. vessels off the coast of New Jersey, had laid the mine that sank the *Pratt*.

In July 1918, the Navy outfitted the *Georgiana III* with underwater listening gear to detect submarines since it was clear many were in the area. It continued to escort ships through the Defensive Sea Area of Delaware Bay. However, it would only be used in that capacity for a few months because the war came to an end. On November 30, two weeks after the Armistice, the USS *Georgiana III* was decommissioned at Essington, Pennsylvania, and returned to Edward Stotesbury. Although the details of the vessel's next change in ownership are unclear, in 1918 Dr. William "Billy" L. Baum, a highly regarded and successful dermatologist in Chicago, member of the Mackinac Cup committee, and commodore of the Chicago Yacht Club, purchased the yacht, by then renamed *Whitemarsh*. Stotesbury may have been the person to rename it because at the time of its sale, he and his new young bride were in the midst of construction of a palatial estate outside of Philadelphia called Whitemarsh Hall. Baum had likely taken notice of the yacht during a trip out east in 1918. He frequented the east coast where he often participated in races. In fact, in 1909 he successfully ran the 670-mile Bermuda Race on his ninety-nine-foot schooner *Amorita*.

Baum arranged for the *Whitemarsh* to be brought into the Great Lakes, where he moored it at the Chicago Yacht Club, creating quite a stir as the first diesel yacht ever home-ported in Chicago. Either Stotesbury had already added a center deckhouse and upper flying bridge or Baum undertook that remodeling because its configuration as the *Whitemarsch* differed significantly from its appearance as the *Georgiana III* or as a patrol boat.

Four years later, avid mariner Robert Hosmer Morse joined the Chicago Yacht Club and took interest in the *Whitemarsch*. As he got to know Billy Baum, he probably had the opportunity to look over the yacht. Morse was the vice president of Fairbanks-Morse, a distribution company that sprang from the E & T Fairbanks Company, a manufacturer of platform scales. Morse's father, Charles, began the company and expanded into a manufacturer and distributor of a number of mechanical and electrical products. In 1922, Morse purchased the yacht from Baum. It remained at the Chicago Yacht Club, but received the new name *Rosinco*. Morse began considering using the yacht to showcase a new diesel engine the company had just begun manufacturing. In 1927, he installed his firm's newest Model 35 Fairbanks-Morse electro-diesel engine. After that and other improvements, appraisers valued the *Rosinco* at $150,000. By that time, Morse had been elected fleet commander of the Chicago Yacht Club and his yacht became the flagship of the club. However, just one year later, that flagship would be at the bottom of Lake Michigan.

## LOST

In mid-September 1928, Robert Morse, his fourteen-year-old son, Robert, three of the boy's friends, and Chicago banker George L. Weed left Chicago for a cruise to Milwaukee. Edward Ellison served as the ship's captain with Harry Marumrud as his chief engineer, plus a steward, a lookout, and two crewmen. After a layover in Milwaukee, Morse decided that rather than return directly to Chicago, he would arrange a car to take him south to Beloit, so he could visit the Fairbanks-Morse plant there. His son, who loved flying, convinced Morse to take him and his friends along and then charter a plane back to Chicago.

On Tuesday evening, September 18, Ellison and his crew began the journey back south, returning with only Weed, who would be able to sleep during the trip and arrive fresh for a day of work on Wednesday. The weather was calm and Weed, the steward, and two seamen turned in for the night, leaving Ellison, Marumrud, and lookout John Larson in control of the vessel. At about 2:45 a.m., the three crewmen felt a tremendous shock as the vessel, cruising full speed at fifteen miles per hour, lurched violently, knocking Ellison to the floor. He quickly got up and throttled down the vessel, then ran out to the deck to see what they had hit. Marumrud rushed below to check for damage and Larson hurried to alert Weed and the other two crewmembers, if the loud thud had not already awakened them. Marumrud returned to the pilothouse to report an enormous amount of water pouring in through a gaping wound in the lower hull. Ironically, the *Rosinco* suffered damage similar to the tanker *Pratt* that had hit a mine a decade earlier. In this case, however, there were no other vessels nearby to rescue those on board as the yacht had done for the sailors on the *Pratt*.

All seven men aboard the *Rosinco* quickly gathered topside. No one had any idea what had caused the damage, but all realized the gravity of the situation because the vessel sat much lower in the water than normal. Ellison knew that the *Rosinco* would sink very soon and hustled everyone to the stern, telling them they would have to jump and swim to the small motor launch or small rowboat that they had been towing behind the yacht. There was not enough time to launch the tender secured to davits at the port side near the stern. The moonlight illuminated the two vessels that now bobbed several dozen yards behind their once-sturdy yacht.

Once everyone made it safely into the motor launch, the crewmen cast off the line that tethered them to the yacht. As they drifted away from the yacht, they watched with utter disbelief as the *Rosinco*'s stern lifted into the air and the vessel slid, bow first, beneath the surface, leaving only a trail of bubbles reflecting in the glow of the moon. Only then did Ellison recall that the ship's canary mascot was still onboard. Marumrud fired up the launch's motor and headed west for shore, towing the rowboat, but after less than a mile the craft began leaking. Everyone started bailing and they managed to keep the boat afloat in those conditions for two hours until they saw an outline against the lightening sky and a scattering of lights that told them they were nearing shore. Ellison used a flashlight and began signaling an SOS, ironically a code developed by his employer's distant relative Samuel Morse, to alert anyone who might see them from shore.

Patrolling the beach early that morning, Kenosha Coast Guard Surfman Paul Berg spotted a small, flashing light offshore. Keeping his eye trained on it, he quickly realized that the pattern of three short flashes, followed by three long flashes, meant someone was in trouble. Running back to his station, Berg notified Commander William McGraw, who quickly ordered the life-saving boat dispatched. It took the station's crew less than a half hour to reach the struggling party. They took the six men safely aboard their vessel and secured the yacht's two boats to take in tow.

In the days following the sinking, Morse, Ellison, his insurance men, and the Coast Guard speculated about what had caused the rupture in such a sturdy, well-built vessel. Originally, Ellison blamed it on "box timber," a raft of sawed wooden beams. Since many docks in the Racine and Kenosha area were being repaired at the time, it was certainly possible that some of the timbers had floated off. Another theory involved a pile-driving barge that had recently been lost and was suspected to be adrift in northern Lake Michigan. The Coast Guard conducted a search that week, but found neither a floating pile of wood nor the barge. They did find a few cushions, life preservers, a captain's hat, and some neckties, all that was believed to remain of the *Rosinco*. Days later, a Racine fishing tug towed in the tender from the *Rosinco*, which they had found adrift.

## FOUND

Diver and side scan operator John Steele found the *Rosinco* in the late 1970s after a commercial fisherman informed him that his nets had snagged on something off Kenosha. Steele, who lived most of his working life in northern Illinois, has been referred to as the "King of the Great Lakes Shipwreck Hunters" for the many discoveries he has made, including the *Cayuga* (detailed in Chapter One) and dozens of other wrecks in the Great Lakes. In fact, he began searching for shipwrecks in 1959 and would continue hunting for them until 1997. Working from his vessel, *RV Hunter*, with a surplus sonar from a Navy submarine, he headed out to the general vicinity of the net snag and began running a search grid, eventually picking something up in 180 feet of water. He and Keith Retslof made the first dive and quickly identified the wreck as the *Rosinco*.

They found the wreck sitting upright on the hard clay bottom in 185 feet of water with an intact hull and deckhouse. A large steel windlass and two

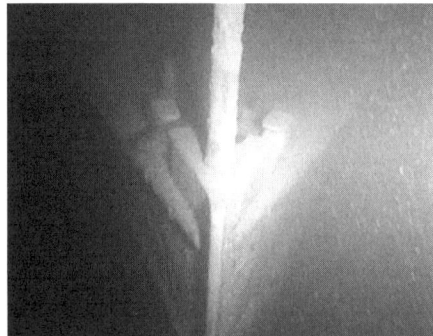

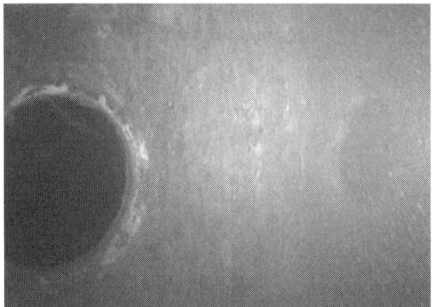

**Underwater images of the wreck show, from top to bottom, the bow, the missing portholes, and a fan mounted inside the deckhouse.** *Video captures by Bradley Friend*

anchor chain chocks rest on the bow deck just forward of the center deckhouse. The square deckhouse window frames still contain intact panes of glass. Wood-framed storm and screen doors remain securely hinged on the aft and port side doorways of the deckhouse. Built-in cabinets and counters within the deckhouse are also intact. A steel gangway platform on the starboard side amidships and a set of steps lead down to the lake bottom. This would have allowed access to the ship's motor launch.

The smokestack stands tall just aft of the center deckhouse. Behind it, three of the four skylights above the engine room are intact. A bank of fifteen storage batteries, still hooked in series and to the engine, are housed in an on-deck locker that surrounds the engine room skylight. When not under diesel power, these batteries supplied power to the vessel's many electrical conveniences, including fans, elegant light fixtures, and telegraph for communication between the engine room and navigation bridge. Most of the railings around the yacht are intact.

A deposit of clay on the stern deck suggested to the discovery team that the *Rosinco* landed on the bottom stern first and scooped up the clay before it settled on the bottom. Fittings for the lifeboat davits remain on the port side near the stern. They likely secured the tender that was forced off during the sinking. A companionway provides access to below-deck areas, but is too narrow for divers with cumbersome gear to penetrate safely.

The divers kept the discovery a secret except from a choice group of friends, and in 1978 Steele, Wally Bissonett, Steve Radovan, and a few others began regularly diving the wreck. At that time, the recovery of artifacts was common practice not restricted by law, and a number of artifacts were taken from the wreck. In his book *The Great Lakes Diving Guide*, author Cris Kohl included images of the beautifully preserved ship's wheel, dishes, and utensils recovered from the *Rosinco* by a diver whose identity he could not disclose. According to Radovan, some years later, George West, who was a regular member of Steele's crew, introduced Elgin, Illinois-based diver Paul Ehorn to the team and invited him to dive the *Rosinco*. Ehorn's involvement would put the *Rosinco* in the news and make it legendary more than two decades after its discovery and one decade after the establishment of the Abandoned Shipwreck Act.

On October 25, 1998, a warden employed by the Wisconsin Department of Natural Resources, apprehended Ehorn for removing a porthole from the *Rosinco*. More than a year after arresting him, in December 1999, the Kenosha County, Wisconsin, district attorney charged him with felony criminal damage and misdemeanor theft to Wisconsin state property, marking the beginning of a criminal case in Wisconsin state court. Law enforcement personnel had taken a special interest in shipwrecks since the enactment of the federal Abandoned Shipwreck Act of 1987 and the resultant stricter laws in Wisconsin mandating penalties for damaging underwater archaeological or historical sites. Per the act, Wisconsin claimed ownership of the *Rosinco* and all other abandoned and embedded or historically significant shipwrecks on its bottomlands. In 1988, the state had provided initial funding to the Wisconsin Historical Society to manage its historic shipwrecks. That year, the society hired David Cooper to serve as state's first underwater archaeologist, a position he would hold for ten years. He began documenting known shipwreck sites and any new finds that shipwreck hunters called to the state's attention. In the process, he wrote National Register nominations for a number of shipwrecks, most in Lake Superior, but the *Rosinco* was not among the wrecks he documented because he was unaware of its location.

Facing criminal charges for the porthole he had recovered, Paul Ehorn hired David J. Haywood, a Lansing, Michigan-based attorney, to represent him. Haywood, as expected, saw the case in much different terms than the State of Wisconsin. He took the position that when Ehorn recovered the porthole in 1998, the wreck was neither embedded in the lake bottom nor listed on the National Register, one of which would have had to be true for Wisconsin to own the wreck. The Abandoned Shipwreck Act, he felt, was not sufficient to claim a blanket ownership over every wreck, and so he took the position that Ehorn had not taken state property.

In August 2000, Ehorn filed an admiralty action in federal court, seeking a declaration that he is the owner of the *Rosinco*. Strategically, if that case could result in the court declaring him owner, then he could not be prosecuted for recovering the porthole. Because public notice is essential to give an opportunity for anyone else with an interest in the shipwreck to come forward, Ehorn published notices in the *Milwaukee Journal Sentinel*, the *Kenosha News*, and in the federal courthouse, then awaited a response. He did not inform the Wisconsin Historical Society directly, which was an omission that would later be used against him. However, the society became aware of the case and, under the leadership of Jefferson Gray, who had replaced Cooper as Wisconsin's underwater archaeologist, prepared a National Register nomination, one of its strategic legal moves to assure that the court would grant ownership of the wreck to the state. The state's nomination made a case for the historic significance of the *Rosinco* based on it being an early diesel-powered yacht, its connection with significant individuals, and the potential that the wreck could yield important archaeological data.

On February 8, 2001, the United States Secretary of the Interior determined that the *Rosinco* was indeed eligible for the National Register and five months later, the *Rosinco* was officially listed in the National Register of Historic Places. However, because of issues regarding the timing of Wisconsin's official response to notice of the suit by Ehorn, in September 2001 the federal court issued a default judgment giving Ehorn ownership of the wreck. The victory would be short lived.

In June 2002, Wisconsin appealed, arguing that Ehorn should have notified the state of his admiralty claim directly. The judge concurred, ruling that the admiralty case must be tried again. Four months later, in October 2002, after the *Rosinco* had been listed on the National Register, the federal court determined that the State of Wisconsin owned the *Rosinco*. Consequently, Ehorn once again faced criminal charges. His salvation came in May 2003, when Wisconsin's district attorney decided not to pursue criminal charges, realizing the difficulty of prosecuting Ehorn for taking the porthole three years *before* the state officially owned the wreck. This complex case, though much simplified here, indicates how contentious the issues over shipwrecks can be. Ehorn recovered artifacts as others before him had done, but he happened to be the only one apprehended for it. In the words of Jeff Gray, "a lot of people speed, only some people get speeding tickets."

Wisconsin, Illinois, and Michigan have all asserted state ownership of shipwrecks through a small number of cases that have been taken to court. The *Rosinco* case, according to Jeff Gray, reinforced the need for pursuing the listing of more shipwrecks on the National Register to solidify state ownership. He realizes that although Congress clearly intended to protect historic wrecks from artifact recovery for personal collections like the *Rosinco* porthole, the wording of the Abandoned Shipwreck Act, as it regards abandoned Great Lakes' shipwrecks that are not embedded in the lake bottom nor listed on the National Register, leaves room for differing interpretations that only a court can sort out.

To attempt to avoid further legal skirmishes, the Wisconsin Historical Society has nominated more than thirty shipwrecks in the waters of Lake Michigan and more in Lake Superior since the *Rosinco* case to assure its clear ownership of them. That tactic may have done as the state intended: There have been few cases of un-permitted artifact recovery since and no other cases contesting ownership. In addition, the Wisconsin Historical Society has cultivated and encouraged what has become a very active community of divers who serve as volunteers on projects to document the state's many shipwrecks. Wisconsin's efforts at preserving its shipwrecks now include installing moorings, creating waterproof dive guides, installing shore-side interpretive plaques, and maintaining a web site dedicated to Wisconsin's historic shipwrecks, all to ensure that divers and the public have access to the wrecks and the information.

Ironically, although Wisconsin could not successfully prosecute the porthole recovery, the case served to set in place procedures that would preserve and protect many other shipwrecks. However, the *Rosinco* case, like that of the *Lady Elgin*, highlighted that the Abandoned Shipwreck Act and individual state laws leave openings for individuals to contest the laws, particularly if the state governments do not take formal action to claim legal ownership of the shipwrecks that fall within their boundaries. Of course, the time and expense of contesting those laws falls to the individuals who choose to either risk being caught taking artifacts or strategically mount a battle for ownership that would give them legal rights to recover artifacts. Many divers would, in time, initiate their own efforts to preserve shipwrecks. Once John Steele began filming shipwrecks, he stopped recovering artifacts and was often was heard to say, "When you dive with a crowbar, you dive alone. When you dive with a camera, you take thousands with you."

**The *Lottie Cooper* pictured at Sheboygan, Wisconsin.** *C. Patrick Labadie Collection - Alpena County Public Library*

# 13

# FROM SURF TO SHORE

For the handful of legal actions that have challenged the Abandoned Shipwreck Act, like those involving the *Sea Bird*, *Lady Elgin*, and *Rosinco*, there are many other cases where the law has been accepted without question. When the City of Sheboygan planned a lakefront development project, it recognized that the state would own any historic resources in the area and so contracted to have an archaeological survey conducted in the waters affected by the project. In fact, a shipwreck was found. That wreck is now legendary as the second shipwreck, after the *Alvin Clark*, to move from surf to shore. It is now the only shipwreck in the Lake Michigan region that everyone, not just divers, can visit.

## FOUND

In early 1990, the City of Sheboygan hired Tidewater Atlantic Research, Inc. of North Carolina to conduct a side scan sonar survey in an area that would be dredged for development of a new public marina within the inner harbor. Tidewater Atlantic Research was established in 1979 to provide historical and archaeological research and cultural management services to state and federal agencies and other institutions needing its specialized skills. Personnel have experience in remote sensing, diving, archaeology, underwater photography, artifact analysis, and conservation. Gordon Watts, the firm's owner and director of the Maritime History and Underwater Research at East Carolina University, served as the project director for the work in Sheboygan.

In July 1990, Tidewater conducted a proton magnetometer and side scan survey as part of a phase one, non-invasive survey. The remote sensing identified six potential targets, which the firm's divers then surveyed. Two of the targets proved to be structures associated with a wooden vessel or vessels, buried in the bottom silt. The other four were inconsequential modern debris. Under a second contract with the city, Tidewater conducted a phase two investigation

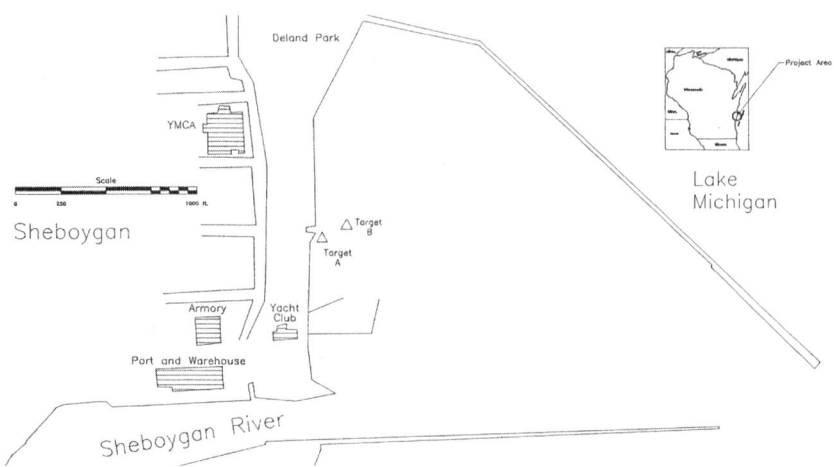

A site map indicates the position of the target that would later be identified as the *Lottie Cooper* as discovered by Tidewater Atlantic Research. *Courtesy of City of Sheboygan*

in September and October 1990 to attempt to identify the shipwreck remains and determine their significance. The firm set up operations at the Sheboygan Yacht Club located inside the protected breakwater since the targets were located only a few hundred feet north of the club's marina.

The divers utilized a twenty-five-foot boat as a work platform, and initially buoyed the sites for easy access and relocation. The proximity to shore allowed them to create underwater baselines correlated to features on land. In this way, divers were able to measure the wreckage. Since the sites were mostly buried, the work began with pre-disturbance mapping, which revealed only a few frames visible above the lake bottom. Then, the firm had to excavate to begin to understand what lay hidden in the sand. They utilized diver-operated induction dredges powered by a 5 hp centrifugal pump for test excavations at two places on one target and four places on the other. The excavations revealed hull planking and structures associated with a single wooden vessel that had obviously broken up since its sinking. One site proved to be a major section of the side of the ship, about ninety-two-feet long. The other site proved to be

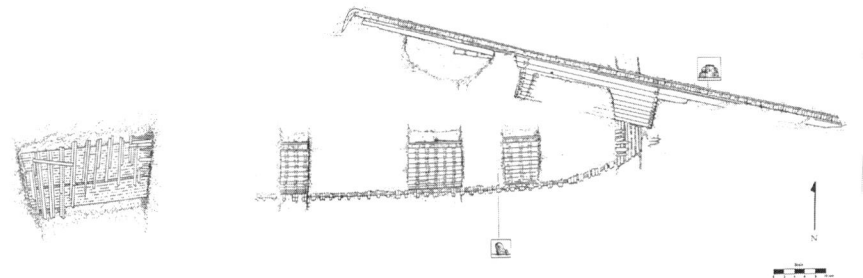

A site plan prepared by Tidewater Atlantic Research after partial excavation of the target. *Courtesy of City of Sheboygan*

two additional hull sections and a long portion of the keel, keelson assembly, and centerboard trunk. They identified one mast step that indicated it was configured as a schooner rig, but recognized that two or three masts would have been normal for that size vessel. Structure associated with the stern seemed to be missing, but divers found the stem attached to the end of the keelson.

The researchers concluded that it was a sailing vessel, about 110 feet long. Due to the shape of the lower hull, they suspected that it might be a scow schooner, which typically was more boxy than a schooner. After discussions with Wisconsin State archaeologist David Cooper, historian Patrick Labadie, and Ken Pott, who had conducted the archaeological investigation of the scow schooner *Rockaway*, Tidewater became convinced the vessel was a scow.

A significant part of Tidewater's work included developing an inventory of all ships lost off Sheboygan, which they numbered at sixty-three. Only eleven of those ships sank or grounded near the location of the wreck, and of those, only two had been scow schooners. The *Blue Bell*, an eighty-three-foot scow, ran aground south of the Sheboygan pier in 1887 and the *R. H. Becker*, a 108-foot long scow, sank in 1908. Tidewater immediately ruled out the *Blue Bell* because the wreck was longer than eighty-three feet. A photograph of the *Becker* at Sheboygan showed features consistent with the wreck and so the firm tentatively identified it as the *Becker*.

The *Becker* was a 140-ton scow schooner owned by the Fredrick's Lumber Company. On May 7, 1908, the scow had difficulty entering the Sheboygan harbor and let go its anchor to avoid going ashore. A tug was able to secure a line to the scow and proceeded to tow it into the harbor. Before the two vessels could reach the safety of the harbor, a large sea struck the *Becker* broadside causing the ship to heel over. It fouled its spars in the south pier and capsized, partially blocking the harbor. A week later, a tug was able to right the scow and tow the broken vessel to the north pier at the foot of Michigan Avenue, where they let it lie out of the way of traffic. The next storm broke it up and it disappeared beneath the surface. Although the site where the *Becker* sank was significantly farther north than the location of the wreck, Tidewater understood that the action of the currents and waves can move entire shipwrecks a considerable distance. Consequently, the *Becker* remained the prime candidate. Further discussions with Ken Pott, as well as Jay Martin, historian for the *Rockaway* project, revealed that scows varied greatly in their designs. They both felt that it would be difficult to conclude that the wreck was a scow until more of the hull could be surveyed.

Part of any archaeological process regarding a shipwreck is to consider whether the wreck could be deemed eligible for the National Register of Historic Places. To be considered, the vessel must meet one or more of four criteria. It must be associated with an historic event, associated with an important person, embody a distinctive method of construction, or be able to yield important information. The broken and only partial remains of this wreck degraded its eligibility, but its construction might reveal important historical data. Tidewater concluded that the wreck could provide significant historic information if further studied.

The firm presented three options for consideration by the City of Sheboygan. The city could alter its marina construction plans to avoid impacting the site, it could relocate the wreck elsewhere in the lake, or it could gather the historic data, then allow the wreck to be destroyed during marina construction. The city decided on the third option. It retained Tidewater to excavate and survey the wreck in place, in an attempt to positively identify the vessel and gather historical information, and then let it be demolish it. The U.S. Army Corps of Engineers and the Wisconsin State Historic Preservation Office agreed that the excavation and study would be of benefit to the public and issued the necessary permits to allow for the work.

The third phase of the project took place in July and August 1992. Surprisingly, data recovered then, two years into the project, revealed that the wreck could not possibly be the *R. H Becker* as previously presumed. With the aid of local historians, Tidewater concluded that the wreck was not a scow, but instead a schooner. Its location within the breakwater suggested that it was the *Lottie Cooper*, a three-masted schooner lost in 1894.

The *Lottie Cooper*, described by the *Manitowoc Tribune* as a handsome three-masted schooner, began its career in the shipyard of Rand and Burger

The *Lottie Cooper* pictured at Sheboygan, Wisconsin. *C. Patrick Labadie Collection - Alpena County Public Library*

in Manitowoc, Wisconsin, built for the firm of Cooper and Jones in Racine. On March 30, 1876, its builders launched the vessel in the river. Co-owner George Cooper named the new schooner in honor of his wife. At 131 feet long and 27 feet wide, the *Lottie Cooper* represented the largest of the three-masted schooners at the time. The vessel initially carried an A1 rating with a value of $11,000. Cooper and Jones added two partners to help underwrite the schooner and enrolled it on April 19 with four one-quarter owners. After fitting out, which took the better part of April, the schooner began its first trip heading up to Two Rivers, Wisconsin, to load a cargo destined for a port south on the lake, a run that would be the model for the balance of its career running from port to port on Lakes Michigan and Huron.

As with most sailing vessels, the *Lottie Cooper* could be difficult to handle in high winds. Consequently it had a couple accidents in its career. Compared to most schooners, these early accidents were relatively inconsequential. For instance, on November 5, 1880, it grounded at Sherman Bay and remained stranded four days until tugboats could release it.

By 1880, Cooper and Jones and their partners sold the middle-aged schooner, by then downgraded to A-2 condition, to Captain Ole Groh of Sheboygan, Wisconsin, for $7,500. Groh often commanded the vessel himself. On August 28, 1884, the *Lottie Cooper* left Detroit in the early morning bound for Drummond Island to load cedar for Chicago and encountered an east wind. At about 9 a.m., the wind veered quickly around and drove the schooner ashore about a mile and a half below Port Sanilac, Michigan, where the vessel filled with about four feet of water, in a repeat of the accident four years earlier. The wrecking tug *Winslow* soon succeeded in raising the schooner. After that accident, the *Lottie Cooper* was downgraded to a B-1 rating and dropped in value to only $3,000. It was still usable, but only in the lumber trade, a cargo that would not be affected if the vessel leaked. As did the original owners, Groh added partners in March 1894 to help financially support his shipping business, including Wm. Lorenz, Eugene O. Pautzer, George B. Matoon, and Watson D. Crocker, of Sheboygan. The owners had the ship outfitted with new spars, sails, and rigging in 1894, and gave it a fresh coat of paint inside and out to try to eke out a few more years of use. However, the new paint job would matter little when the *Lottie Cooper* suffered another tragedy just one month after its refurbishing.

## LOST

On April 8, 1894, the *Lottie Cooper* took aboard 230,000 board feet of lumber from Pine Lake near Advance, Michigan, a village on Lake Charlevoix. It was destined for Matoon Manufacturing Company in Sheboygan, the vessel's home port. Skilled dockwallopers filled the schooner to capacity, first loading boards through the square hatches on deck, then topping it off inside by wrangling more boards through the lumber ports on the sides of the vessel just below the deck. To complete the load, they stacked the deck full with more boards and lashed them down with ropes. Captain Fred Lorenz commanded the schooner with five crew, including William Huhme, Charles Esbach, Angust Pegelow, Barney Haynes, and Edward Olson, most from Sheboygan.

The *Cooper* made good time crossing northern Lake Michigan, then proceeded south along the lake's western shore. When the bright spring sun sank below the tree line on the distant western shore, a heavy wind from the southeast began blowing. Later that evening, the wind increased to a fierce gale, lashing the water of Lake Michigan into an angry sea. The *Lottie Cooper* struggled on under half sail and had nearly reached its destination, when just north of Sheboygan, the winds took a toll on the old vessel and it began taking on a large amount of water. First Mate Huhme discovered that water covered the cabin and forecastle floors.

Just before midnight that Sunday, the schooner made it into the breakwall at Sheboygan, but became sluggish and unwieldy to handle. Lorenz knew he could never maneuver his way into the harbor in that condition. He was forced to lower the sails, set the anchor, and try to signal a tugboat to tow them in. At about 1 a.m., as some crew secured the anchor, others lit torches. However, no one on shore saw the lights and the crew had to spend a terror-filled night on the flooding schooner. Every huge wave that dashed over the boat drenched the frightened men.

Overnight, the companionway to the fo'c'sle washed away and the bulwarks followed. When a gray, dismal morning dawned, Lorenz realized his schooner would not last much longer. No longer worried about a tow, the crew raised a flag at half-mast to signal their distress, hoping for rescue by the Life-Saving station. Captain Nequette, the commander of the Life-Saving station saw the flag and promptly responded. He commanded his crew to launch the station's surf boat, but also called into service the tug *Sheboygan,* better suited to make it out of the rough waters of the harbor. However, before either crew could reach the stranded vessel, the *Lottie Cooper* lurched and keeled over within their sight. The Life-Savers watched as most of the schooner's crew scrambled into the rigging. They saw one man grab hold of several loose boards from the deck cargo, which floated away from the capsized hull, but as the rescuers headed toward him, a big wave upset the boards and forced the man underwater. No one saw him surface. Turning their attention to the five men left clinging to the wreckage, the Life-Saving crew decided to abandon the surf boat and climbed aboard the tug to effect a rescue. They quickly bore down on the schooner and one-by-one pulled the exhausted survivors from the wreck over the next agonizing thirty minutes.

After the five crewmen had been taken to the Life-Saving station, the rescuers learned that the seaman they had seen disappear was fifty-year-old Edward Olson. He had a wife and two teenaged children in Arendal, Norway, and had been working to earn enough money to bring them to America.

At the station, the five survivors, whose bodies were badly bruised from their horrible ordeal, changed out of their wet clothing, had a much needed meal, and got a good night's rest. The next morning, they saw that the deck load had washed away as the surf pounded the *Lottie Cooper* and pushed the hulk toward the beach. Groh and his partners carried no insurance on the vessel, which was worth, at that time, less than half the value of its cargo.

By April 18, what was left of the *Lottie Cooper* began to break up and wash ashore. When the weather cleared nearly a week later, on the morning of April 24 the crew of the schooner *Joseph Duvall* raised the valuable anchors and chains from the wreck, but deemed the schooner too badly damaged to be raised. Wrecker Matthew Carr was hired to salvage the lumber. On April 26, he cut a hole in the bottom of the schooner, but could only recover some of the cargo. Two months later, in mid-June, another furious storm struck. The *Lottie Cooper* was so badly twisted and contorted by the raging surf that after the storm abated, watchers on shore saw some of the framework protruding ten feet above the water. The storm did one good thing; it washed more of the cargo to the beach where the vessel's owners employed a gang of men to gather it up. Two months later, Edward Olson's body washed ashore near the mouth of the Black River, south of Sheboygan.

While Tidewater excavated and mapped the wreck of the *Lottie Cooper* in September 1992, the firm proposed an alternative to destroying the wreck. It encouraged the city to consider raising the remains and featuring the wreck as an outdoor display to educate the public about Sheboygan's maritime history. The city agreed. After the survey was completed that fall, Zaretzke Marine lifted the remains using a crane and recovered, much to everyone's surprise, a windlass and centerboard not previously discovered. The structures were transferred to temporary storage on the waterfront pending decisions about an eventual display. By the following year, the concrete pad and supports were in place, and the *Lottie Cooper* was positioned in its new home in Deland Park, part of the Harbor Centre Marina. It now sits in full view of the lakefront where the schooner frequently sailed during its eighteen-year career. It includes an eighty-five-foot-long surviving section of the keel (the ship's backbone), the centerboard trunk, and portions of the port and starboard sides arranged in a position that, despite the missing pieces, allows visitors to understand how it was once configured.

The hull planking inside and out is made of oak and the planks taper

**A crane lifts a side of the *Lottie Cooper* out of the water in 1992.** *Courtesy of the City of Sheboygan*

and curve upward toward the bow and stern. The frames, or rather ribs of the ship, can be seen through gaps where planks are gone. The edges of the hull planking are beveled so that caulkers, some of the most highly skilled shipyard workers, could drive a rope-like material called oakum into the groove between the planks. This would have prevented the ship from leaking. There are holes located about halfway up the side of the ship, called salt ports. Crewmembers would regularly pour salt down these holes into the bilge, where it mixed with water to form brine that helped preserve the bottom of the ship.

Near the top of the existing structure on the starboard side is a square window-like opening that served as a lumber port through which boards up to sixteen-feet long could be loaded directly into the hold. A large U-shaped hole near the top represents the place where salvors chopped the hold to remove the cargo of timber. Although the masts are long gone, several chain plates, part of the rigging to support them, exist on the wreck. These once held deadeyes, through which the shrouds securing the mainmast upright were threaded.

The centerboard was once housed in the narrow watertight box called the centerboard trunk, and could be raised and lowered by means of a winch and chain on deck. In the display, it is positioned next to the trunk so that it can be seen. Weighing over a ton, the centerboard of the *Lottie Cooper* could be suspended as far as twenty feet below the keel to prevent the vessel from slipping sideways through the water when sailing into the wind improving stability and maneuverability. Because Great Lakes schooners served many small communities located on relatively shallow waters, they needed to be able to lower their centerboards while under sail and raise them when they entered shallow harbors, rivers, and canals.

The windlass is prominently placed in the outdoor display. It is a spool-like winch that was mounted crosswise on the foredeck of the ship and was used to raise the anchors. The anchor chains passed through hawse pipes (oval, metal-lined openings in the bow), then wound around the windlass. The crew manually cranked the ratcheted windlass to lift the anchors, which could weigh several tons. The laborious task could require several hours depending on how much chain was let out. Consequently, the anchors were dropped only when absolutely necessary. It was certainly necessary to lower them on that stormy day in April of 1894, which set in motion the chain of events that would, a century later, result in this magnificent lakeside attraction.

In December 2011, sixty-four-year-old Cliff Larsen, a Sheboygan native then living in North Carolina, and the great-grandson of one of the crewmembers, Albert Haynes, contacted officials at the City of Sheboygan and offered to donate a commemorative plaque to add to the *Lottie Cooper* display. "They deserve to be remembered," Larsen told a reporter from the *Sheboygan Press*. "I just thought there should be something honoring the crew."

Larsen never met his great-grandfather, who died a few years before Larsen was born in 1947. "He was originally from Omro, Ireland, and served as the ship's cook. I heard a lot of stories about him and the *Lottie Cooper* was one of the biggest," he recounted. Apparently Hayes, whose real name was Albert,

**The author visits the *Lottie Cooper* in the Deland Park in Sheboygan, Wisconsin.**
*Photograph by Taya and Cella Van Heest*

not Barney as newspapers had reported, broke his leg in the ordeal when he went overboard. After that he never sailed again, working instead as a carpenter for the rest of his life. Larsen said his family considered the site of the *Lottie Cooper*'s demise a monument. "We periodically would drive by where it sank," remembered Larsen.

As with the wreck of the *Alvin Clark* (detailed in Chapter Four), the *Lottie Cooper*'s wooden timbers likely will not remain structurally sound forever, but supporting braces and periodic maintenance by the city may extend its life beyond the twenty-five years the *Alvin Clark* graced the world. The *Lottie Cooper* offers a legendary opportunity for divers and landlubbers alike to see a shipwreck up close and personal and is worthy of a pilgrimage to Sheboygan, Wisconsin, to view these historic remains.

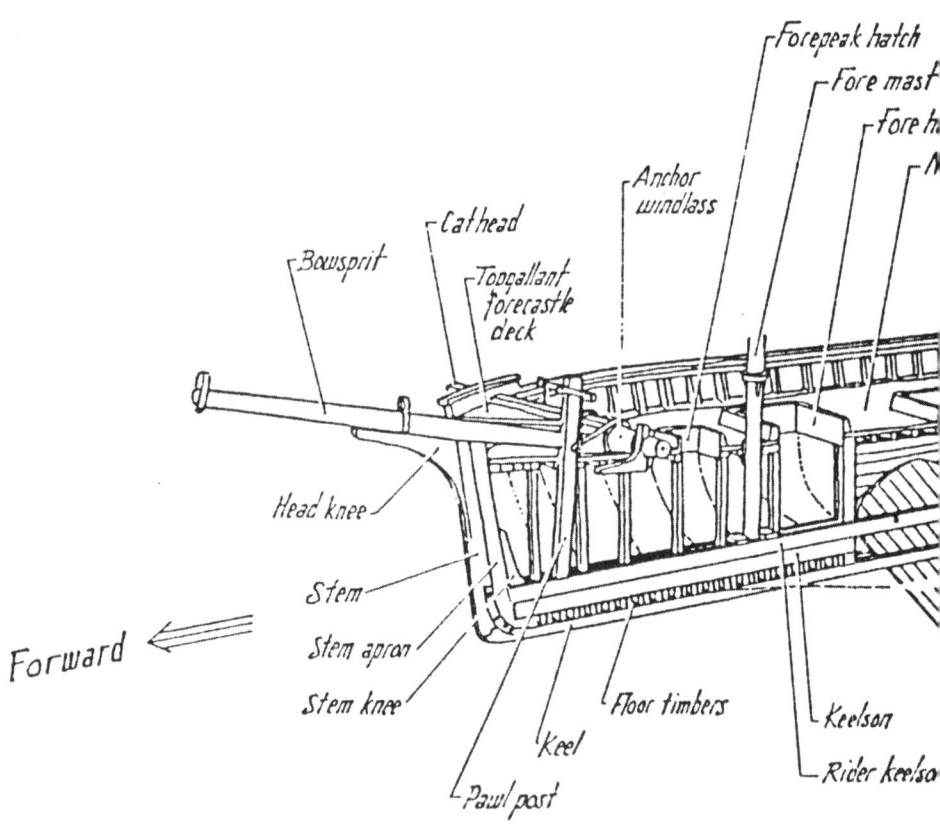

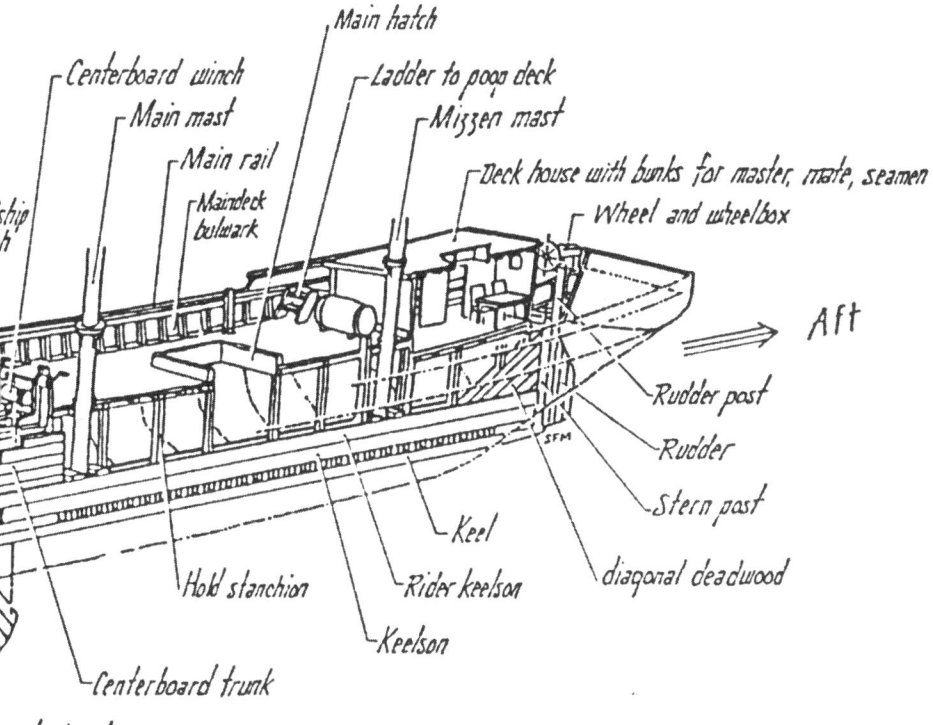

Main hatch

Centerboard winch

Ladder to poop deck

Main mast

Mizzen mast

Main rail

Deck house with bunks for master, mate, seamen

Maindeck bulwark

Wheel and wheelbox

ship h

Aft

Rudder post

Rudder

SFM

Stern post

Keel

diagonal deadwood

Hold stanchion

Rider keelson

Keelson

Centerboard trunk

Center board

The recovery of the *Lottie Cooper* allowed archaeologists the opportunity to study the vessel in detail. Historian C. Patrick Labadie prepared this half-section drawing of the schooner. *C. Patrick Labadie Collection - Alpena County Public Library*

A bow-on view of the *Three Brothers* taken just a few years prior to its sinking.
C. Patrick Labadie Collection - Alpena County Public Library

**14**

# SHIFTING SANDS

The *Three Brothers* ranks among legendary shipwrecks in Lake Michigan because of the circumstances of its discovery. Unlike the other shipwrecks described in this book, no one set out to specifically find it, nor accidently stumbled upon it. The *Three Brothers* simply revealed itself in 1996. The wreck quickly became, for some time, the biggest tourist attraction in Michigan. By some estimates, tens of thousands of people have visited it.

The *Three Brothers* began its career as the *May Durr*. The Milwaukee Shipyard Company built the steamer in 1888 for John Spry of his namesake lumber company in Chicago to haul his product. At 162 feet long, the traditional, wooden-hulled lumber hooker was average sized for that vessel type, but compared to a similar sized schooner, it could carry significantly more lumber, up to 530,000 board feet. The Frontier Engine Works of Buffalo, New York, built a steeple compound engine specially for this vessel. In a move in 1892 that likely expressed both his satisfaction with the steamer and a talent for promotion, Spry renamed the vessel *John Spry* after himself and his company. When the steamer reached middle-age in the mid-1900s and John Spry no longer had a use for it, he sold it to Charlevoix brothers William, James, and Thomas White who owned the William H. White Company in Boyne City, Michigan. The brothers renamed it *Three Brothers* after themselves and used it to haul their company's lumber. They had the new name painted on its stern at the shipyards in Manitowoc where they also had it recaulked soon after the purchase. In this capacity, the vessel hauled lumber often between Lake Charlevoix and the Whites' sawmill in Tonawanda, New York, and on to other ports as well.

## LOST

On September 27, 1911, the *Three Brothers* took on board a $4200 load of hardwood at Boyne City destined for Chicago. The lumber hooker set out south

**The *Three Brothers* pictured soon after its build when it carried the name *May Durr*.**
*C. Patrick Labadie Collection - Alpena County Public Library*

under the command of Captain Sam Christopher with a crew of twelve men. Weather in September is usually calm, but as the vessel approached the light ship positioned to mark North Manitou Island, the wind began blowing, waves built up, and the twenty-three-year-old hull began to take on water. The crew fired up the pumps that they carried for just such an occasion, connected their fire hose, and ran it up from the lower deck over the stern to discharge the water.

Captain Christopher headed south intending to take shelter in the bay at South Manitou Island, but the water poured in so fast, the crew could not keep up with the flow. Soon it flooded the hold and coal bunkers. To keep steam up, the crew fueled the boilers with kerosene in a last-ditch attempt to reach the island. In this condition, the captain steamed right into the shallows at South Manitou Island about 200 yards east of the Life-Saving station.

Although Christopher probably hoped the vessel would sit high and dry in the shallows, the floor of the bay sloped steeply downward. When the steamer hit the beach, the bow split open and knocked the pilothouse loose. Then, the stern sank until only the top of the smokestack was visible. As it did, the deckload of lumber began to wash away. The crew climbed up the sloping deck or struggled in the water to reach the bow, the only portion of the ship that remained above the water. There they prayed and waited for rescue with waves lashing at them from all sides.

Captain Kent of the Life-Saving station at South Manitou watched the events unfolding and immediately took action to rescue the crew from the sinking steamer. The Life-Saving crew launched the lifeboat and rowed out to the steamer. One-by-one they managed to get everyone into the boat and safely ashore. After eating a hot meal and drying their clothes, Christopher and his crew began to strategize how to salvage their vessel. They telegraphed a request for the assistance of the wrecking tug *Favorite* and lodged with the life-savers until it could arrive several days later. When it did, the wreckers surveyed the remains of the *Three Brothers*, but by then judged it to be beyond salvage value. They removed some hardware, then transported the *Three Brothers'* crew to the mainland. The *Favorite* returned the next spring to salvage the machinery, but the wreck had already slipped beneath the surface into deeper water.

Over the next several decades, the landscape of South Manitou Island changed. In time, the remote outpost became a vacation destination. The Life-Savers were replaced by park rangers. A spit of sandy beach formed near the Life-Saving station. As each year passed, the land grew until it became a five-acre beach where tourists flocked to sun themselves and swim. Locals called the beach Sandy Point. While some were content to lounge on the beach, others combed the waters around Sandy Point in the 1970s and 1980s searching for the wreck of the *Three Brothers*. Although more than sixty years had passed, they figured it lay there somewhere just waiting to be discovered. However, despite their best efforts, the wreck remained elusive.

## FOUND

That changed in 1996. Park rangers David Nagel and David Wilkins of the Sleeping Bear Dunes National Lakeshore motored out to the island on April 30 to prepare for the influx of tourists in May. As they entered the bay, they were surprised to see that over the winter, Sandy Point had eroded away to nothing. Incredulous, they cruised their boat over what used to be solid land, and they saw a dark shape under the clear water. After a couple more passes, they realized it was a shipwreck. Soon thereafter, the Park Service contacted divers with the Manitou Passage Underwater Preserve Committee, which had been established in 1988. Its boundaries extend from the Sleeping Bear Dunes National Lakeshore on the mainland and encompass the water surrounding North and South Manitou Islands.

The sand had preserved the *Three Brothers* remarkably well over the prior eighty-five years since its sinking. Obviously the ship's presence at that spot beginning in 1911 had altered the currents in the area, causing a slow, almost imperceptible, buildup of sand inside and around the wreck until Sandy Point had fully formed. Over that time, the locals probably forgot that the *Three Brothers* had been lost there. In fact, a number of divers went looking for the wreck and had difficulty understanding why they could not find it considering the detailed information that had been recorded at the time of the grounding.

The wreck of the *Three Brothers* can be seen in this satellite image just offshore in the center, right hand side. Captured in the early 2010s, this image shows how the sand has remained scoured out around the hull since shifting in 1996 to reveal the wreck.

A severe storm over the winter of 1995-1996 had probably washed away the point, consequently revealing the shipwreck.

The sand that surrounded the wreck washed away, but the ship was still filled with sand. Only the upper works, including the pilothouse and cabins were missing, but this damage occurred at the time of its accident. Otherwise the shipwreck, at the time of its appearance, was remarkably intact because the sand covering protected it from damage by storms or ice. Even some items of clothing and other personal affects littered the site. Two fire hoses dangled over the stern, evidence of the crew's struggle to pump out the vessel just before it was beached. On the stern transom, the painted name was clearly visible: *Three Brothers* of Buffalo.

Michigan's state archaeologist at the time, John Halsey, became interested in the discovery and traveled from Lansing to dive the site. The wreck posed an unusual opportunity and a dilemma. If studied, it could provide valuable historical information. However, its location at the island, a popular vacation destination, meant that both divers and non-divers could flock to it out of interest and curiosity. Its location in shallow and clear water near shore meant that even snorkelers could reach the site easily. This would give many more people the opportunity to see a shipwreck in person, but the heavy visitation could affect the condition of the wreck. Despite the laws making artifact recovery a felony, Halsey feared some artifacts might go missing anyway. He considered making the site off limits, but knew this would create an uproar among divers. Instead, he decided that the shipwreck could be a test case to see how a new-found wreck would hold up to heavy visitation and whether the laws would curtail pillaging.

The Manitou Passage Underwater Preserve committee, led by Tom Stoltman and Jed Jaworski, teamed up with archaeologist Hawk Tolson and resource manager Ken Vrana from Center for Maritime and Underwater Resource Management (CMURM) and the Sleeping Bear Dunes National Lakeshore to document the site even as divers and snorkelers began visiting the wreck.

Although underwater archaeologists prefer to document a shipwreck before others come near it in order to record its condition upon discovery, that was impossible with this wreck. News traveled quickly. Hundreds of people made the trip to South Manitou Island specifically to see the shipwreck. The Park Service attempted to track the number of people by having divers register before diving the wreck, something not possible with most shipwrecks. The presence of their office so close to the site, and the fact that most visitors arrived at the island on the regular ferry, allowed them to do this more easily. Yet many others took private boats to the island and chose not to register.

The documentation team logged hundreds of hours on the wreck that summer to create a detailed archaeological drawing of the steamer and capture video and photographs. Tourists and other divers had the opportunity to see the dive team at work, something that added greatly to their visit. Although most divers respected the site, their touching and moving of artifacts at times frustrated the archaeologists. This book's author had

Jack Van Heest swims between the port and starboard sides of the bow, which have separated significantly since the wreck became uncovered. *Photograph by the author in 2012*

**Sand remains atop the stern deck of the *Three Brothers* where the capstan and two sets of bollards remain.** *Photograph by the author in 2012*

the opportunity to visit the wreck that year during September, and by then, four months after its appearance, the name on the back had already faded from the many hands brushing it to get a clearer look. In addition, boaters had dragged anchors across the wreck trying to moor to it, and that had damaged the fragile superstructure.

The Park Service estimated that during the island's three busiest summer months, at least 1200 divers visited the site. Many more swimmers and snorkelers peered down into the clear water to catch a glimpse of it. CMURM gathered some economic statistics and estimated that the visitors to the wreck brought in an additional $180,000 to the local community in that three-month period alone, proving that a shipwreck can be an economic boost to a community.

In October 1996, soon after the South Manitou Island transit ferry's stopped running, Ken Vrana returned to the wreck to assess its condition after a summer of heavy visitation. He was disappointed to see that many artifacts had been removed or relocated. The fire hoses that lay over the stern were still there, but the brass nozzles had been taken. Likewise, the brass fittings on the steam engine were missing. He found a pair of rubber boots and jeans in tatters, probably from handling, and a number of personal items were missing. Park Service rangers presumed that a diver or divers operating out of a personal boat after park rangers vacated the island had taken the artifacts. Vrana acknowledged that the looting was not as bad as it might have been before the establishment of laws to protect shipwrecks because most divers wish to see the wrecks in an authentic condition. But for Vrana, even the relocation of an artifact contributes to a loss of information. "Those artifacts are clues to the past," he told a reporter in late October 1996.

The following year, the Manitou Passage Underwater Preserve Committee became concerned that pressure from the sand inside the wreck would force the sides outward because they were longer supported by the protection of a sand covering. The committee applied for a permit to dredge the interior of the wreck as a protective measure. The Department of Environmental Quality denied the permit on the grounds that the work could damage the hull, further destabilize the structure, and expose any artifacts that might lie hidden in the sand. In the face of that denial, all the committee could do was hope for the best as divers and snorkelers continued to visit the site with great regularity over the next many years.

As with the wreck of the *Francisco Morazan* on the opposite side of the island, the *Three Brothers* claimed the life of a visitor. On August 23, 2003, experienced salt water diver Laura Krause, of Benzie County, died of "dry water drowning," caused when a muscle spasm in her throat cut off her air supply. The *Three Brothers* was her first shipwreck dive in freshwater.

Since the *Three Brothers* became exposed, it has remained visible and accessible, though it has decayed considerably. The sand that once covered it has not built up again. Fortunately, the archaeological team was able to gather a significant amount of historical information before visitation and exposure to the surrounding water altered the site. Today, the *Three Brothers* on the east side of South Manitou Island and the *Francisco Morazan*, which lies just a few miles from it on the south side of the island, remain two of Lake Michigan's most visited shipwrecks.

**A thick layer of algae covered the *Three Brothers* in 2012, but no zebra mussels were present.** *Photograph by the author in 2012*

A bow view of the *H. C. Akeley,* possibly at Cleveland, is one of two known photographs of the freighter. *C. Patrick Labadie Collection - Alpena County Public Library*

# 15

# CONVOLUTED CIRCUMSTANCES

Among the stories of vessels gone missing in southern Lake Michigan, the *H. C. Akeley* stands out as legendary for the convoluted events that led to its demise and for the similarly confusing circumstances that led to its discovery and its identification. For more than a year, the *H. C. Akeley* was misidentified as the *Chicora*, which has clouded the history of the *Chicora*. At the time of this book's publishing, the *Chicora* is still missing.

The search expedition that eventually led to the discovery of the *H. C. Akeley* began as the "Quest for the *Chicora*" in 1998. Lost in a January 1895 winter storm on a run from Milwaukee, Wisconsin, to St. Joseph, Michigan, the *Chicora*'s mysterious disappearance ignited interest in finding its wreckage that has not waned for more than a century. The committee to establish the Southwest Michigan Underwater Preserve, under the leadership of this book's author, mounted the expedition in order to solve the historical mystery and generate publicity in the hopes that the state would officially designate the area between New Buffalo and Holland, out to a depth of 130 feet, as the state's tenth underwater preserve.

Searching for shipwrecks lost for decades can be a daunting task: It is time-consuming, costly, and weather dependent. In the Great Lakes, there is little potential salvage return. Treasure like that found on the *Lady Elgin* is extremely rare. Most ships carried such cargoes as iron, stone, grain, lumber, or fruit. Typically divers with financial resources to acquire costly side scan equipment search for shipwrecks as a hobby, often keeping the results of their efforts a secret. The preserve committee planned to take an unprecedented approach to its search effort. Since the "Quest for the *Chicora*" was designed to call attention to the proposed preserve, the group would announce the plans publicly, hire the services of a side scan operator, host an event to raise money to fund the expedition, and keep the media informed of its work. In the event of a discovery, the group would document the wreck, then release the results of its work to the public. In the spring of 1998, the committee hosted a film festival that helped raise $5000 for the search, and partnered with David Trotter, the Great Lakes' most legendary shipwreck hunter and explorer.

David Trotter, who has since been immortalized in the book *Shipwreck Hunter* by Gerry Volgenau, is a diver and retired Ford Motor Company executive who has been operating side scan sonar equipment for decades and had found many dozens of long-missing Great Lakes shipwrecks. He provided his side scan sonar and expertise, and the committee provided the boat, the manpower, and conducted the research to develop a probable search area. Since none of the crew survived the sinking of the *Chicora,* the only data available to suggest where the ship went down were newspaper accounts that indicated where debris washed ashore. Since debris from the ship was found from Saugatuck down to Benton Harbor, the search area encompassed over one hundred square miles off western Michigan.

The search area represented an immense amount of bottomland, especially considering the sonar Trotter used at the time could only cover about two square miles per day. Despite the coverage made in 1998 and 1999, the *Chicora* remained elusive. However, the attention the search garnered did as it intended: The State of Michigan officially designated the Southwest Michigan Underwater Preserve in December 1999. Of course, committee members still wished to locate the wreck and therefore raised more funds to conduct a third expedition in the spring 2000. However, the group still did not locate the *Chicora* within the 130-foot depth boundaries of the preserve. To further narrow down the search area, the group enlisted the expertise of Arthur Allen, a scientist with the U.S. Coast Guard Research and Development Center in Groton, Connecticut, who studies drift theory to aid the Coast Guard in its search and rescue operations. Allen is able to make predictions as to where objects drift in the water given certain wind and current conditions.

Although Allen had never applied this technology to finding a long-missing ship, the process was certainly viable. To create a drift model, he needed a digital simulation of the wind, currents, and waves as they existed in 1895. Allen collaborated with David Schwab at the Great Lakes Environmental lab in Ann Arbor, a division of the National Oceanic and Atmospheric Association (NOAA), to create the simulation. Recent weather records are easy to obtain because the National Climatic Data Center, a division of NOAA originally formed in 1870 by Congress as the National Weather Service, keeps computerized logs all weather conditions around the country. However, Schwab needed weather data from 1895 Fortunately, he was able to find hour-to-hour handwritten accounts of wind velocity and direction for the entire month of January 1895 for the ports of Chicago, Milwaukee, and Sault Ste. Marie, which gave him enough information to generate a computer model. Art Allen then generated a series of computer simulations in hundreds of locations to predict where the *Chicora* might have sunk that would have brought the debris to the positions on shore as historically recorded.

Allen and Schwab's work resulted in an unexpected conclusion: The *Chicora* likely went down in very deep water, significantly beyond the boundaries of the preserve and much deeper than safe sport diving depths. None-the-less, the group mounted yet another expedition in 2001.

## FOUND

On May 25, 2001, the searchers persistence and diligence paid off when they discovered a massive shipwreck in 275 feet of water off Saugatuck, Michigan. Although the sonar image indicated the wreck was just over 200 feet long, matching the length of the *Chicora*, it did not offer proof. At the time, the wreck ranked among the deepest wrecks discovered in the Great Lakes, making the prospects of getting divers down difficult and dangerous. Ultimately, because the wreck was outside the boundaries of the preserve and beyond safe sport diving limits, members of the preserve committee formed a separate organization to document and identify the wreck. In time, the new group would incorporate as the charitable, nonprofit Michigan Shipwreck Research Association (MSRA).

MSRA realized that the size and shape of the wreck matched three other vessels besides the *Chicora* that were presumed lost off western Michigan: the passenger steamer *Michigan,* the barge *Hennepin,* and the bulk freighter *H. C. Akeley.* MSRA would need to see the wreck firsthand to identify it.

The organization turned to Guy Meadows, who operated the University of Michigan's MROVER, a remote-operated vehicle with a camera. Meadows was interested in assisting with the site survey, but could not schedule the dive until October 2001. Anxious to identify the wreck sooner than that, MSRA

**A side scan image of the wreck of the *H. C. Akeley* captured in May 2001.** *Author's collection*

deployed a small, non-maneuverable drop camera on the wreck. Watching through a remote monitor, the team captured video that revealed a wooden-hulled vessel. However, after less than one minute at that depth, the housing ruptured. The brief video helped rule out the *Michigan* because it was clad in iron, but it was consistent with the design of the *Chicora*, *H. C. Akeley*, and *Hennepin*. However, historical accounts indicate the *Hennepin* was lost off South Haven and the *H. C. Akeley* was lost off Holland. The location of the wreck fit with what had been presumed about the loss of the *Chicora*.

The October 2001 MROVER operation had to be canceled due to bad weather. Because the public had funded the search that resulted in this discovery, MSRA felt obligated to announce the discovery of the shipwreck. Although the team stressed that the wreck had not been positively identified, the media took liberties. Soon, everyone assumed that the *Chicora* had finally been found. MSRA continued to seek proof.

After another cancellation of the MROVER in the spring of 2002, MSRA enlisted the services of technical divers from western Michigan with the training and equipment to make the deep dive. Their dives indicated that the shipwreck was clearly a bulk freighter, not the passenger steamer *Chicora*. Only one bulk freighter had been lost off the shores of western Michigan: the *H. C. Akeley*, and the wreck matched the size and appearance of the *Akeley*.

The *H. C. Akeley* was built at Thomas W. Kirby's Mechanics Dry Dock in the busy commercial port of Grand Haven, Michigan, for Healy C. Akeley. The 230-foot steamer cost over $110,000 and was launched in the spring of 1881 to be used in the grain and iron ore trades in a partnership between Kirby and Healy Cady Akeley, who named the vessel after himself. Born in Stowe, Vermont, in 1826, and later becoming a lawyer, Akeley moved to Grand Haven in 1858, where he was instrumental in developing the lumber and shipping indus-

**A plan and side view of the wreck of the *H. C. Akeley*.** *Drawing by the Author*

tries. After serving in the Civil War, Akeley returned to Grand Haven and became one of the major stockholders of the Grand Haven Lumber Company, justice of the peace, circuit court commissioner, newspaperman, U.S. customs collector, bank director, mayor of Grand Haven, and owner of the world's largest shingle mill.

Thomas Kirby was a prominent maritime man in Grand Haven. His Mechanics Dry Dock & Shipyard on the north bank of Harbor Island in the Grand River had been responsible for the construction of more than a dozen important Great Lakes vessels. He also operated a line of wrecking tugs, manufactured pumps for use in the wrecking business, and through his firm, Kirby, Furlong & Company in Grand Haven, owned and operated the *General Halbert E. Paine,* a 150-foot-long, steam-powered, propeller-driven passenger vessel. Each business fed the others and so when on November 19, 1879, his vessel *General Halbert E. Paine* sank at the entrance of the Grand Haven harbor, his wrecking tug used his pumps to salvage the wreck. Although the ship was beyond repair, he used its boilers and single-cylinder, low-pressure engine to power his newest vessel, the *H. C. Akeley,* then in construction.

The *Paine* had originally been built as the USS *Trefoil* on the east coast in 1865 as a United States dispatch boat. It had been brought into the Great Lakes by a Racine operator who renamed it *General Halbert E. Paine* and converted it to a passenger steamer after an accident that required a significant rebuilding. Although the *Akeley* received the older engine, Kirby reinforced its hull with his newly patented hog rods, turnbuckle-like straps that reinforced the hull across its width and diagonally from the underside of the deck to various points in the lower hold.

Kirby and Akeley put the *H. C. Akeley* under the command of forty-three-year-old Captain Edward Stretch, an experienced and highly regarded shipmaster. Stretch was born in Ireland in 1838, moved to the United States as a young man, and married Sarah Portsmouth in 1864 in Cook County, Illinois. Their first child died at birth and their next children, a daughter and son, were twelve and ten years old at the time their father took charge of the *Akeley.* Stretch would command the vessel for its entire career, and, in fact, even served as a spokesman at one time for his employer, Thomas Kirby. An 1882 advertisement in the Marine Directory promoted the usefulness of Kirby's patented hog rods by including the text of an August 1882 letter from Stretch to Kirby in which he wrote, "I have sailed the steamship *H.C. Akeley* during the seasons of 1881 and 1882, in the grain and iron ore trade, and have been in many gales of wind with her. She is provided with your patent hog rods and I consider them a splendid improvement in ships and no ship ought to be without them, whether built of iron or wood, for when the ship strains the most, the rods are the most useful; that is when rolling in the trough of a heavy

**This photograph of the _H. C. Akeley_ during construction in Grand Haven, Michigan, is one of only two known images of the steam freighter.** _Tri-Cities Museum Collection_

sea said strain is taken from the ship's bilges and beam ends. A ship can't strain herself in a beam sea, besides they prevent a ship from hogging."

Little more than a year later, and only three years into his command of the _Akeley_, Captain Stretch may have reconsidered the usefulness of Kirby's hog rods for they were no match for the storm he encountered that November—the same storm that nearly sank the _Rockaway_ off Kenosha—and would sink dozens of vessels including the _H. C. Akeley_.

On November 9, 1883, the _H. C. Akeley_ took on board 54,000 bushels of corn in Chicago destined for Buffalo, New York. The freighter departed on Sunday, November 11, in the wee hours of the morning. Edward Stretch commanded the freighter with a crew of seventeen men with John Kingston as first mate and John Driscoll as chief engineer. The wind blew moderately out of the southwest as the _Akeley_ headed northeast following the main freighter lanes that run up toward the Manitou Islands. Just a few hours into the journey, the wind clocked around until it started blowing strong out of the west. About seven hours into the run, when near the point where the Chicago to Grand Haven course intersected the St. Joseph to Milwaukee course, the crew of the _Akeley_ heard the sound of a distress whistle. In the distance, they could see two vessels. As they neared the site of the trouble, Wheelsman Samuel R. Martin spotted the familiar tug _Protection_ bobbing out of control near a two-masted schooner that had capsized and was almost three-quarters of the way submerged. He would later learn that the schooner was the _Arab_, which had grounded at St. Joseph two weeks earlier and was being towed to Milwaukee by the _Protection_. At about 4 a.m. that morning, despite the _Arab's_ crew having run the pumps constantly, water had overcome the schooner and it capsized. Captain Anderson of the _Protection_ had come about to pick up the struggling crew and had succeeded

220

in saving ten of eleven members of the crew. However, in backing up, the tug's propeller became fouled in the tow cable. Now the tug bobbed at the mercy of the violent water with its eight-man crew, plus the ten men from the *Arab*, all frightened and undoubtedly glad to see the substantial-sized *H. C. Akeley*.

Stretch ordered the wheelsman to take the tug in tow. The operation was made even more difficult because the wind shifted again, and now blew strong out of the northwest building waves to near ten feet in height. With the tow hawser finally in position, the *Akeley* and its consort fought their way northeast, taking waves on their sides. Just when the crewmembers thought the storm couldn't get any worse, the gales of November blew in with winds that exceeded fifty miles per hour. By 4 p.m. that Sunday, the *Akeley*'s rudder gearing gave out, probably due to the strain of towing the tug in the rough seas. The freighter rolled so fearfully that the cargo shifted and the pony feed pipe from the port boiler broke. Chief Engineer Driscoll changed the throttle from right to left so as to hold the water in the port boiler, but found he could not feed it that way, and keep the boiler supplied. He and Second Engineer James Connell labored to repair the pipe, and by evening thought they had a solution. However, at about 11:30 p.m. as Connell sent steam running between the two boilers, he heard the guy-chain snap on the smokestack and dodged out of the way just as the massive metal tube broke loose, crashed down onto the aft cabin, and rolled into the lake. With the engine completely disabled now, Captain Stretch ordered the raising of the sails—there for just such an emergency—and the ship was able to maintain its nose into the wind for a short time. Soon, though, the wind ripped the sails into tatters. Stretch had no choice but to order an anchor set to try to wait out the storm. The operation took the better part of an hour, but once secured both the *Akeley* and the *Protection* rode much better in the water. Unfortunately, overnight, the waves got worse. At 4 a.m. on November 12, a giant whitecap swept one of the *Akeley*'s two lifeboats overboard. The *Protection*'s crew struggled with their propeller all day trying to make their tug operational and finally succeeded at 6 p.m., as darkness fell. Captain Anderson signaled the crew of the *Akeley* to set them free. As he motored forward he shouted across the water, "We'll coal up in Grand Haven, and return to tow you in." As those on board the *Akeley* watched their only hope steam off, they saw the *Protection* suddenly lurch sideways and turn broadside into the waves. The engine had obviously failed again. From their anchored position, they watched helplessly as the tug drifted east toward shore and to an unknown fate.

With nothing to do but wait, hoping the lake would calm, the crew tried to get some rest as the *Akeley* remained at anchor yet another night. When morning dawned and they saw the condition of the ship, they knew it would not stay afloat much longer. Early that afternoon, they spotted their salvation on the horizon. A schooner, which they would later learn was the two-masted

*Driver,* bound from Chicago to Grand Haven, sailed straight for them. Uncertain how much longer the *Akeley* would remain afloat, at about 1:30 p.m. on Tuesday, November 13, Captain Stretch gave what would be his last command, telling the crew to launch the remaining lifeboat, "Go aft and look out for yourselves." With not enough room in the boat for all, Stretch and five others remained on the *Akeley*, probably hoping against hope that it would support them until the schooner arrived.

## LOST

On board the *Driver*, Captain David Miller, his brother Daniel, and the crew spotted the sinking freighter, saw a lifeboat full of men nearby, and adjusted their sails to bear down on them. "Good God, Dave, she is foundering," Daniel hollered to his brother when he saw the big ship's mast crack and fall over. Then they watched as the freighter heeled over, the bow rose up, and it plunged stern first to the bottom. Miller was able to maneuver his way toward the lifeboat and when near enough, Daniel and one other man launched their yawl. They managed to row over to the small boat and take three of the men on board to lighten their load. While pulling back toward the *Driver*, the yawl capsized, dumping the five men into the water. They were able to right it and climb aboard. Both boats and all the men made it back to the safety of the schooner. Although they spent some time searching for the six men who had remained on board the *Akeley*, they found no one dead or alive in the water. Captain Stretch, First Mate John Kingston, steward John Babbitt, cabin boy Willie Stanley, and two deckhands went down with their ship. The surviving crewmembers later estimated that the *Akeley* sank between nine and fifteen miles off Holland.

In the ordeal that played out over three days in 1883, the *Arab* and the *Akeley* both sank, and seven men died. The tug *Protection* eventually grounded at Saugatuck, and after a tremendous ordeal near the beach, all but one of the crewmembers of the *Arab* and *Protection* were saved by the local life-savers. For his heroics, Captain Miller of the *Driver* was later awarded a medal. It would be nearly a month before Edward Stretch's body washed ashore. It was sent to Chicago on board another ship just in time for his funeral held at his brother's home on West Polk in Chicago. He was buried at Calvary Cemetery.

On October 12, 2002, the MROVER operation took place as a collaboration between MSRA, the University of Michigan , and NOAA, which supplied the Research Vessel *Laurentian*. Haunting underwater video of the *H. C. Akeley* offered testimony to the events that played out on Lake Michigan 118 years previously. The aft deckhouse, all five hatch covers, and the forward pilot-house are missing, swept off when the ship sank. The corn cargo still fills

A postcard drawing depicts the final moments of the **H. C. Akeley**. *Mason County Historical Society Collection*

the hold, coming to within two feet of the underside of the deck. Only the base of the smokestack is present, confirming survivors' accounts of its collapse. The forward and aft masts lie fallen on the deck in a tangle of wire rigging. The main mast fell to the port side and lies up against the port rail on deck. A buildup of clay on the aft deck indicates that the *Akeley* plunged stern first just as the crew of the *Driver* reported. When it hit bottom, it must have stirred up the sediment, which then landed on its deck. The port anchor chain trails off on the hard sand bottom about three hundred feet north. The end disappears into the sand. The force exerted by the *Akeley* and *Protection* on the anchor must have been so strong that it embedded the anchor fully in the lake bottom. The wreck rests eigh-

teen miles off Saugatuck, *not* Holland as the survivors reported. Perhaps if Captain Stretch had lived, he might have provided reporters with the correct location of the wreck.

MSRA technical divers made another dive on the wreck in November of 2002. They observed the words: "Johnston....Ferrysburg, Michigan" on a gauge on the boiler. Undoubtedly the Johnston Boiler Works in Ferrysburg, Michigan, serviced the

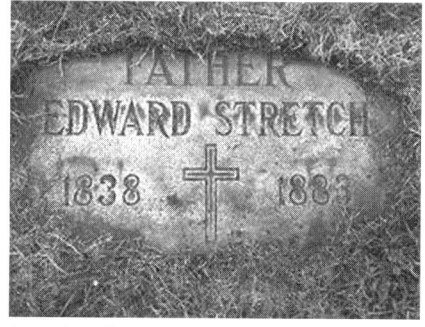

Captain Edward Stretch's body was recovered several weeks after the accident and buried in Calvary Cemetery. *Courtesy of Barbara Patch*

A close-up of a gauge on the boiler of the *H. C. Akeley*. *Photograph of Robert Underhill*

machinery recovered from the *General Halbert E. Paine* before it was installed in the *Akeley*. Incidentally, research on General Paine, the man after whom the vessel was named, revealed a twist of fate as relates to the discovery of the *H. C. Akeley*. General Halbert Eleazer Paine, a Civil War general who later served as a Wisconsin Republican congressman, is most noted for lobbying for Congress to establish the National Weather Service in 1870. Ironically, without the data collected and archived by the National Weather Service, now the National Climatic Data Center, the wreck of the *H.C. Akeley* would not have been found. Paine's foresight changed the way the weather is tracked and predicted and established the tools to help researchers and agencies like NOAA, the U.S. Coast Guard, and shipwreck hunters discover lost ships.

The discovery also brought about the establishment of MSRA, which has dedicated itself to research, exploration, documentation, and the creation of

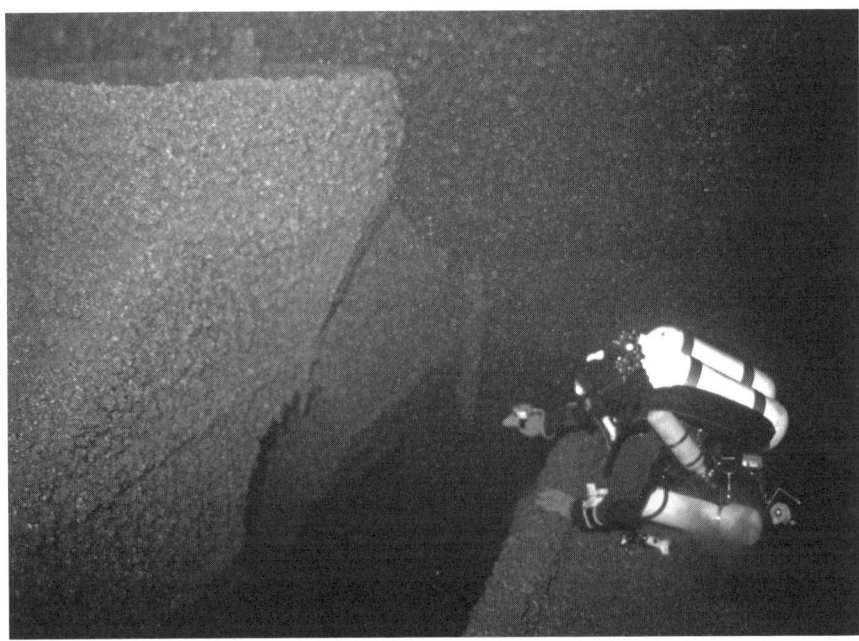

Diver Jeff Vos examines the boiler near the stern of the *H. C. Akeley*. *Photograph by Robert Underhill*

**A video capture shows the bow of the *H. C. Akeley*.** *Video by John Janzen and John Scoles*

educational programs and materials. MSRA would continue to work with David Trotter, as well as a new partner, to find several vessels lost off the shores of western Michigan, a few of which have become legendary.

**Jeff Vos secures a mooring line on the massive wood stock anchor at the bow of the *Michigan*.** *Photograph by Robert Underhill*

# 16

# A NEW HERO

The forty-three-day ordeal that took place on board and around the steamer *Michigan,* stranded in the ice off the coast of western Michigan in 1895, was an amazing battle of man against Mother Nature. The discovery of the wreck of the *Michigan* off Holland, Michigan, 111 years later in 2006 ignited a new interest in this story of perseverance, dedication, and responsibility that made both the steamer and its youngest crewmember, George Sheldon, legendary.

The Michigan Shipwreck Research Association became interested in the *Michigan* when it realized the similarities with another, even more famous, ship lost in Antarctica. There are few who are not familiar with Ernest Shackleton's 1914 expedition attempt to be the first expedition to cross the South Polar continent. After eleven months, Shackleton and his crew of twenty-seven men became hopelessly trapped in the ice and abandoned the damaged *Endurance* to proceed on foot. One month after leaving their schooner, increased pressure from the ice splintered the hull and sent it to the bottom. It would be more than six months later, after living on ice floes, that a small group, led by Shakelton, overcame insurmountable obstacles to safely reach home. As familiar as most people are with this epic voyage through several books and a feature film, most people have no idea that a similar epic event played out thirty years earlier on Lake Michigan on the steamer *Michigan.*

The propeller steamers *Michigan*, its nearly identical sister ship *Wisconsin,* and the sidewheel steamer *City of Milwaukee* were conceived by the Goodrich Transportation Company as passenger and cargo steamers to serve the Detroit Grand Haven and Milwaukee Railroad Company between Grand Haven and Milwaukee. The propellers were each 204 feet long with a beam of 35 feet and a capacity of 13,000 tons. Frank E. Kirby of the Detroit Dry Dock Company, the man who had a hand in the planning of the *David Dows*, and who would later design the ill-fated *Chicora* and the *Ann Arbor No. 5*, designed the vessels to serve year-round, whereas the *City of Milwaukee* would be used largely for summer tourist transportation. Kirby employed iron in the construction of the propellers, one of the first such uses on the Great Lakes. He constructed the *Michigan* with a double iron hull and iron deck, believing that this material would allow it to better withstand service in the icy winter months. He also fabricated them with five watertight compartments. The *Michigan* was launched August 20, 1881, in Wyandotte, Michigan. The 123 spacious cabins were said to be the grandest on the lakes, decorated without regard to cost, with the finest velvet carpets, furniture, and oil paintings. The *Michigan* cost $160,000.

Fifty-four-year-old Captain Redmond Prindiville was put in command of the *Michigan*. He and his brother John, along with multiple siblings, were born in Ireland in the 1820s, and relocated to Chicago with their parents in 1835. The two boys began their careers as schooner captains, engaged in both lake and international, maritime trade. In Chicago, they were founders of the Chicago Yacht Club and owners of a very successful fleet of tugs. Keeping in the tradition of their Irish-Catholic families, both men, despite spending so much time on the water, had large families. Redmond and his wife, Mary, had ten children.

**A single image, rejoined from two photographs that have for years been divided for archival purposes, shows the *Michigan,* on the left, and the sidewheel steamer *City of Milwaukee* docked in Grand Haven, Michigan, the vessels' home port.** *C. Patrick Labadie Collection - Alpena County Public Library*

The *Wisconsin, Michigan,* and *City of Milwaukee* operated successfully in the cross-lake service under Goodrich until the Detroit, Grand Haven and Milwaukee Railroad Company decided that it would be more financially prudent to own and operate its own vessels. With the loss of that contract, Goodrich opted to sell the three steamers to the railroad company in May 1883 for continued operation on the same line. Prindiville stayed on as captain of the *Michigan.* By 1884, the railroad had renamed the route the Grand Trunk Line.

The *Michigan* had its first brush with disaster on November 23, 1884, when on a westbound crossing it encountered a furious northwest gale. Captain Prindiville decided to return to Grand Haven, but when the ship was crossing the sand bar, a wave dashed it into the south pier. The sixty-five-foot Goodrich tug *Arctic,* built for berthing, towing, and rescue work, came to its rescue and towed it into port.

One year later, another fierce winter would result in the end of the *Michigan*'s short career. By December, the lake had begun to ice over, something that had not happened for almost a decade. This severe weather, oddly, was later attributed to a volcanic eruption on the other side of the world. In August 1883, Mt. Krakatoa in Indonesia had erupted killing 30,000 people and sending a plume of ash into the atmosphere. Eighteen months later, the world was still feeling the weather effects of one of the mightiest volcanic eruptions ever. However, by January, the weather in western Michigan started to improve

**Chicago FIRSTS:**

By Earle Harvey

The FIRST RAILROAD ENGINE ARRIVED BY SHIP IN CHICAGO, OCTOBER 10, 1848

REDMOND PRINDIVILLE HELPED UNLOAD THE ENGINE FROM THE BRIG BUFFALO. LATER HE HAD THE HONOR OF NAMING HER "THE PIONEER"

HARVEY.

**A newspaper illustration of Captain Redmund Prindiville.** *Author's Collection*

and locals hoped that the worst of winter was over.

Taking advantage of rising temperatures that might loosen the pack ice, on January 20 the steamship *Oneida*, also owned by the Detroit, Grand Haven and Milwaukee Railroad Company, was sent to cross the lake on a regular cargo run carrying 717 tons of flour, a crew of twenty, and a few passengers. However, conditions were worse than anticipated and the vessel became trapped by the ice the next day approximately seven miles north of Grand Haven. The *Oneida*'s First Mate Martin and ten men left the stranded vessel to hike across the ice to shore, then returned with gear to try to break it free. By January 23, the steamer had drifted north with the pack ice to a point off Muskegon and those on board had already eaten all the food. Over the next two weeks the wind pushed the stranded steamer farther north and everyone was compelled to subsist on the cargo of bran flour and water.

By February 7, the vessel had used up all its fuel struggling to break free of the ice. Watchers on shore reported its position then at about five miles off shore. Although the passing steamer *Pere Marquette No 2* tried but could not break the *Oneida* free, it did drop several tons of coal on the ice for the *Oneida*. The crew fired up the boilers and commenced trying to break free, but by then the ice had opened up several seams in the vessel and it began taking on water. The crew had to run the pumps almost continually to keep up with the incoming water. Something had to be done, or the *Oneida* would sink.

## LOST

The Detroit, Grand Haven and Milwaukee Railroad Company decided to send one of their other ships to rescue the trapped *Oneida*. Managers chose the *Michigan*, confident that the steamer's double iron hull could break the ice and set the *Oneida* free to steam back to port. Captain Prindiville quickly assembled a crew of twenty-nine men to join him. On Monday, February 9, 1885, they left the *Michigan*'s winter port in Grand Haven, conveniently during a lull in the snow. Joseph Russell served as first mate and George Sheldon, the youngest member of the crew at twenty-one, served as porter.

Sheldon had been born the third of four boys to Scottish immigrants Cornelius and Laura Sheldon in Stowe, Vermont, on October 22, 1863, just four months after his father enlisted as a private in Vermont's First Heavy Artillery Regiment. Cornelius was among the fortunate solders who returned home: He saw his toddler son for the first time when he mustered out in June 1865. When Sheldon was in his teens, his father moved the family to Spring Lake, Michigan, where Sheldon soon began working as a laborer and then joined the Detroit, Grand Haven and Milwaukee Railroad Company on the steamers.

The first few miles were clear steaming as Prindiville headed the *Michigan* out a good distance, then turned starboard and headed north. He made it to a point off White River where the *Michigan* spent several hours searching in vain for the *Oneida*. Blasts from the horn revealed the vessel's position to those on shore. It is unknown how long the *Michigan* steamed, cutting through the thin, patchy ice, but it must have been about twenty miles out when another fierce northeasterly gale hit that evening, pushing the *Michigan* in the opposite direction—south into the ever-building ice pack. The storm raged for three days and temperatures plummeted to twenty degrees below zero. By the time the storm abated on February 11, an official from the Grand Trunk Line headed to Pentwater in an attempt to locate the missing *Michigan*, but could not see it from shore. Great worry arose for the *Michigan*.

On board the *Michigan* the crew was safe; however, the frozen lake had entrapped the steamer far from shore. Winds pushed it and the pack ice south. Days later, the *Michigan* had moved forty miles south of its location when the storm hit. Prindiville could no longer search for the *Oneida*: He had to focus on keeping his vessel and crew safe. However, the ice held the steamer firmly in its grip and within a week Prindiville had to ration the food down to just one meal per day. With no relief in sight, the captain chose seventeen of the hardiest men to walk to shore and arrange for a tug to rescue them, leaving just a skeleton crew to bring the ship in should the ice release its grip. Among the shore crew was George Sheldon, who promised Captain Prindiville that, if possible, he would return to the trapped ship with news from shore, and more supplies.

The crewmembers left the *Michigan* on February 17. The temperature was ten degrees below zero as the party, armed with axes, pikes, ropes, and rations, began their trek at about 7 a.m. With nothing but a compass to lead them in the direction of land, they trudged through deep snow and ridges of ice for the better part of the day. The arduous trip was complicated when clerk W. D. Kenny almost gave up after he tumbled down a ridge of ice. Encouraged and aided by First Mate Russell and George Sheldon, he continued on. Near day's end, the crew finally reached shore in Allegan County's Casco Township, just north of South Haven. The half-frozen crew had covered over twelve miles in ten hours on their hike, only to face one last remaining obstacle before they could rest: to climb the steep bluff. After their trek across the ice, this seemed an insurmountable task. They had all they could do to struggle up the rocky ice-covered bluff, but once they reached the top, they saw a farmhouse.

Owner Levi Thomas must have been surprised when these nearly frozen sailors showed up at his door. He and other locals took the men in for the night. The following morning, Thomas took the crew by sleigh to the train station at Brăvo for the trip north to Grand Haven where their journey had begun. Meanwhile, back on board the *Michigan*, Captain Prindiville and the twelve remaining crewmembers did not have much to do except pass the time. Music, cards, and games helped during the long, cold hours. They waited for four days not knowing whether their crewmates had made it to shore. Then on Saturday, February 21, their patience was rewarded when they spotted a man on the ice walking toward the ship. As he got closer, they recognized George Sheldon. Seeing the hearty young man raised the spirits of the crew.

Once safely on board, Sheldon recounted his journey. He had reached Grand Haven with the other crewmembers the prior Wednesday and informed company officials of the predicament. The company set in motion plans to send a tugboat to the rescue, while Sheldon took the train back south with food and fuel to resupply the stranded crew. Sheldon brought news from home, food, books, oil, and even a few bottles of whiskey. For a crew who had been trapped for more than a week, it must have felt like Christmas morning. After two good nights' rest, the young porter again set out alone on the morning of Monday, February 23, with a bag of letters from the crew to their families and a dispatch from the captain to his superiors. After another arduous trek across

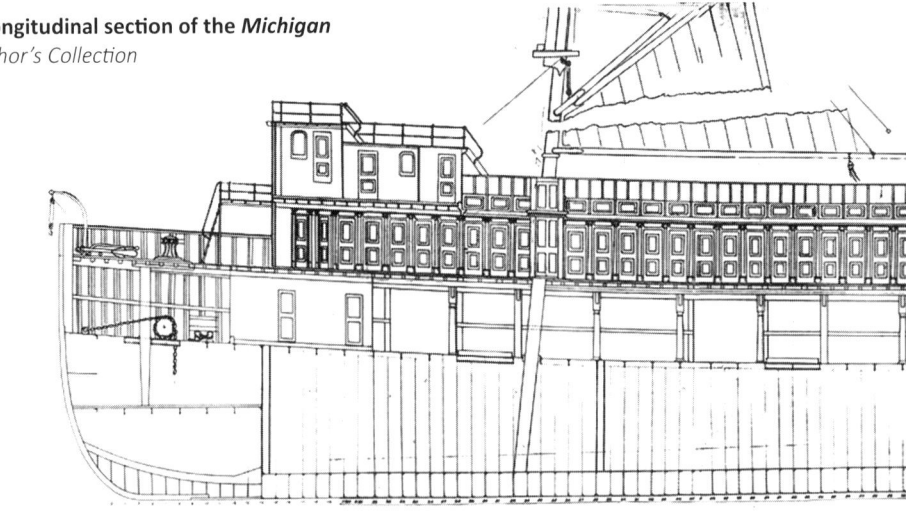

**A longitudinal section of the *Michigan***
*Author's Collection*

the frozen lake, Sheldon again made the journey north to Grand Haven by train to deliver his packages. With the stamina of an ox, he once again traveled back south to the lakeshore in Casco Township with supplies given him by the company and rounded up some locals to assist him.

Departing from the Thomas' property again, Sheldon set out on Wednesday, February 25, leading the group of six Casco residents on a twelve-to-fifteen-mile hike to the stranded schooner towing sleds loaded with provisions. The Casco men had planned to return the next day, but the weather suddenly took a turn for the worse and no one could leave the ship. By Saturday, February 28, the weather had let up enough that the Casco men could head in. Captain Prindiville gave them one of his four lifeboats to drag along behind them as a precaution in case they encountered open water.

With enough supplies now to last out the winter if need be, Prindiville, Sheldon, and the remaining skeleton crew settled in, looking forward to the time when the ice would thaw and allow then to steam back to Grand Haven. The ice did not loosen its grip, though, and the weather worsened, this time with a strong wind out of the south. The *Michigan* began drifting northward in the ice. February turned to March. One week passed, then another. Reporters watching the ordeal from land speculated the steamer would reach Grand Haven "after a while." However, by mid-March, the shifting ice was beginning to take its toll on the iron hull. Captain Prindiville had to consider that they might need to abandon the ship.

On Wednesday, March 18, 1885, he saw and heard things that indicated his vessel would not last until the ice melted. The pressure on the *Michigan*'s hull had become incredible. The crew could hear the iron hull buckling throughout the night and all the next day. In the lower compartment on the port side, the iron was

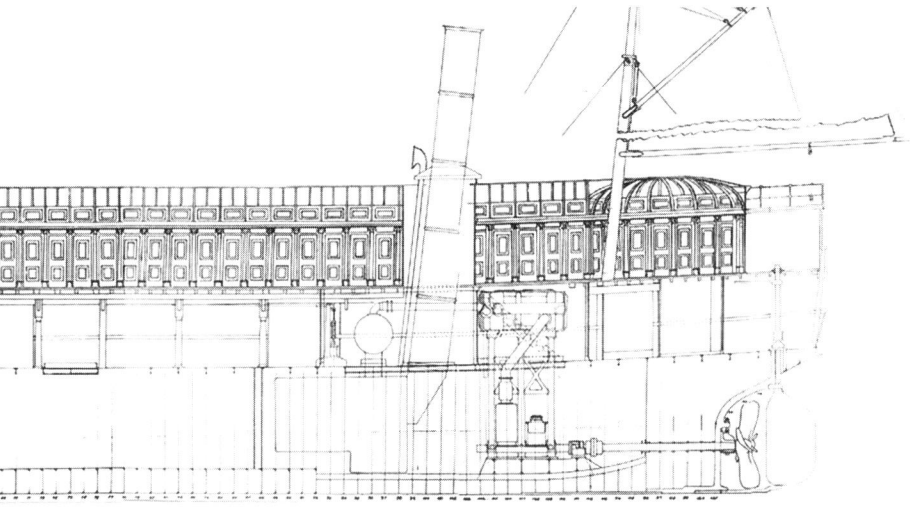

**Although often referred to as the "Ice Crusher," the tug _Arctic_ was unable to break its way through the ice that trapped it on its rescue attempt of the _Michigan_.** *William Lafferty Collection*

bent in all conceivable shapes. Finally, the seams gave way and water began rushing in. The crew attempted to stanch the flow with the pumps, but time was against them. Fortunately, Prindiville had spotted a tugboat about four miles distant. He recognized the familiar silhouette as the _Arctic,_ which had rescued he and his crew once before and which had undoubtedly been sent out to rescue them again. Unfortunately, it appeared that the _Arctic_ had also become trapped by the ice.

As the _Michigan_'s hull buckled and the ship showed every sign of succumbing to the ice on Friday March 19, Captain Prindiville made the difficult decision to abandon ship and try to reach the safety of the tug. Some of the crew launched a lifeboat to tow for safety, while Prindiville gathered up the ship's papers. The ice held as they set out for the _Arctic,_ but by 4 p.m., when they had traveled about a quarter-mile toward the _Arctic,_ the ice finally stove-in the _Michigan_'s hull, filling the vessel with water and sending it to the bottom in about 300 feet of water, according to the captain's calculations.

The _Michigan_'s crew reached the _Arctic_ by nightfall after a painful and dangerous trek across the buckling and shifting ice. They spent the next two days with the crew of the _Arctic,_ in the safety of the warm tug, waiting for the ice to relinquish its grip. The _Arctic_'s crew had already been trapped for several days and was running short of provisions. Consequently, the crew of the _Michigan_ could not remain on board. On the morning of Monday, March 23, they headed for the shore some fourteen miles distant, under the competent leadership of George Sheldon, who had become familiar with the conditions on the ice.

More than halfway to shore, the cook Charles Robinson became so exhausted, he gave up on the ice, but told the others to go on without him. Although hesitant to leave him, Sheldon felt responsible for guiding the others to shore. After an arduous trek, he and his crewmates finally touched solid land for the first time in forty-three days, near Holland. Prindiville and the others continued on, but Sheldon headed back out on the ice and after some searching found the near-dead cook, and carried him to shore. Thanks to Sheldon's bravery, the entire crew lived to tell their incredible story of patience, stamina, and heroism while icebound on Lake Michigan.

The *Arctic* remained trapped for many more days. After more than a week, its crew abandoned the tug and struggled across the shore to safety. However, the tug's owner, Captain Kirby, did not want to lose his stout vessel or his crew. On March 31, he assembled a relief party to return to the tug with a boat on skis and 150 pounds of provisions to last six more weeks if need be. Because of his familiarity with the conditions of the ice, George Sheldon offered to lead the group on the trek out to the stranded tug. They reached the tug, but did not have to brave the weather very long. On April 3, the *Arctic* steamed in on its own power, with George Sheldon among its crew. The *Grand Haven Tribune* acknowledged Sheldon as "the porter who has proved himself such a hero."

Not until Sheldon reached Grand Haven did he learn the full story about the *Oneida*. As luck would have it, the *Oneida,* the original ship that the *Michigan* had been sent out to rescue, had actually managed to work its way out of the ice on the very day that the *Michigan* left to rescue it. Had technology included ship-to-shore communications at that time, the useless, costly expedition on the *Michigan* could have been avoided.

Ironically, the Grand Trunk Line used the *Oneida* to replace the *Michigan*. Captain Prindiville sailed for a few more years, then settled down to a more peaceful life as a loan agent for Northwestern Mutual Life Insurance with offices in Chicago, living to the age of eighty-seven. He was buried in a plot in Chicago's Calvary Cemetery under a giant boulder engraved with the family name Prindiville. The brave and hearty George Sheldon married a Van Drezer girl from Grand Haven but lived only another five years, passing away of rheumatism in 1890 in Mt. Clemens, Michigan, where he had gone to partake in the mineral baths to try to regain his health after the ordeals of the winter of 1885. He was buried in the Van Drezer family plot in the Forest View Cemetery in Grand Haven, alongside May Sheldon, a girl born in 1887 who died in 1889. It is believed that Sheldon and his wife suffered the death of their own infant just two years before Sheldon died.

## FOUND

With a good understanding of the sinking of the *Michigan* from newspaper accounts and the hope that it had remained in good condition on the bottom in deep water, MSRA began to develop a probable search area. Captain Prindiville had reported that his ship had gone down between fifteen to twenty miles off Holland's harbor. This provided a general idea of where to begin the search; however, a different newspaper account indicated that it had taken the crew only about two hours to reach the *Arctic* and another six hours to reach shore, which seemed too short a time to have traveled that far over ice. MSRA increased the overall search area to encompass an area between ten and twenty-two miles off shore.

As it had since 1998, MSRA retained the services of side scan operator David Trotter, who in 2003 provided the equipment and expertise to search for the *Michigan*. Trotter had acquired a new 50 kHz sonar that would allow the sonar to "see" out on both sides much farther than his 100 kHz sonar. He could cover almost one square mile per hour with the new sonar. MSRA began searching in the middle of the probable search area, but did not find the wreck. In 2004, MSRA continued its quest. On May 24 the plotter recorded an unusual target in 270 feet of water. The wreck appeared to be about 200 feet long, the size of the *Michigan*. The darker-than-usual plot suggested a ship made of metal, like the *Michigan*'s lower hull. Exploratory dives a few weeks later revealed a modern barge, probably scuttled for the insurance money.

MSRA continued the search for the Michigan in 2005 for a period of ten days. The team divided the remaining search area into quadrants of about six to eight square miles, representing an area that could be covered in one long day. Beginning with the quadrants closest to shore, the team made incredible progress in four days, but found nothing. In reviewing newspaper accounts for additional clues, a quote previously overlooked indicated that it may have taken the crew longer to reach shore than the other account had indicated. It seems that the crew spent an entire day hiking to shore, then had to rest somewhere along shore overnight before setting out for the train station the next day. If this account was true, then Prindiville may have been correct in his calculation. With those new insights, the team moved the search farther off shore. By the last day of the search, all but three quadrants had been covered without finding the ship.

A side scan image, captured in May 2005, convinced MSRA and David Trotter that they had found the *Michigan*. *Author's collection*

MSRA arbitrarily chose to continue the search in the quadrant closest to shore, which turned out to be a good decision. On the first lane of the day, the sonar plotted a target which appeared to be about 200 feet long and made of metal. Hopes were higher this time, but

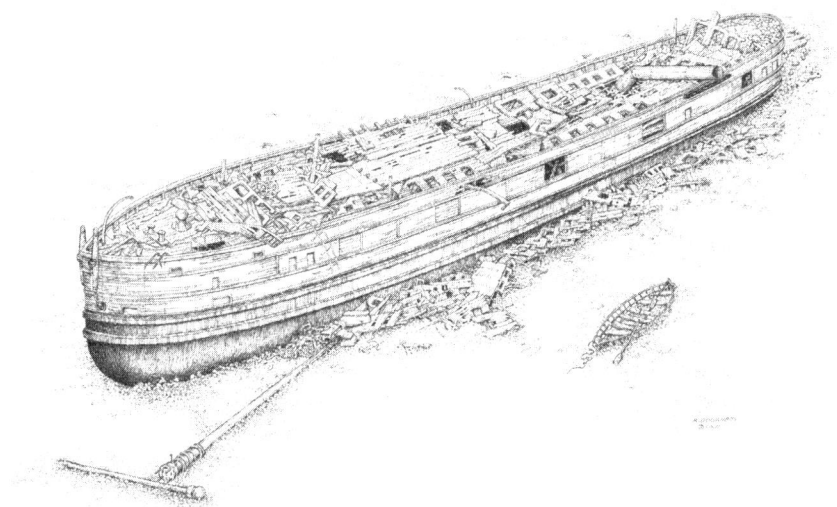

**An artist's rendition of the wreck of the _Michigan_. The upper works probably collapsed upon impact with the bottom. One of the ship's four lifeboats remains in the sand.** _Drawing by Robert Doornbos_

only a closer look at the wreck in person could confirm its identity.

In June 2005, MSRA technical divers Jeff Vos, Todd White, and Bob Underhill geared up for a dive to investigate the target. They had studied the construction drawings found of the _Michigan_ to plan their dive. Each wore a drysuit and double tanks containing mixed gas, a special blend of air containing less nitrogen and oxygen to avoid the intoxicating and toxic effects of the gases under extreme pressure. They all carried two dive computers, two lights, two knives, an oxygen and Nitrox tank to breath during decompression, and an argon tank to fill their drysuits. They entered the water and headed down

**Jeff Vos hovers near the _Michigan_'s wheel, which is still intact although the pilothouse collapsed around it.** _Photograph by Robert Underhill_

the anchor line secured near the wreck in 275 feet of water, where they would plan to spend twenty minutes on the bottom. Although it was very dark at the bottom, the divers could begin to see the outline of an upright vessel when they reached 200 feet. Zebra mussels could be credited with this extraordinary visibility. While an environmental nuisance, the mussels have had a mixed effect for divers. As filter feeders, they have cleared the water, but they attach to most every wood and metal surface and obscure the detail on shipwrecks.

Reaching the wreck at the stern, they immediately realized the ship was a passenger steamer, likely the *Michigan*. However, finding proof of the wreck's identity would be their main goal. They saw that the hull was intact, but the smokestack, cabins, and pilothouse that once sat on top of the main deck had collapsed. First, they made their way to the rail to look for the name board as pictured in photographs of the *Michigan*. Although they found a long, slender board at the right spot, the paint had been scoured off by the action of the silt in moving water. Moving forward toward the bow, they saw a double wheel standing intact among the collapsed pilothouse. Seeing that made them suspect, for the moment, that the vessel was not the *Michigan* because the construction drawings did not indicate that kind of a wheel, designed to afford more leverage in high winds. Continuing forward, they encountered the ship's capstan, used to help raise and lower the anchors. Round, domed capstan covers like these were usually engraved with the ship's name, but zebra mussels covered the surface. They brushed it off and after the silt cleared, they found their proof: the name MICHIGAN was engraved on the cover.

Before heading back, they filmed the sturdy wood stock anchors in place at the bow just as they would have been secured, considering the *Michigan* had no need for them. Heading aft along the starboard side toward the down-line, the divers peered into the cargo openings. Some had doors in place, but others were open. The temptation to go inside was great, but with bottom time almost used up and over an hour of decompression before they could deliver the good news to the crew waiting topside, they returned to the down-line.

During subsequent dives on the *Michigan*, the team documented the wreck's condition. Over the century it has spent underwater, it has nestled down into the soft sand bottom. The stern deck exhibits quite a bit of sand and clay buildup, which suggests that the ship impacted the bottom stern first and, like a spoon, scooped up some of the bottom in the process. The upper cabins, smokestack, and mast all lie fallen in the direction of the port side toward the stern, indicating that the initial impact on the bottom caused a massive collapse. Had the joints waterlogged and decayed over time, the structures would have fallen more haphazardly.

After becoming familiar with the outside of the vessel, the divers opted to venture inside through an open cargo hatch on the port side near amidships. Since the *Michigan* carried no cargo, the main cargo deck was empty. Three openings spaced out in the floor with winches mounted over them would have provided the means to load cargo into the lowest deck. The divers ventured down through one opening, and as expected found it also empty. They bottomed out at 290 feet, which meant that they were deeper than the lake bottom: The ship had sunk into the bottom at least fifteen feet. Swimming up through the floor opening, they headed forward toward where they expected to find the galley, a crew cabin, and the fo'c'sle. On the port side, the galley wall had partially fallen. Inside, they saw a stove. Wooden racks lined one wall. White porcelain dishes still sat in the rack where they would have been when the crew abandoned ship. The crew likely spent a lot of time in the galley to take advantage of the heat from the stove, probably playing cards and musical instruments there. Across the hall, the door to the crew room had come off its hinges and blocked access into that room. Debris in the passageway also blocked access forward to the fo'c'sle. To get there, they had to swim back to the port side hatch, exit the cargo deck, then swim forward to the bow.

On the port side of the forwardmost deck, they found a stairway leading

A work bench and shelves inside a workroom on the main level near the stern show brass lanterns that would have been kept lit during the crew's ordeal on the stranded steamer. *Photograph by Robert Underhill*

**The author visits the grave of Michigan porter George Sheldon, a "new" hero.**
*Photograph by Ross Richardson*

down to the fo'c'sle. Inside, they found the gears below the capstan, as well as bilge pumps to use in the event of water seepage. Peering down into an opening in the floor, they spotted the chain locker in the lowest, most forward area of the ship, filled with chain.

During another dive, they entered the open port-side hatch and swam aft, where they encountered a wooden grill that separates the cargo space from the engine room. The engine still exhibits red paint, indication that there has been little movement of the water to scour it off. Behind the engine room, a companionway runs from side to side. There, a wall-mount signal bell on a ceiling joist would have allowed the officers to signal the engine room crew. On the after-side of the companionway are three rooms, the center one appearing to

240

be work room. Several oil lamps sit on a work bench with six more secured in a shelf along the side of the room. Two oilers on the floor would have held lantern fuel. Undoubtedly the young porter George Sheldon spent time in this room. He would have been in charge of maintaining and filling the lanterns to provide light during the long ordeal. The two rooms on either side of the workroom contain bunks, potentially one where Sheldon slept. Behind those three rooms are two stalls with swinging doors. A bench inside each contains a hole, obviously crude toilets that must have discharged directly into the lake.

The discovery and survey of the *Michigan* served as a time capsule providing a glimpse of what life aboard the vessel must have been like during the six weeks the crew remained trapped. Since its discovery, the story of the *Michigan* has been told in a children's book written by this book's author, and in a documentary film, and has been the subject of numerous lectures to both adults and school groups. In these recountings, George Sheldon, a young man who passed away more than a century ago, has become known as the hero he was. One pastor in western Michigan even delivered a sermon based on the behavior of this young crewman, who now lives on as a source of inspiration for numerous young people.

An aerial view of the three vessels used to protect the in-water work areas during construction of the Palisades Power Plant. The *Ann Arbor No. 5*, cut down to a barge, is pictured in the center. Herald Palladium *Archives*

# 17

# REWRITING HISTORY

The stories of sinking ships usually include stormy seas, foggy nights, or deadly collisions accompanied by heroic rescues and tragic losses. However, for every ship that met its end in dramatic circumstances, there are dozens of other vessels that were simply scrapped when they became too old for service. That was the case, according to written records, of the car ferry *Ann Arbor No. 5*. Therefore, the discovery of the aft half of the *Ann Arbor No. 5* on the bottom of Lake Michigan off South Haven, Michigan, made it a legendary shipwreck.

**FOUND**

In September 2004, MSRA had the privilege to begin working with internationally acclaimed author Clive Cussler in a joint venture project to search for the wreck of Northwest Airlines Flight 2501, a DC-4 lost off South Haven, Michigan, in 1950. All fifty-eight passengers and crew died when the plane, enroute from New York to Seattle, disappeared in the southern basin of Lake Michigan. The accident ranked as the worst commercial aviation disaster in the United States at the time, but the wreckage was never found, and the cause of the disaster was never determined. The mystery piqued Cussler's interest. The highly successful writer has admitted to "loving the challenge of solving a mystery," and acknowledged that "there is no greater mystery than a lost shipwreck."

To satisfy his curiosity, he founded the National Underwater and Marine Agency (NUMA) as a nonprofit, volunteer foundation dedicated to preserving maritime heritage through the discovery, archaeological survey, and conservation of shipwrecks. In between writing more than forty best-selling novels, among them the Dirk Pitt, NUMA Files, and Oregon Files series, he has organized expeditions to search for some of the world's most famous lost vessels. He has found many dozens of ship and plane wrecks. Among his most famous discoveries are the Confederate submarine *Horace L. Hunley*, and the *Carpathia*, the ship that rescued *Titanic* survivors.

The search for Flight 2501 marked Cussler's first expedition in the Great Lakes. MSRA provided the local connection, the search boat, and conducted the research to attempt to develop an appropriate search grid. Cussler provided the services of marine archaeologist and side scan sonar expert Ralph Wilbanks and boat pilot Steve Howard, who traveled to western Michigan to work with MSRA beginning in September 2004. Wilbanks had been working with Cussler for over a decade on several high-profile expeditions, and was responsible for locating, with Cussler, the *Hunley*, which during the Civil War became the first submarine to sink an enemy warship.

The initial search area encompassed approximately twenty square miles of high probability area off South Haven presumed to contain the airplane's remains. Wilbanks used a high-frequency 500 kHz Klein side scan sonar capable of locating small pieces of aluminum and four engines, all that was believed would remain of the airplane. During the first week, the sonar plotted several anomalies that could indicate airplane remains, but subsequent dives revealed nothing but rocky bottomlands and an uprooted tree. Another small target inspected by MSRA divers proved to be an intentionally scuttled Chris-Craft.

In the spring of 2005, Wilbanks returned for a month-long expedition. Each day the weather allowed, he and his crew motored out to the search area and deployed the sonar, a three-foot-long, torpedo-shaped device tethered by cable to the on-board computer. He set it to run about forty feet off the lake bottom. Then he proceeded at about four miles per hour covering the designated search grid by running lanes. On one particularly calm day that month, the boat suddenly lurched. Wilbanks immediately realized that the sonar had plowed into something on the bottom. After he recovered his gear and found that it had not been damaged, he deployed the sonar again, maintaining it much higher off the lake bottom, and ran patterns around the object. The sonar image revealed a shipwreck about 100 feet long and almost sixty feet wide in 160 feet of water. It appeared to stand just over forty feet off the bottom. There existed no records of a ship having been lost in the immediate area, so the team could not even venture a guess what it might be.

The following week, MSRA divers Craig Rich, Jack Van Heest, Bob Underhill, Jeff Vos, Todd White, and this book's author made a dive to the wreck

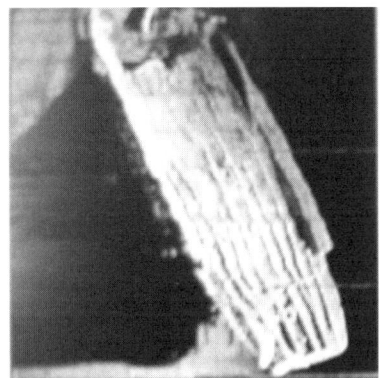

**Side scan image of the *Ann Arbor No. 5* captured with a 500 kHz Klein side scan sonar.** *Courtesy of Ralph Wilbanks*

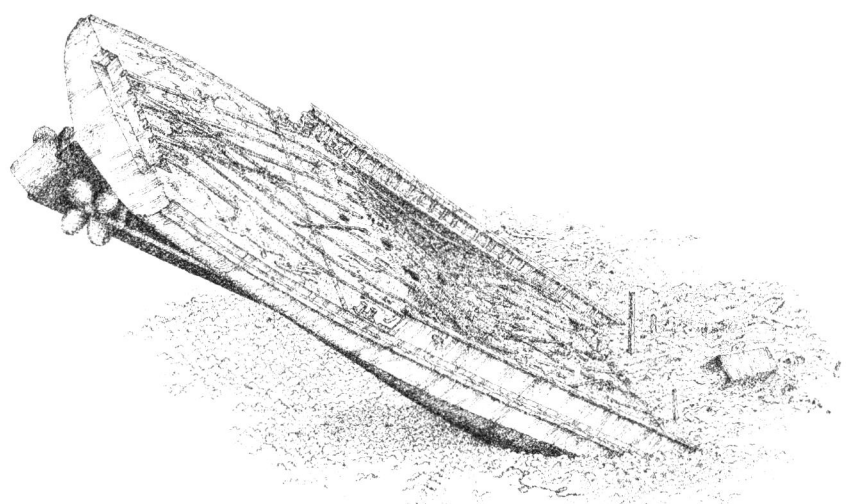

**An artist's rendition of the wreck of the aft section of the *Ann Arbor No. 5* as it is plunged into the lake bottom.** *Drawing by Robert Doornbos*

to try to identify it. The dive revealed the aft half of a massive steel ship, plowed into the bottom on a steep angle. The severed end is buried in the lake bottom and the stern of the vessel hovers at a thirty-degree angle off the bottom. Two twelve-foot-diameter, four-bladed propellers flank the rudder. Because of the angle, the divers could actually swim under the propellers and the rudder. An opening at the severed end allowed access into the

**Jack Van Heest hovers under the stern of the *Ann Arbor No. 5*.** *Photograph by the Author*

**A view looking at the side of the *Ann Arbor No. 5* shows a pair of bollards near the stern and indicates the angle on which the wreck rests.** *Photograph by the author*

"flicker," the crew's quarters aft of the engine room, so named because in rough seas the electric lights there would flicker. The most recognizable features on the wreck were train car rails that ran along the deck of the vessel. Indicative of a carferry, these rails posed an interesting dilemma. There existed no records of a carferry sinking in southern Lake Michigan.

Only four carferries have gone down in Lake Michigan: The *Pere Marquette No 18* sank off Milwaukee. The *Lakeland* sank off Sturgeon Bay, Wisconsin; the *Milwaukee* sank off Milwaukee; and the carferry *Barge No. 2* sank in Indiana waters. Only one carferry, the *Ann Arbor No. 5*, was used in the vicinity where the wreck was found, but records indicated that it had been scrapped, not sunk. Still, that seemed the only possible candidate.

The *Ann Arbor No. 5* became famous in 1910 as the "Bull of the fleet," a nickname given it because it was the biggest, most powerful carferry yet launched for the Ann Arbor Railroad Company. By then carferries had been operating for more than thirty years in the Great Lakes. Before the carferry, Lake Michigan posed an obstacle to railroad transportation. Railroad companies overcame this through break-bulk shipping. Loaded trains would arrive by track to the water's edge, where the boxcar cargo was transferred into ships for the lake crossing. On the other side, the cargo would be once again loaded into train cars. At first, this inefficiency was overlooked because of the great benefits brought by the railroads. However, it soon became obvious that this service was too labor intensive.

In the mid-1800s, the United States' railroad industry saw a new technology taking root in Scotland in the Firth of Forth that could prove useful. Specialized railcar ferries were designed to carry train cars across the River Forth that spills out into the North Sea. The first application in the Great Lakes was at a crossing of the Detroit and St. Clair Rivers. In 1881 larger boats were soon designed and began crossing the stretch of water separating Michigan's upper and lower peninsulas at the Straits of Mackinac.

In 1892, attorney James M. Ashley, governor of Montana and president of the Toledo, Ann Arbor & North Michigan Railway, developed a plan to expand his business and expand the range of the carferry. He engaged the noted naval architect Frank E. Kirby to design a ship capable of carrying loaded railcars across the open waters of Lake Michigan between Frankfort, Michigan, and Kewaunee, Wisconsin. On November 24, 1892, the *Ann Arbor No. 1* became the first carferry to cross Lake Michigan. That unique looking ship with rather high sides departed Frankfort, Michigan, to begin a crossing to Kewaunee carrying four coal-filled railroad cars.

Although Kirby's *Ann Arbor No. 1* had a wooden hull, it incorporated most of the features that eventually characterized all Lake Michigan carferries. Key features were a broad, flat car deck with four sets of track and an open stern for loading cars. Other railroad companies followed Ashley's lead and in time, multiple railroads employed the use of carferries on the Great Lakes. The sinking of two carferries would prompt a redesign, however. Both were lost due to water cascading over the open stern deck and flooding the engine room. In 1909 the *Marquette and Bessemer No. 2* sank in Lake Erie, and a year later the

**The *Ann Arbor No. 5* as a carferry.** *Author's Collection*

*Pere Marquette 18* sank in a storm off Wisconsin. The design of the *Ann Arbor No. 5* would solve that problem. It was the first carferry to be equipped with a sea gate to close the open stern. Built at Toledo Shipbuilding Company in Toledo, Ohio, the *Ann Arbor No. 5* was the largest ferry on the lakes and the one designed primarily to break ice on Lake Michigan. At 360 feet long and 56 feet wide, with two triple expansion engines, four Scotch boilers, and individually controlled twin propellers, it could carry thirty railroad cars. The sea gate would become a key feature in every subsequent carferry.

The operation of the carferry involved backing the ship into the slip using the twin props to maneuver into position, carefully aligning the rails on the ship's car deck with the rails on the dock apron. Once in position, the apron was lowered, locking the vessel in place. Then the railroad cars were pushed into place using empty flat cars called idlers because the locomotives were too heavy to cross the apron. The train cars had to be sequentially loaded beginning in the middle and then side to side to keep the ship in balance. The deck crew then jacked up the corners of each car to take the weight off the springs and chained them to the rail so they could not rock independently of the ship. Blocks and clamps were employed to keep the cars from moving forward or back. On one occasion, the process of loading resulted in disaster. In May 1909, the *Ann Arbor No. 4* capsized in Manistique, Michigan, because the crew failed to exercise due caution for balance while loading cars filled with iron ore.

In addition to freight cars, the carferries carried passengers and were built with staterooms, dining quarters, and a variety of public spaces. When the Great Depression brought an end to most of the package freighters, the Ann Arbor and Pere Marquette lines actively promoted the passenger business and planked over their car deck to carry automobiles. Passengers and vehicles became a major source of revenue for those two lines.

The *Ann Arbor No. 5*'s career was long and rather uneventful. After more than fifty years of service, the ship was retired in the mid-1960s. The heyday of carferry service would continue beyond the usefulness of the *Ann Arbor No. 5*. The Ann Arbor Railroad experienced its busiest year for passenger service in 1971, boasting nearly 30,000 passengers and 11,000 automobiles. However, the early 1970s also marked the beginning of the end for the carferries. By then, all the railroad companies were convinced that carferry service was no longer practical or profitable. Improvements to the Chicago railway system reduced transit time. The evolution of diesel power led to trains of up to one hundred cars, more than could be handled by the twenty-five- to thirty-car-capacity ferries. Crew and fuel costs also became prohibitive and after fifty and sometimes more years in service, the ships themselves were outdated.

In 1966, the Ann Arbor Transportation Company sold the *Ann Arbor No. 5* to the Bulk Food Carriers of San Francisco. It was swapped back and forth for a number of years in the government's ship exchange program. Bultema Dock & Dredge Company purchased it from the Maritime Commission in 1967 for $27,775 and towed it from Frankfort, Michigan, to Manistique with the tug *Muskegon* on December 1. The company cut the ship down to a barge by removing its smokestacks, engine, and upper works. With a contract to work on the laying of a massive, eleven-foot-diameter water intact pipe in trenches below the lake bottom to bring cooling water to the Palisades Nuclear Power Plant, under construction south of South Haven in 1969, Bultema utilized its "new" barge. Divers partially sank it, along with two other barges to be used as a temporary breakwater to protect the in-water work area during the pipe laying. By then, the *Ann Arbor No. 5*'s hull was old and it broke up during the harsh winter of 1969-1970. Records indicated that Bultema scrapped out the vessel and took it off the ship's registry. Although the *Ann Arbor No. 5* was presumed to no longer exist, clearly a piece of it still existed eight miles off shore in deep water.

Scattered throughout history are the incredible stories of valuable objects thought destroyed by fire, war, or decay, but which then miraculously turned up—sometimes centuries later. There are several accounts of famous paintings lost, which later resurfaced. One example, the painting "Toilet of Bathsheba" by Italian artist Giorgio Vasari was thought to have been lost in the bombardment of Berlin, but was found in 1965 in private ownership. Ford Motor Company's twenty-millionth vehicle, a 1931 Model A Ford Town Sedan, was believed to have been destroyed in a museum warehouse fire in the late 1930s, but was found more than forty years later stored in a garage in northern Michigan. Likewise, in 2004, technicians at Sweden's public television station unearthed a complete original recording of a 1969 Jimi Hendrix concert long thought to have been destroyed due to storage limitations. The *Ann Arbor No. 5* marks the first time in the Great Lakes history that a vessel—believed to have been scrapped—has turned up. MSRA set off to determine how it got there and why its sinking had not been recorded.

## LOST

Media coverage about the discovery of the carferry wreck brought several people out of the woodwork, so-to-speak. Diver Bud Brain from Chicago, one of the team who helped raise the schooner *Alvin Clark* in 1969, informed MSRA that he had dived on a barge at that spot sometime in the 1970s after it had been found by commercial operator Dick Race, also in the course of searching for Northwest Flight 2501. Race never identified or publicized the discovery of the wreck. Then, Holland resident Robert Love contacted MSRA. His recollections shed light on the true fate of the *Ann Arbor No. 5*. Love's grandfather, Carl Johnson, served as helmsman on the *Ann Arbor No. 5* from

**This aerial view shows the sagging stern of the *Ann Arbor No. 5,* damaged during the winter storm of 1969-1970.** *Author's Collection*

age fourteen to fifty-six, along with his brothers Carl, Richard, Johnny, Raymond, and Harry. Love learned what became of the *Ann Arbor No. 5* from a friend, local marine contractor Kenny Cartier, who in the 1980s showed Love movie footage that he shot when employed by Bultema to help transport the *Ann Arbor No. 5* from the Palisades Power plant to a scrapyard. Cartier recalled that the film showed the aft portion of the *Ann Arbor No. 5* sinking.

Contact from John Bultema Sr., the last owner of the ship, who was then eighty-three and living in Muskegon, provided an even more detailed account of the sinking. Bultema had started Bultema Dock and Dredge in his home town of Manistee, Michigan. Over the years he tackled a number of complex marine construction projects around the Great Lakes. His plan to partially sink three barges in the configuration of a "C" as a breakwall won him the project to lay water intake and discharge pipes for the new Consumers Power plant at Palisades Park. Bultema's son, John Bultema Jr., then just twenty years old and fresh out of commercial diving school, worked on the Palisades Project.

"We were supposed to be done in one year," Bultema Jr. recalled. "But the job didn't get done in time."

The three barges had to spend the winter in Lake Michigan and storms were severe that year. In the spring, the company discovered that the *Ann Arbor No. 5* had broken in three places. Even in that condition, it could still provide protection for the work area, so Bultema kept it in place with the other two barges until the work could be completed that summer. Bultema was able to refloat the other two vessels, but it would not be so easy to remove the *Ann Arbor No. 5*.

Bultema Jr. spent many weeks in the water with torches, cutting up the first two sections of the wreck and loading the scrap onto barges for removal. However, the management team decided to try to save time by raising the stern portion, pumping it out, and towing it to a scrapyard. "We were attempting to bring it to Holland," Bultema recalled, "but the seas picked up."

Bultema recounted the final moments of the vessel, "I had my wet suit on all day and we had a pump on board, to try to keep it afloat." They towed it out into deep water, then headed north toward the Padnos Scrap Yard at Holland. "Then one of our big pumps shut down," he recalled, "and I couldn't get it working."

Water began filling the barge and Bultema scrambled to secure the expensive pump to the crane that extended from the tug. "Then everyone began screaming at me to forget about the pump and get off the barge," he later recalled.

Just in the nick of time, with water up to his knees, Bultema hopped onto the arm of a crane and was safely transferred to the tug where he watched the barge go down. "It was like the movie *Titanic*," he continued. "The stern stood up and as it did, I could see her shaft and props and the water was boiling up. I could even hear it and feel it when she hit bottom."

Bultema Dock and Dredge alerted authorities to the sinking of the stern section of their barge by issuing a formal "Notice to Mariners." It took seven years for NOAA to update the Lake Michigan chart, but the agency only added an unidentified shipwreck icon at a random spot off South Haven. The actual location of the *Ann Arbor No. 5* is four miles south of the icon.

Long thought to have been destroyed, the wreck of the *Ann Arbor No. 5* is evidence that history can be incorrectly recorded. Today the lost barge is an exciting dive site and one of Lake Michigan's few remaining carferries.

A view from the top of the A-frame on the *Hennepin* that served to lift the unloading boom. Horizontal strips of wood created a makeshift ladder so crew could reach the top of the A-frame for maintenance. *Photograph by Robert Underhill*

# 18

# REVOLUTIONARY DISCOVERY

Before the discovery of the shipwreck *Hennepin*, very little had been written about the vessel. At the time of its loss in 1927, its last enrollment document indicated that its engine had been removed and it served as a barge. However, when MSRA divers first laid eyes on it, they immediately realized it was no ordinary barge. Now legendary as the world's first self-unloader and the model for what has become the most prolific vessel type on the lakes today, the *Hennepin* is listed on the National Register of Historic Places.

The *Hennepin* began its career as the *George H. Dyer*, built by Milwaukee's Wolf and Davidson shipyard, the largest shipbuilder in the region. It was launched in October 1888, and named in recognition of William Wolf's son-in-law. Originally fitted with three masts and the salvaged engine from the steamer *William T. Graves*, lost off North Manitou Island in 1885, the *Dyer* was built for hauling cargo. With a 1600-ton single cargo compartment, and a value of $85,000, the *Dyer* was rated A-1 at the time of its building.

The *Dyer* changed hands many times in its life, several in the first decade. At ten years old it was sold to a Michigan partnership to transport package freight for the Soo Line Railroad through the Great Lakes from Buffalo, New York, to Gladstone in Michigan's Upper Peninsula. The ship was renamed *Hennepin*, after the Minnesota County where the Soo Line Railroad was headquartered. During the early afternoon of Thursday, June 27, 1901, the *Hennepin* caught fire when a blaze at a warehouse along the old Blackwell Canal at Buffalo spread while the vessel was being loaded. No one was injured, but the fire destroyed the entire upper works and damaged the engine and boilers, resulting in a $30,000 loss. After the fire, the Milwaukee, Wisconsin-based Lake Shore Stone Company purchased the *Hennepin* and in 1902 had it rebuilt with "an elevator belt to handle crushed stone," according to the notes written in the 1930s by Milwaukee maritime historian Herman Runge.

**The *George H. Dyer,* as it appeared near the time of its build.** *William Lafferty Collection*

The *Hennepin* transported limestone from the firm's Belgium, Wisconsin, quarry north of Milwaukee until 1920. Only once did it cause a death. On April 6, 1918, crewman Frank Fierstein was crushed to death while unloading stone in the early morning at the dock in Milwaukee. In looking at his mangled body, the captain thought he may have been trying to clear a track with a shovel and gotten drawn into a large pulley. When the company had fully mined its Belgium quarry, it chartered the boat to its primary competitor, the Leathem D. Smith Stone Company. The *Hennepin* remained in the employment of Smith's company until it again became redundant after Smith purchased the larger, all-iron *Andaste* in June 1923.

The *Hennepin* then became the property of Construction Materials Company, the brainchild of Jacob Sensibar, a northern Indiana engineer who had acquired a national reputation with his novel land reclamation projects for Chicago's lakefront. He operated several aggregate and sand supply yards throughout Chicago and in 1922 purchased 1100 acres of limestone-laden property several miles up the Grand River from Grand Haven, Michigan. The company erected a screening and crushing plant at Ferrysburg on the Grand River. Sensibar used the *Hennepin* to haul crushed stone from Ferrysburg to its supply yard just below 92$^{nd}$ Street on the west bank of the Calumet River at South Chicago, as well as to various other harbors on Lake Michigan.

For the next three years the *Hennepin* traveled between Grand Haven and Chicago until the beginning of the 1926 navigation season, when its engine, originally built in 1870 for the *William T. Graves*, became unfit for further service. Rather than invest in repowering the old craft, the company had the engine removed and planned to tow the *Hennepin* from place to place, the same fate as many older vessels. On June 22, 1926, Construction Materials surrendered the vessel's final enrollment document, listing it as a barge. For the 1926 season, the tugs *Ufasco* and *Lotus* were employed to tow it between Ferrysburg and South Chicago. That would mark the beginning of the end for the *Hennepin*.

## LOST

On the rather warm evening of August 18, 1927, the forty-foot tugboat *Lotus* headed slowly up the Grand River returning to its home port in Ferrysburg, Michigan. The tug had departed from its port the day before, bound for Chicago, towing the *Hennepin* loaded with a cargo of crushed stone. As the *Lotus* neared the dock on the north side of the Grand River, the tug's Captain Anderson blew the steam whistle to get the attention of workers near the dock. To those waiting, it was clear something was very wrong. They could see the familiar faces of the crew of the *Hennepin* and its captain, sixty-eight-year-old veteran seaman Ole Hansen, but the *Hennepin* was nowhere in sight. Realizing their concern, Hansen shouted across the water to explain what had happened. "We lost her, boys. She died a hard death."

Hansen later told reporters from the *Grand Haven Tribune* that he blamed a "stiff nor'wester" for causing his barge to sink. All the crewmen had been able to transfer to the tug *Lotus* and make it safely back to Grand Haven. He indicated the *Hennepin* went down in 203 feet of water off South Haven.

**The *Hennepin* unloading in Muskegon in the configuration of the vessel at the time of its loss.** *Great Lakes Marine Collection of the Milwaukee Public Library*

## FOUND

Nearly eight decades after the sinking of the *Hennepin*, the Michigan Shipwreck Research Association (MSRA) set out to find and document the ship that Captain Hansen lost in 1927. MSRA felt that finding the *Hennepin*, unlike other vessels lost in more mysterious circumstances, would be a simple matter of searching exactly where Captain Hansen reported he lost his ship. Hansen's report of 203 feet, however, seemed almost too specific considering the crude tools used for measuring depth at that time. Considering that perhaps the newspaper had made an error, MSRA expanded the search area to encompass waters from 190 to 230 feet deep.

Since 1998, MSRA had been working with David Trotter to conduct side scan survey expeditions in Lake Michigan. Keeping detailed records of the hundreds of square miles scanned in eastern Lake Michigan, MSRA knew that almost half of the *Hennepin*'s probable search area had already been covered during prior expeditions, which had narrowed down the search area considerably. In July 2006, Trotter covered the balance of the *Hennepin*'s search area extending east, north, and west of areas already covered. Running lanes in a pattern much like mowing a lawn, the 50 kHz torpedo-like sonar was towed 100 feet below the boat sending acoustical signals out to each side. The team completed the remaining search area in just four days, but found nothing, or so it appeared.

To be thorough, MSRA reviewed the rolls of sonar paper to check for any targets that might have been overlooked by the boat crew. As the paper unrolled, an unusual splotch appeared. Although indistinct, it appeared to be a shipwreck in 230 feet of water, but divers would need to visit the site to determine if it was the *Hennepin*.

Soon thereafter, MSRA's dive team, Bob Underhill, Jeff Vos, Todd White along with the author, made exploratory dives. The depth required specialized equipment and the use of tri-mix, a special blend of gas that lessens the narcotic effect, called nitrogen narcosis, that can occur when breathing nitrogen under pressure. Bottom time at that

**Side scan image of the *Hennepin* captured with a 500 kHz Klein sonar.** *Courtesy of Ralph Wilbanks*

**A video capture looking up at the A-frame as the author and Robert Underhill ascend from a dive.** *Video capture by Todd White*

depth is limited to approximately twenty minutes, requiring another forty-five minutes for decompression, a process involving stops at various levels on the ascent to allow the body's tissue time to release compressed gases. If a diver does not properly decompress after a deep dive, nitrogen bubbles can form in the bloodstream and cause mild to severe pain in the joints. This affliction, called the bends, can be debilitating and sometimes fatal. For this dive, in addition to double tanks on their backs, each diver carried two tanks slung from his chest. One contained Nitrox, a mixture of nitrogen and oxygen, and the other, pure oxygen. These tanks would be used in sequence during the decompression to provide an additional quantity of breathing gas as well as hasten decompression. Both mixtures breathed in sequence at the appropriate depths help rid the body of compressed nitrogen more quickly. Complicating the dive, each diver carried a video or still camera.

In the case of many shipwrecks, particularly those in deteriorated condition, it can take multiple dives, sometimes extending over years, to make a positive identification. Divers must measure size, locate unique structural features, and dig around twisted debris to locate official registry numbers or manufacturer's marks that could be matched to historical records. However, after just one dive, the divers confirmed the wreck as the *Hennepin*. The extraordinary water clarity provided in excess of seventy-foot visibility with ambient light even penetrating to the bottom.

**The wheel of the *Hennepin* is pristine although the pilothouse that surrounded it was forced off during the sinking.** *Photograph by Robert Underhill*

The wreck is fairly intact and looked identical to the last known photograph of the *Hennepin*. The name *G. H. Dyer* is engraved on a capstan cover, offering proof of its identity. Apparently after the name change, the cover was never replaced. The wreck sits upright on the bottom with a slight cant to the starboard side. The bow, midships, and boiler house are intact; however, structure aft of the boiler house is significantly damaged. There are six hatches between the fo'c'sle and the boiler house. The hatch covers are missing, which allowed a direct view into the empty cargo hold. There are two possible reasons the hatches are gone. The crew may not have "dogged down" the hatches during the return trip. This undertaking is time consuming and crews often avoided the process if weather was calm. If that was the case, then the covers would have simply floated off during the process of sinking. If the crew had secured the hatches, then pressure from the buildup of water in the sinking process might have forced them off. There seems to be little damage on the hatch coaming, so the former scenario is more probable.

The forward mast is still standing, although it is canted a bit to starboard due to the angle at which the hull rests. The aft mast has fallen almost completely to the starboard side and rests perpendicular to the deck. The smokestack has toppled and lies perpendicular to the deck toward the port side opposite the aft mast. There are several points at which the divers could reach the fo'c'sle in the bow where the crew slept: through a ladder from a small square hatch on the fo'c'sle deck, through a steep ladder-like stair just behind where the pilothouse stood, or by swimming down into the first cargo hatch and traveling forward. The walls that divided the forward cabins have fallen. No personal possessions were left behind in the ship, except a pair of boots. Several small wooden boxes may contain tools.

Just below the ladder behind the pilothouse that leads down to the crew quarters, divers found a large utilitarian bell half buried in the muck that has partially filled the cabin area. Photographs of the *Hennepin* show the bell mounted atop the pilothouse roof. It is apparent that it fell from its mount and became lodged beneath the ladder. About fifty feet off the starboard side of the wreck the divers discovered a flat, wooden structure with the bell's bracket still mounted upon it. Clearly this is the roof of the pilothouse, which must have been forced off during the sinking by the pressure of the trapped air as water rose within that structure. There is no information about modifications made to the *Hennepin* when it was converted to a barge in 1926, except one photograph taken while under tow. The wreck provided additional data. The photo indicates that upper pilothouse had been removed, leaving the *Hennepin* with only one wheel in the lower pilothouse for docking. Although the pilothouse came off during the sinking, the wheel is in pristine condition. In fact, there exists a smaller wheel that is mounted in front of the big wheel connected to the hub. This

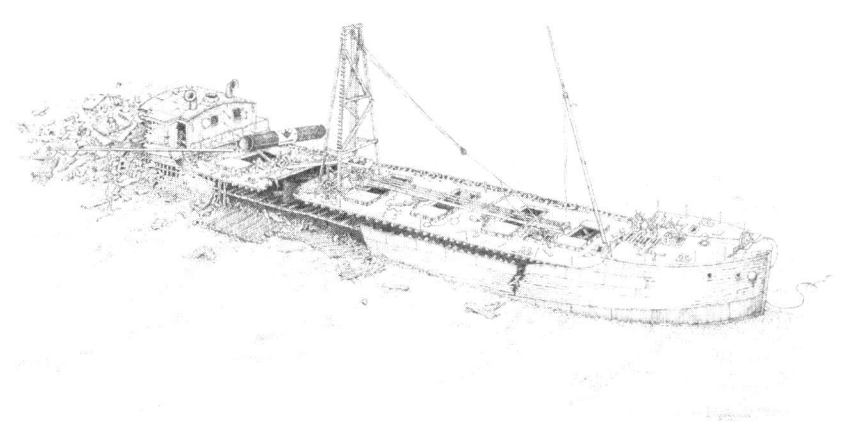

**The wreck of the *Hennepin* as it appeared in 2008 when discovered by MSRA.** *Drawing by Robert Doornbos*

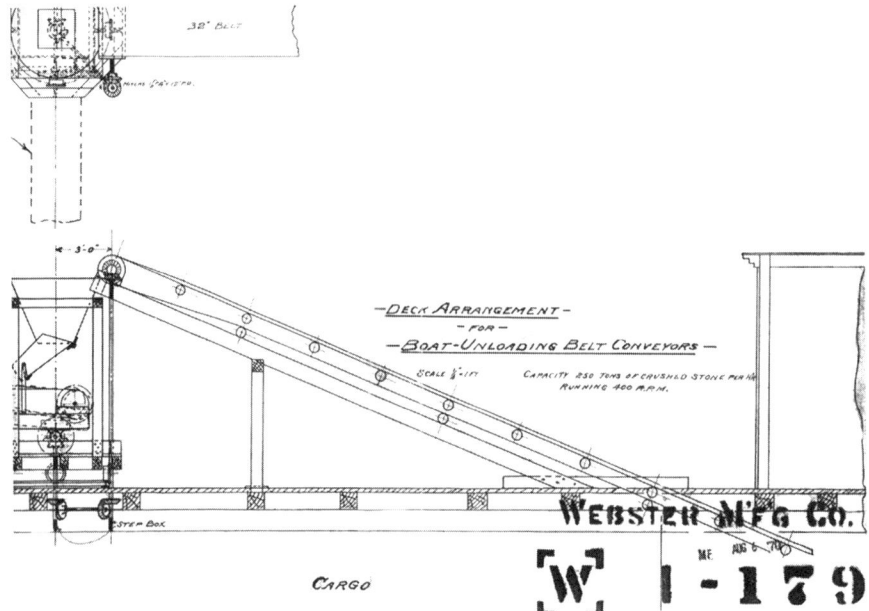

**A construction drawing by Webster Engineering of the conveyor system designed and installed on the *Hennepin*, marking its conversion in 1902 to a self-unloading freighter.**
*William Lafferty Collection*

unusual wheel configuration might represent manual and steam power steering side-by-side, another innovation installed on the *Hennepin*. The conversion also involved removing the solid rail around the fo'c'sle, probably to facilitate towing. A post and rope railing replaced it to provide basic protection for the crew at the bow, but the rope has disintegrated after its long submersion. A large winch for towing exists on the forward deck around which a steel tow cable, or hawser, is still coiled. The hawser still runs tautly forward through an oval steel fairlead at the bow, and pays out to the lake bottom about fifty-feet forward of the hull, where it came to rest after the *Lotus* cut it loose.

Additional changes made by Construction Materials Company to convert the vessel to a barge are apparent at the stern. Of course the engine no longer exists, but there is only one rather than two boilers. With no engine, it is likely the vessel needed only one boiler to provide steam for the auxiliary equipment like the towing winch.

Between the fourth and fifth hatches stands the massive A-frame as pictured in photographs of the vessel after its rebuild in 1902. It is constructed of wood and still intact after over a century since its installation and over eight decades underwater, a testament to its sturdy construction. A steel cable runs from the top of the A-frame and connects to the forward end of a boom, which runs parallel down the length of the ship. Roller mechanisms evenly spaced down the boom suggest it once held a belt, but that would have decayed during its long submersion. Portions of the starboard hull have fallen outward, revealing a below-deck conveyor system as well. An electric motor at the base of the A-frame likely supplied the power for the conveyor. Undoubtedly, this equipment was part of the 1902 elevator belt installation referred to in the one description of the vessel. However, the equipment had all the appearance of a modern self-unloading vessel.

The discovery of construction drawings prepared by Chicago-based company Webster Engineering shed light on the conveyor belt system. Webster was hired to design a state-of-the-art quarrying operation for Lakeshore Stone Company in Belgium, Wisconsin, complete with a pier into Lake Michigan for loading stone. To transport the quarry's output, Webster engineered an unloading system to be installed on the *Hennepin*. The Milwaukee Dry Dock Company, a consolidation of Wolf and Davidson, the original builders of the ship, fabricated and installed Webster's unloading system for the *Hennepin*. The plans indicate that inclined walls within the hold dispensed cargo onto

An image of Captain Ole Hansen accompanied his obituary, which made reference to his serving as captain when the *Hennepin* sank, an unfortunate legacy. Milwaukee Sentinel

conveyors below deck that ran the length of the ship. The conveyors moved the cargo into a hopper where it was transferred to an inclined conveyor, up to the conveyor boom on deck, which swung over to deposit the bulk material on land. This advancement was unique because the ship would no longer require massive shore infrastructure at major harbors to unload its cargo. The *Hennepin* could discharge its stone not only in a small harbor, but along a river, into a construction caisson, or into trucks, something not possible before this development. Although most popular accounts indicate that the steel vessel *Wyandotte,* built in 1908, was the first self-unloader, clearly the *Hennepin's* equipment predated it by six years, making the *Hennepin* the world's first self-unloader. The discovery of the wreck helped solidify its proper place in the history of the self-unloaders.

The discovery of the wreck also led to a correction being made regarding the sinking. The condition of the wreck suggested that the ship sank gently, rather than in a "stiff nor'wester," as Captain Hansen reported. A review of archival weather records indicated that winds were, in fact, light that August day in 1927. The discovery of an oral history in the archives of the Loutit Library in Grand Haven provided evidence of what really occurred during the *Hennepin's* final hours. Vern Verplank, a now-deceased Spring Lake, Michigan, resident and former *Hennepin* crewmember, had apparently spoken with several crewmembers who survived the sinking of the *Hennepin*. In a tape-recorded session, he reported what he learned about the sinking.

Verplank recalled being told that on August 18, 1927, after the *Hennepin* unloaded its gravel in Chicago, Captain Albert Anderson of the *Lotus* directed his crew to secure the hawser that ran from the *Hennepin* to the tug. With an empty hold, the *Hennepin* rode high on the return trip to Grand Haven. "The old hull was taking on water as she typically did and all ten of her bilge pumps were running," Verplank recounted.

The first few hours of the return trip were uneventful, but around 10:30 a.m. Hansen noticed the pumps weren't keeping up with the incoming water. Verplank blamed Chief Engineer Abe Lyons, "He was notorious for slacking, and must not have kept the pump filters cleaned." Any attempts to clean the pumps at that point would have been futile because they would have been submerged.

By 2:30 p.m., Captain Ole Hansen realized the ship would sink. "Captain Hansen called out to abandon ship," Verplank continued. "Abe Lyons grabbed the distress whistle and blew it four or five times to get the tug's attention." It was going down slowly, so Ernie Casperson, the cook, had time to take the beef out of the cooler. Lyons saved the big brass clock from the engine room. Other crewmembers probably grabbed their own possessions. They launched the lifeboat in calm seas and rowed away from the *Hennepin* with no panic or pandemonium.

As the big ship wallowed deeper in the water, the crew of the *Lotus* finally released the hawser. "Everyone watched as the *Hennepin* sank beneath the waves," Verplank described. "The whole galley house floated right up from the ship. The *Lotus* rammed into it to break it up so it would not pose a hazard to any other ships."

With nothing to do but wait out the return trip, Hansen must have realized the sinking of the *Hennepin*, valued at over $100,000, meant a huge loss for the Construction Materials Company, which still had enormous quantities of gravel to transport to Chicago. At sixty-eight years of age, he probably did not want to have his good reputation marred by such an avoidable mishap. When the tug reached its home port, Hansen likely invented the tale of the "stiff nor'wester" to shift blame from himself and his crew.

Today self-unloaders, the dominant type of vessel on the Great Lakes, represent a multi-million-dollar bulk cargo industry. They deliver dozens of products like iron ore, coal, and sand to virtually every conceivable destination throughout the Great Lakes still using systems modeled after the very first self-unloading system installed on the *Hennepin*. Because of the discovery of the *Hennepin* and the research that ensued, the ship took its place on the National Register of Historic Places in 2009. The *Hennepin*'s revolutionary equipment remains on exhibit 230 feet beneath Lake Michigan as a reminder of the roots of an industry still flourishing after more than a century.

The cable used to tow the *Hennepin* is still in place, passing from a winch, past the capstan (which bears the engraved name *Dyer*) and forward through a fairlead and out onto the lake floor. *Photograph by Robert Underhill*

**The *Pizzazz* pictured just a few weeks after it sank.** *Photograph by Deb Chase*

## 19

# LESSONS LEARNED

Some may scoff at a modern yacht being listed among legendary Lake Michigan shipwrecks. The *Pizzazz* has been included for the very fact that it is modern. It serves as a salient reminder that the sinking of a ship is not something that could only happen in a former century: Marine accidents can occur any time and safety measures are essential to prevent deaths. The *Pizzazz* is also notable as the only ship sinking on Lake Michigan that has been captured on videotape and one of the few cases in which the captain of the lost vessel has later dived on the wreck himself.

The *Pizzazz* was a classic sixty-five-foot, Chris-Craft "Constellation," built in 1966, one of only four of that sized model. The roots of Chris-Craft began on Point du Chene, in Algonac, Michigan, a small town on the St. Clair River, where Christopher Columbus Smith built his first boat in 1874 at only thirteen years old. Destined to spend a life on the water like the explorer he was named after, Smith continued to build boats for friends, then customers. His boats soon became known as "punts" or "skiffs." His reputation as a master boat builder grew and along with his brother Hank, he began producing boats full-time in 1881. As demand for their dependable crafts increased, the duo increased production, laying a groundwork for their future as builders of "standardized" runabouts. In 1910, the brothers joined with other partners to form the Smith Ryan Boat & Engine Company. By 1924, the company had located to the Detroit area and became known for sleek racing boats. At that time, the company name was changed to Chris-Craft and continued to operate independently until Shields & Company and National Automotive Fibers acquired it in 1960. Then, the company was renamed Chris-Craft Industries, Incorporated. Just prior to that, Chris-Craft had introduced the "Constellation" model.

The Constellation, affectionately called "Connies" by their loyal owners, was perhaps the most sought-after, flush deck motor yacht of the time. It was

**The *Pizzazz*, a sixty-five-foot Chris-Craft Constellation during the time it was owned in Florida.** *Author's collection*

designed for the most discriminating yachtsman, superbly fashioned in every detail, built to give unexcelled performance, and styled for lasting beauty. The model ranged from fifty-five feet to sixty-six feet, so *Pizzazz* was one of the larger vessels of that style. It was fabricated with a double, mahogany-planked hull on oak frames at a time when the company was transitioning to fiberglass. The Constellation was developed with three key principles: seaworthiness, comfort, and performance. It became the flagship of the Chris-Craft Corporation and, as described by one owner, "a floating optical attraction."

Chris-Craft reduced the rolling of its large cruisers by building the Constellation models with a hard chine. In addition, its six-foot freeboard offered excellent protection and safety in the rough waters. The twin diesel engines produced 672 horsepower and could propel the yacht at speeds up to 24 knots and carry 650 gallons of fuel. The *Pizzazz* was originally painted in the traditional Chris-Craft colors of Midnight Blue and Snow White with the classic gold scroll *Chris-Craft* triple C arrows adorning both sides of the bow. The interior was generously finished in mahogany. Three large, double staterooms could accommodate six people very comfortably, with additional berths for crew. A spacious lower-level salon and aft deck provided space for entertaining and relaxing.

In 1966 when the average annual family income was little over $7000, a first-class stamp was five cents, a gallon of gas sold for thirty cents, and a washing machine cost about $160, the sixty-five-foot Constellation ran about $100,000. The *Pizzazz*'s first owner purchased it new and operated it for the first forty years of its life, keeping it moored in Fort Lauderdale, Florida. As it aged, he made numerous updates, including a new $150,000 electrical system, new fuel and water tanks, satellite television, GPS, and many other modern amenities as they became available.

In 2006, Tim Pearl of Haslett, Michigan, purchased the aging Constellation and had it brought into the Great Lakes, docking it in Saugatuck, Michigan. He had intended to use it personally for cruising as well as offer charters on the vessel, which caught the immediate attention of anyone who saw the gorgeous yacht. Pearl established a limited liability corporation, Pizzazz Charters. However, before he booked his first cruise, Pearl decided to take an extended trip. He hired Holland, Michigan-based boat captain Tim Marr to sail the *Pizzazz* to northern Lake Michigan where he and his family would meet up with the yacht.

Captain Tim Marr, a burly forty-six-year-old former Special Forces operative, holds a 100-ton master's license. In addition, he is a professional

**Interior views of the *Pizzazz* show its luxurious accommodations.** *Author's collection*

boat mechanic, a scuba diving instructor, the owner of a retail scuba shop, and a charter boat operator. Over decades of diving, he has visited numerous shipwrecks in the Great Lakes. However, he could never have imagined that he would be shipwrecked himself.

On July 23, 2008, Marr piloted the *Pizzazz* out of the channel at Saugatuck and headed north toward Charlevoix. The air was hot, the sky dull, and the seas were running one to three feet. *It would be a comfortable and safe run*, Marr thought, *particularly for a boat of that size*. The beautiful, forty-two-year-old motor yacht, with mahogany planking and teak decks, ran well under Marr's hands.

Marr's fifteen-year-old son and namesake, Tim Marr Jr., accompanied him on the run north. Tim is no stranger to Lake Michigan; he is a certified diver and first mate, who regularly worked alongside his dad. The father and son had intended to spend a few days together in Charlevoix before the yacht's owner arrived. The three-foot chop they set out in on Tuesday morning would have more than enough to make a cruise on a smaller boat annoying and unpleasant, but the big yacht *Pizzazz* took the waves comfortably and made good headway north along Michigan's western shore. Marr calculated they would reach Charlevoix, 220 miles distant, by late afternoon on Wednesday.

## LOST

The *Pizzazz* was about one mile off Little Sable Point when Marr saw a freak wave in the distance. "Get up here Junior," he called to his son, who was down in the salon playing on his Xbox. "There's a huge wave heading our way!"

Marr held the helm steady as his son rushed to join him, and steered perpendicular to the freak wave building from the north. *Pizzazz* reared upward and glided nicely over the wall of water. Marr and his son both breathed an audible sigh of relief, but when the onslaught of water cleared from the windshield, they could see several more unusually large waves. *My God*, Marr thought, *I've never been in such big waves—they're over ten feet high.*

Marr had heard of rogue waves before, but had never seen one. For centuries salt water sailors have told stories of encountering monstrous waves, some towering nearly a hundred feet high. However, until recently, oceanographers have discounted these reports as tall tales—embellished stories of mariners with too much time at sea. Scientists have discovered strong evidence indicating that massive rogue waves do exist, and not just on the ocean. They describe a rogue wave as being twice the size of other waves occurring at the time. Rogue waves seem not to have a single, distinct cause but occur where physical factors such as high winds and strong currents cause waves to merge to create a single, exceptionally large wave.

Marr had also heard of the legendary "Three Sisters," a series of massive waves mariners have reported encountering on Lake Superior. A first rogue wave hits the ship, and before washing off, a second, then third, wave hits, overloading the ship with tons of water. Such a phenomenon was implicated in the sinking of the *Edmund Fitzgerald* on Lake Superior in November 1975. Now the Marrs faced a similar situation on Lake Michigan.

Marr maintained his composure and reassured his nervous son that a boat this size could handle rough seas like they were experiencing. The boat rode over the second wave just like it did the first. However, when the third wave hit, Marr's confidence turned to fear when he heard a loud cracking noise.

Rather than ride up the wave, *Pizzazz* plowed right through it. As Marr gripped the wheel and tried to see out through the cascading water, he realized the boat was not handling normally. When the water cleared, he could see and feel the boat angling down at the bow. He stepped to his right to glance down into the salon and saw what no one ever wants to see on a boat: Water was rushing in, filling the lower cabins. In a heartbeat, Marr knew the boat would sink. His only thought was for Tim. With one hand on the helm, he groped around the bench seat for the bag that he knew contained the life jackets and struggled to pull one out and wrap it around his terrified son. They both fumbled with the clasps, but were able to secure it. Only then did it occur to Marr that the jacket was rather thin, not the expensive personal flotation devices he kept on his own boat. "Go out back and wait for me," Marr directed when he saw how high the water in the salon was. "But don't jump in till I tell you."

Tim is a good swimmer, but his dad saw the fear in his eyes. This was every parent's nightmare—a situation he had no control over that could result in the loss of his child. Captain Thomas Fountain of the schooner *Wells Burt* (detailed in Chapter Eight) must have felt the same panic rising for his son when their ship began sinking. The *Pizzazz* was angling more steeply down by the bow and water was working its way up the steps toward the pilothouse. Marr was able to radio a distress call, "Mayday! Mayday! Abandoning ship!" After a verbal scuffle with the Coast Guardsman, who thought it was a crank radio call, Marr provided the coordinates for his position. Worried that after he and his son abandoned ship, the yacht might roll over on top of them, Marr intentionally kept the throttle engaged. He hoped that the boat would continue to move forward, giving them enough time to swim away from the sinking hulk.

As the Marrs were preparing to abandon ship, a lakefront homeowner, Cindy Jurik, spotted the struggling boat and quickly called the Coast Guard, only to learn they had already received Marr's Mayday call and had dispensed a rescue vessel and chopper. With no other way to help, Jurik grabbed her video camera, intent to capture whatever happened next on film.

On board the *Pizzazz*, water began lapping at Marr's ankles. He quickly grabbed another life jacket, threw it over his shoulders, and hurried aft to join his son. Seconds later, he gave the go-ahead for Tim to jump. "Swim hard," he hollered to his son, still afraid the boat would roll over on him.

Tim hit the water hard and fought his way to the surface. The thin life jacket did little to keep his head above water and he had to tread frantically. With no time to secure his own life jacket, Marr jumped seconds later but landed in the trough between waves. As he surfaced and gasped for breath, he was pounded by the next wave, and took in a gulp of water. Seeing his dad choking and struggling with the life jacket that was a tangled mess around his shoulders, Tim forgot about his own troubles and worried for the safety of his dad, who had, up until then, seemed invincible.

Tim managed to swim the twenty feet that separated him from his father. By then, Marr had coughed out the water, but was still fighting the life jacket.

A lakefront homeowner captured video of the *Pizzazz* sinking, which was aired on the nightly news.

Tim tried to help fasten it, but it was too tangled and every wave made it worse. They were so busy with their struggle, neither saw the *Pizzazz* slip beneath the waves, but Cindy Jurik on shore had captured it all on video.

A small piece of the hull bobbed to the surface near Marr. In desperation to stay afloat, he grabbed onto it, ignoring the pain when bent nails tore into his flesh. Able finally to catch his breath by holding onto the floating wood, Marr tried to calm his son by reminding him they were within sight of shore, "We're going to make it—we can swim."

Even though the life jackets did not provide much flotation, Tim now felt a surge of confidence, but he still worried for his father. "I wasn't willing to leave my dad's side," he later recounted.

Just as they began to swim east toward shore, they crested a wave and saw their salvation appear. About a quarter-mile distant, a boat was heading their way. However, their hopes were dashed when they saw it turn away from them. A few minutes later, it turned around. "Hold on, Tim, I think they've seen us."

Craig Cather, the captain of the forty-six-foot Sea Ray, *Upwords and Onwords*, had in fact, spotted two people jumping from the sinking ship. He was trying to negotiate his way toward them without the same thing happening to his boat, and hoping they could hold on until he got there.

It would take Cather thirty minutes to reach the Marrs. He managed to bring his boat close enough to fish the two men out of the water. Despite the relatively warm water and their proximity to shore, Marr later admitted, "It's a good thing the other boat picked us up. I wasn't really sure we could make it."

Keith Pearson, a captain and salvage master of TowBoat U.S. Chicago, sees the outcome of a number of boat accidents and sinkings each year. "A captain's job is to stay out of trouble, but occasionally, like with these rogue waves, there are things you can't anticipate." He reminds boaters, "More often than not, when there's a massive hull breach, you have less than a minute before you find yourself in the water." The Marrs had double that time, and yet it was not enough to prepare to safely abandon ship.

Survivors Tim Marr Sr. and Jr. taken just after the sinking of the *Pizzazz*. *Photograph by the author*

Once the Marrs made it back to shore, reported the sinking to owner Tim Pearl, arranged a ride back home, watched their ordeal play out on the nightly news, and got some rest after their near-death experience, Tim Marr had a chance to contemplate what had happened. He wanted to find out why the *Pizzazz* sank in waves that, although high and closely spaced, should not have caused such destruction. The answer, he figured, lay on the bottom of Lake Michigan.

Marr contacted a friend and diver, Bill Miklosz, who he knew had a Humminbird side scanning bottom finder, a sophisticated device that many divers now use to find shallow-water shipwrecks. He gave him the coordinates of *Pizzazz*'s last known position. Before the search could begin, a piece of the pilothouse cabin washed ashore and Marr, on behalf of the owner, retrieved some equipment mounted on it. Then Holland residents and yachters Chuck and Shirley Cooper found an expensive deck chair floating in the lake that they presumed was from the *Pizzazz*. They recovered it and gave it to Marr to return to the owner.

## FOUND

On September 27, 2008, little more than one month after the sinking, Miklosz and his friend Gordon Chapman were able to locate the wreck of the *Pizzazz* after about a hour. It rested in seventy feet of water, some distance from the location Marr provided. They suited up and made a dive, capturing video and still images so that Marr would know what to expect when he dived it. Their dive revealed significant decay at the area of the bow, where Marr had reported the water rushing in. Shortly thereafter, Marr and a friend headed out to take a first hand look at the wreck and retrieve some of Marr's personal possessions. This would mark one of the few occasions where a captain has dived on his own sunken ship.

As he suited up for his dive, Marr recalls feeling a grudge toward the vessel. It had nearly killed him and his son, and had taken with it a lot of expensive items including a laptop computer, mapping software, a GPS, a handheld radio, an Xbox, two bags of clothing, and $1000 cash that Marr had brought along on the trip, all which he had learned insurance would not cover.

Marr realized the power of the lake when he saw the wreck. Everything above the main deck had been sheared off, including the railings, the salon roof, pilothouse, and aft cabin. He knew immediately that he would not find his cash. He had stowed it in his laptop case left in the pilothouse. The case would have washed out when the pilothouse broke away and now probably lay several hundred feet away from the wreck. Swimming down through the remains of the salon stairway, he was able to find the Xbox that his son had been using when he spotted the first big wave, but of course it was waterlogged. In a forward cabin, he recovered the duffle bags containing their clothing. On his way out, he grabbed some liquor bottles that the owner had asked him to retrieve.

**This image, captured a few weeks after the *Pizzazz* sank, shows the damage the waves did to the lower hull at the port side of the bow. Water quickly poured in at this breach.**
*Photograph by Deb Chase*

Changing roles from salvor to investigator, Marr began surveying the wreck. At the bow, he saw how the waves had torn off the deck rails and boxes bolted to the deck. This had created openings through which the water had poured into the boat. In the lower hull near the bow, some of the outer planking had been torn off in the sinking and Marr saw the rotted condition of the frames to which the planks had been secured as reported by Miklosz and Chapman. With his bare hands, he pushed on the frames and they deteriorated at his touch. He knew immediately that dry rot had been the culprit in this sinking. Had the vessel's structure been maintained to the same degree as its cosmetic appearance, it would have likely survived the rough seas.

Some weeks later, Marr returned to the wreck with technical diver Todd White to attempt to recover the propellers and anything else salvageable. Halfway down to the wreck, they encountered near blackout conditions and a stronger current than they had ever experienced. That same current had probably contributed to the development of the rogue waves that had sank the yacht two months earlier. Not willing to tangle with the power of Mother Nature, Marr and White abandoned the dive and chose not to return to the wreck.

The following summer, local divers Deb and Paul Chase dived the wreck for a second time after having visited it soon after it had been found in 2008. To their surprise, after only one year underwater, the entire vessel had broken down into an indiscernible pile of twisted wood, metal, and wiring. Considering that many shipwrecks at a similar depth of water have remained semi-intact after more than a century underwater, it is evident that the dry rot hastened the decay of the *Pizzazz*.

The sinking of the *Pizzazz* is now a topic of conversation among boaters and has alerted many to the potential of dry rot and the possibility of rogue waves on Lake Michigan. Undoubtedly, charter boat cap-

**Just one year after the *Pizzazz* sank, the wreck had already broken up badly, the victim of age, dry rot, the submerged environment, and the action of the waves.** *Photograph by Deb Chase*

tain and diver Ralph Ripple of Wisconsin had heard of the accident, but likely did not think of it three years later when taking a group of divers out to a shipwreck on a regular charter excursion. On that August afternoon in 2011, he had just anchored his twenty-eight-foot boat *Diver's Delight* on the wreck of the carferry *Milwaukee* seven miles northeast of Milwaukee, when he spotted three monstrous waves at least ten feet high. He, his two crewmen, and ten divers braced for the hit. "The first two waves swamped the boat and third rolled it over," Ripple recalled. "It wasn't violent, but there was nothing you could do to stop it." The fiberglass boat did not sink, and the survivors were able to climb aboard the overturned hull. Ripple's EPIRB emergency beacon automatically activated when it hit the water and sent a distress signal and his location via satellite to authorities. Ripple called his wife with his waterproof cell phone and she called the Coast Guard. Still, it would take two hours before they were rescued.

Each year recreational boats sink on the Great Lakes but rarely make it into the media. *Pizzazz* became legendary largely because it was captured on video and then shown on the nightly news and on the web. The incident serves as a reminder that shipwrecks are not just a thing of the past. The Marrs skirted death in the twenty-first century because another boater happened to be at the right place at the right time and took it upon himself to affect a rescue. Marr lost about $5000 in personal possessions, but he did not lose that which is most precious: his son. He is confident they could have endured many hours in the water and easily made it to shore *if* they had worn good life jackets, rather than the ones kept on board the *Pizzazz*. He therefore feels compelled to pass on the lesson he learned: "Spend the money necessary for 'type one' personal flotation devices for everyone on your boat and bring yours along when traveling on someone else's boat, rather than trust they will be properly equipped. Stow the PFDs in an accessible place near open deck and put yours on and secure it at the first sign of trouble. Lives may depend on it."

This rendering depicts the *Thomas Hume* as it looked in 2010 when surveyed by MSRA and the dive team from Chicago.
*Painting by Robert Doornbos*

**20**

# MYSTERY SOLVED

The career of the three-masted schooner *Thomas Hume* ended on May 21, 1891, under mysterious circumstances that baffled even the most experienced lake men. More than a century after the *Hume*'s loss, the *Thomas Hume* held rank as one of the more mysterious Lake disappearances. Its loss was even attributed to the "Michigan Triangle," an area between Ludington, Benton Harbor, and Manitowoc, Wisconsin, in the book *Weird Michigan*. One web site prophetically noted, "Until sport divers confirm that the wreck of the *Hume* lies somewhere at the bottom of Lake Michigan, there will remain a doubt in some minds that the vessel ever sank." In fact, divers did find the *Hume*, and finally laid to rest the wild rumors. An archaeological investigation, the lake's most comprehensive completed without removing any artifacts, resulted in solving the mystery of the *Thomas Hume*'s sinking. It also provided an enormous amount of archaeological data about Michigan's important lumber transportation history through a museum exhibit, book, and documentary film, all which served to position this shipwreck as legendary.

The *Thomas Hume* began its career christened as the *H. C. Albrecht*, in honor of its master and part-owner, at its launching on Saturday, April 16, 1870, in Manitowoc, Wisconsin. It made its maiden voyage on Monday, May 2, 1870, heading around the tip of Door County and into Green Bay to load lumber at Menominee, Michigan, for Chicago. The *Albrecht*'s first cargo would define most of its career, but Albrecht had an eye on the burgeoning grain trade. The *Albrecht* had been designed to carry 16,000 bushels, a relatively large capacity for a vessel its size. Captain Albrecht initially concentrated on the grain trade, especially Chicago to Buffalo with return trips of coal loaded at Buffalo or Cleveland. He also carried iron ore from Lake Superior and lumber from Menominee to Chicago and Michigan City, Indiana. However, near the end of the *Albrecht*'s second season on the lakes, the blaze that consumed a good portion of the

No definitive photographs of the *H.C. Albrecht/Thomas Hume* have been found, although the schooner docked at the Hackley & Hume mill sometime after 1881, when the firm was founded, could be the *Hume*. The Hackley & Hume Company owned five schooners in addition to the *Hume*, three of which also had three masts: the *Rouse Simmons, S. A. Anderson,* and *Cape Horn*. The schooner in this image matches the construction of the wreck of the *Hume*, but may also be the *Cape Horn*. However, it definitely does not match the construction of the *Rouse Simmons* or the *S. A. Anderson*. *Lakeshore Museum Center Collection*

growing metropolis of Chicago in 1871 altered the nature of the lumber trade on Lake Michigan and affected the career of the *Albrecht*. Chicago become the nation's leading lumber market, with over a hundred lumberyards distributing over a billion board feet annually, mostly from Wisconsin and Michigan. Following the fire there arose a sudden huge demand for pine not only to rebuild the city itself, but to slake the demand for lumber in the West. Albrecht found this a favorable time to put the *H. C. Albrecht* on the market so that he could build an even larger craft.

Captain William Walsh of Chicago purchased the *Albrecht* for $15,500 to use in transporting lumber to Chicago. In 1878, he sold it to Hackley & McGordon of Muskegon, Michigan, one of the largest lumber companies in that town, to add to its growing fleet of vessels to transport its product to market. The company grew by following a pattern of vertical integration, controlling the production of its lumber by owning its own timberlands and mill and con-

**Thomas Hume, after whom the schooner was renamed in 1884, was a one-quarter owner in the lumber business and the vessel.** *Lakeshore Museum Center Collection*

trolling the transportation of its logs to market. Following its first year of service for Hackley & McGordon, the *Hume* went into dry dock at Muskegon to have new keelsons installed.

With the death of James McGordon in 1880, Hackley dissolved the partnership and formed a new one on June 18, 1881, with his chief bookkeeper, thirty-three-year-old Thomas Hume, under the name Hackley & Hume. Thomas Hume had been born on June 15, 1848, in Beechfield, County Down, Ireland, and had followed family to America in 1870, where he took a job scaling logs in the woods. Charles Hackley had seen the tally work of Hume, and in 1873 had offered him the position of bookkeeper. Over the eight years he had employed Hume, Hackley saw that in the rough, wild town of Muskegon the young man operated with well-founded principles, a good religious commitment, and a love for home and family. Coinciding with that new partnership, Hume acquired McGordon's one-quarter interest in the schooner *H. C. Albrecht*.

Just two years later, in November 1883, the *Albrecht* had a partial rebuild in Grand Haven, consisting of new deck frames, stanchions, stringers, rail and shelf pieces, and some new planking. At this time, it also had a third mast installed, converting the vessel to a two-and-after, instead of a fore-and-after. Although it seems counter-intuitive, adding a third mast was actually a cost-saving measure. The conversion, though expensive, reduced labor costs because three smaller sails could be handled by fewer crewmembers than required to operate two larger sails. The schooner's new silhouette warranted a new name. The company renamed it the *Thomas Hume* when it reentered service in March 1884. Over the next six years, the *Hume* carried lumber exclusively to Chicago. Incidentally, it must have encountered the scow schooner *Rockaway* (detailed in Chapter Six) often, because the *Rockaway* regularly carried lumber out of Muskegon as well.

On average, the *Thomas Hume* transported around 260,000 board feet of lumber per trip. Generally, it laid up over the winter at the Miller Brothers shipyard on the North Branch of the Chicago River at Chicago Avenue. There, it often had its hull recaulked.

The start of the 1890s signaled a change in the lumber industry. Railroads carried increasingly more cargo and the existing stands of pine in Michigan's Lower Peninsula had nearly been depleted. Hackley & Hume began seeking buyers for its schooners. By mid-May, 1891, the *Thomas Hume* had made 408 round trips delivering almost 100 million board feet of lumber since it began service for Hackley and Hume. This amount of lumber was so much that it could have built 31,000 average-sized homes. However, the *Thomas Hume*'s 409th return trip would end its career.

## LOST

On May 21, 1891, Captain Harry Albrightson and a small crew sailed empty out of Chicago on the *Thomas Hume* after having just unloaded a cargo of lumber the previous day. The vessel proceeded back toward Muskegon, Michigan, alongside one of Hackley & Hume's other schooners, the *Rouse Simmons* (which would later become famous as the "Christmas Tree Ship"). The wind shifted and waves built, prompting Captain Miller of the *Rouse Simmons* to return

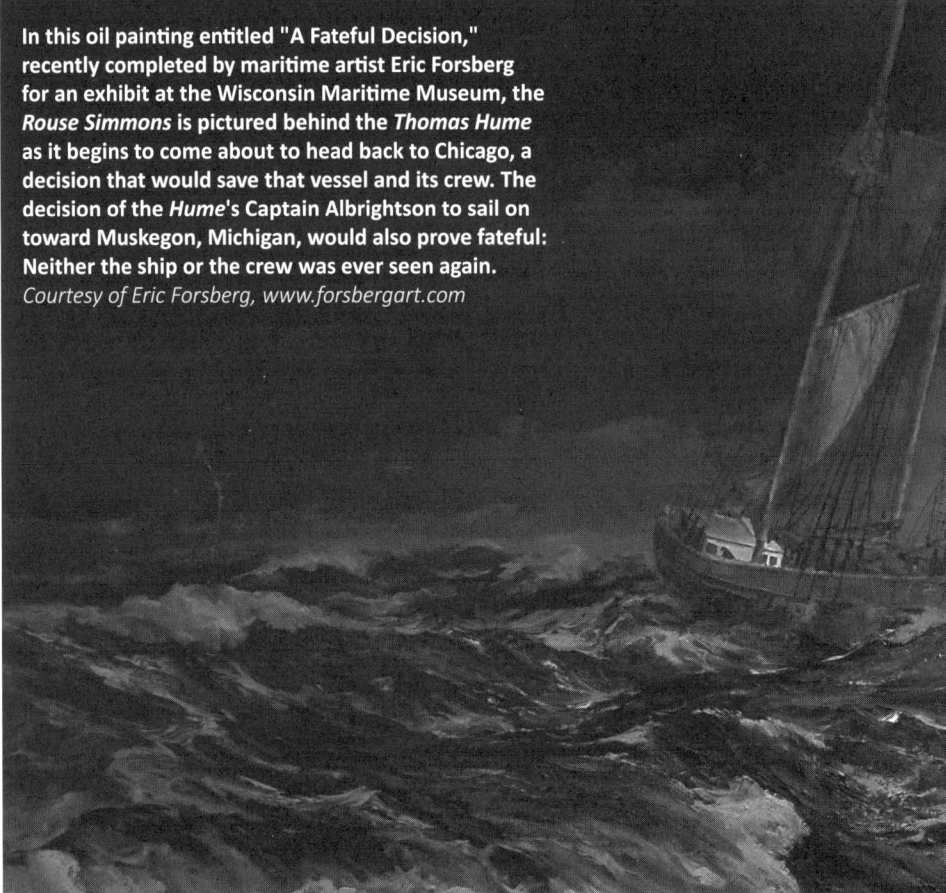

In this oil painting entitled "A Fateful Decision," recently completed by maritime artist Eric Forsberg for an exhibit at the Wisconsin Maritime Museum, the *Rouse Simmons* is pictured behind the *Thomas Hume* as it begins to come about to head back to Chicago, a decision that would save that vessel and its crew. The decision of the *Hume*'s Captain Albrightson to sail on toward Muskegon, Michigan, would also prove fateful: Neither the ship or the crew was ever seen again.
*Courtesy of Eric Forsberg, www.forsbergart.com*

to Chicago to wait out the blow. The *Thomas Hume* continued on, but never reached Muskegon. Thomas Hume and Charles Hackley were shocked to learn that their staunchly built vessel had gone missing. In fact, they expected the schooner had taken shelter and would soon show up. However, when it didn't, they told reporters. The *Muskegon Chronicle* on May 28, 1891, reported that "efforts to find any traces of the boat were unavailing, so this morning her owners abandoned all hope." Thomas Hume wrote to his wife, who was vacationing in Belfast, explaining the disaster, "We don't mind the loss of the boat very much, but don't like losing the seven men on board her."

The mystery thickened. A wild and woolly suggestion originated that the *Hume* might have been sailed to some obscure port, been repainted, and renamed. Others, including Charles Hackley, presumed that a steamer had rammed and sunk the schooner and the captain, fearful of the repercussions, sailed away. Three months later, a bottle washed ashore near Benton Harbor, Michigan. Inside a note signed by Frank Maynard and Wilbur Grover may have explained the *Hume*'s disappearance:

"We the undersigned are the passengers of the Thomas Hume. The schooner's hold is rapidly filling with water and we have no hope of escape. We are on the St. Joseph course and have been drifting for hours. We have friends in McCook, Neb. and Elkhart, Ind. Please notify them of our fate."

Most people, including the vessel's owners, believed the note to be the work of pranksters. They knew that the *Hume* regularly sailed from Chicago on the Muskegon course. One newspaper even noted that lumber schooners didn't carry passengers and found it "improbable that men hailing from Nebraska and Indiana could determine that the vessel was on the St. Joseph course."

## FOUND

The story of the mysterious disappearance of the *Thomas Hume* was the last thing on the minds of commercial aircraft salvors Al Olson and Taras Lysenko of A&T Recovery as they piloted their boat *Brigantine* slowly back and forth across southern Lake Michigan on July 25, 1995. They stayed focused on their tasks of maintaining a straight heading, keeping an eye on the plotter, and making sure the cable and tow fish did not become entangled in anything. Lysenko and Olson were conducting search operations that day, just as they had done many hundreds of days previously, like when they discovered the *Wells Burt* back in 1987 (Chapter 8). Using a 100 kHz Edge Tech side scan sonar, the men were looking for a downed military airplane presumed lost in that general vicinity during a training mission in the 1940s. The transducer on the tow fish emitted pulses of sound shot horizontally across the lake bottom, which reflected off any objects that project above the bottom. The strength and travel time of the pulses were recorded and processed into an image that printed out on the paper plotter.

On that spring day, Olson and Lysenko watched as the plotter stylus pulsed back and force, beginning the outline of an anomaly. They immediately realized it was something of substantial size at about 150 feet deep at the far western edge of Illinois waters. Familiar with the kind of image that a small, single-engine plane would make, they quickly realized this anomaly was too big to be an airplane. To the untrained eye, the image appeared to be little more than a smudge, but Olson and Lysenko had interpreted many dozens of side scan images. Based on the size and shape, they realized they had discovered a schooner and it appeared to have three masts.

The company later turned the wreck over to Chicago sport divers Tom Palmisano, Jeff Strunka, Bob Schmitt, and also Bud Brain, who, incidentally, was mentioned previously for his work on the *Alvin Clark, David Dows,* and *Sea Bird*. After many dives over several years, in 2006, they announced to the media they believed the wreck to be the long-lost *Thomas Hume*. Their video revealed one of the most intact shipwrecks in Lake Michigan. Realizing the vessel's significance to Michigan's lumbering history, and hoping that an archaeological survey might positively identify the wreck, this book's author, on behalf of the Michigan Shipwreck Research Association, (MSRA) contacted the four Chicago divers to propose such a survey. They agreed to a joint venture project. The team then invited the Lakeshore Museum Center in Muskegon, Michigan, curators of the historic homes of Charles Hackley and Thomas Hume, to join in the partnership. Executive director John McGarry and collection manager Dani LaFleur had experience in underwater archaeology. In turn, the Michigan Humanities Council agreed to fund the project.

Researchers find it exciting to study history through written records. Divers find it extraordinary to actually see the object of their study in person, walking the decks, so to speak, just as a crewman did more than a century prior. The first dives on the wreck, located just a quarter-mile west of the Michigan border, revealed its extraordinary condition. Visibility provided ambient light down to the bottom and divers could see the entire length of the wreck. It sits upright, on an even keel. The deck is intact; only the aft cabin is missing, likely forced off during the sinking Three hatches provide access to the hold. The hull is intact, offering no evidence of any collision. Two bilge pumps appear to have been in use when it sank. The only visible damage is in the area of the deck cabin, which is missing—probably forced off during the sinking—and the three masts, which have all fallen to the starboard side.

The first task involved looking for clues to confirm the identity as the

**A view of the bow shows the port side anchor fallen off its cathead mount, probably dislodged upon impact with the lake bottom.** *Photograph by Robert Underhill*

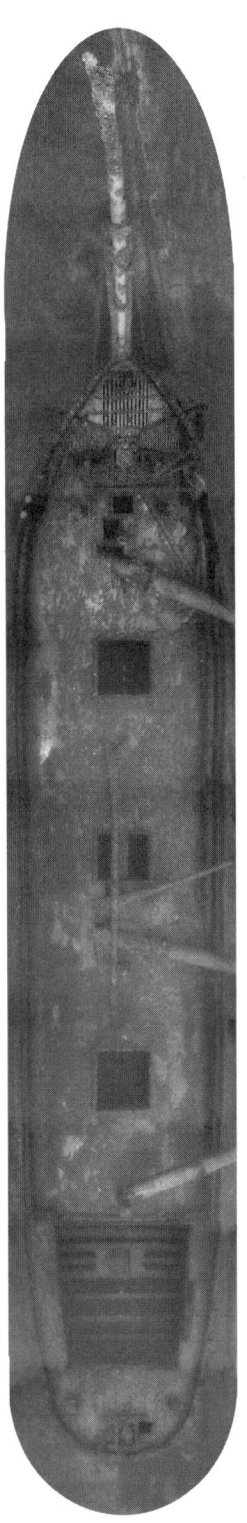

*Hume*. Typically vessels of that period had their registration number carved into a main beam; however, the number could not be found on the wreck. This may be the result of the 1883 installation of new deck beams. The builder probably did not carve the numbers into the new timber. The wreck is 126 foot long and 25 feet wide, which matched the enrolled dimensions of the *Hume*. Metal rigging lies in the sand off the starboard side of the wreck confirming what was known of the *Hume*'s construction. There is no cargo on board the vessel, which is in keeping with the *Hume*'s last trip. Name boards affixed to the starboard and port hull are the right length to carry the name *Thomas Hume*, but the paint has worn off. So far, everything pointed to the wreck being the *Hume*.

During the next many dives, the team explored the interior of the wreck, which unlike nearly every other shipwreck in Lake Michigan contained absolutely no sand or silt in the interior. This is likely because it sits on a very, hard clay bottom. Most of the other shipwrecks in lower Lake Michigan, like the *Material Service, Wells Burt,* and *David Dows* have sunk into the soft bottom and filled with sand and silt. The lack of sediment allowed the divers to swim through the hold of the ship and see it much the same way as the crew did when walking through the empty hold. The fo'c'sle in the bow where the crew slept and the area below the aft cabin contained all manner of personal items and ship's wares jumbled on the starboard side. Likewise, many galleywares, ship's equipment, and personal possessions remained in the lower hold on the starboard side underneath where the cabin had been located. This indicated that when the schooner capsized, the cabin broke off, and the ship's wares fell into the hold. This enormous collection of artifacts rivaled the few other Great Lakes shipwrecks that had been the subject of extensive excavations and would in-

**A photomosaic of the deck of the *Thomas Hume* was stitched together from video.** *Video by Jeff Strucka, graphic by author*

deed be worthy of a detailed archaeological investigation.

While much has been recorded about Michigan's lumbering industry, little is known about the shipment of lumber and life aboard the lumber schooners. This shipwreck could potentially provide some of that data. To conduct a thorough archaeological investigation, artifacts would need to be recovered as had been done on the *Rockaway* twenty years previously. Artifact preservation is one of the most important considerations when planning the recovery of material from a submerged site. Organic and inorganic materials taken out of a wet environment and exposed to air decay at a fast pace unless stabilized. However, conservation is a time-consuming and expensive process, often costing more than the excavation. In order to limit costs and leave many artifacts for divers to observe in their environment on the wreck, the team considered the possibility of recovering only a few items that could yield important data and offer interpretive value in a museum exhibit.

A permit from the State of Illinois would be necessary even for limited recovery work and the team knew this could be difficult to obtain since very few permits had been issued over the previous decade. Budget reductions

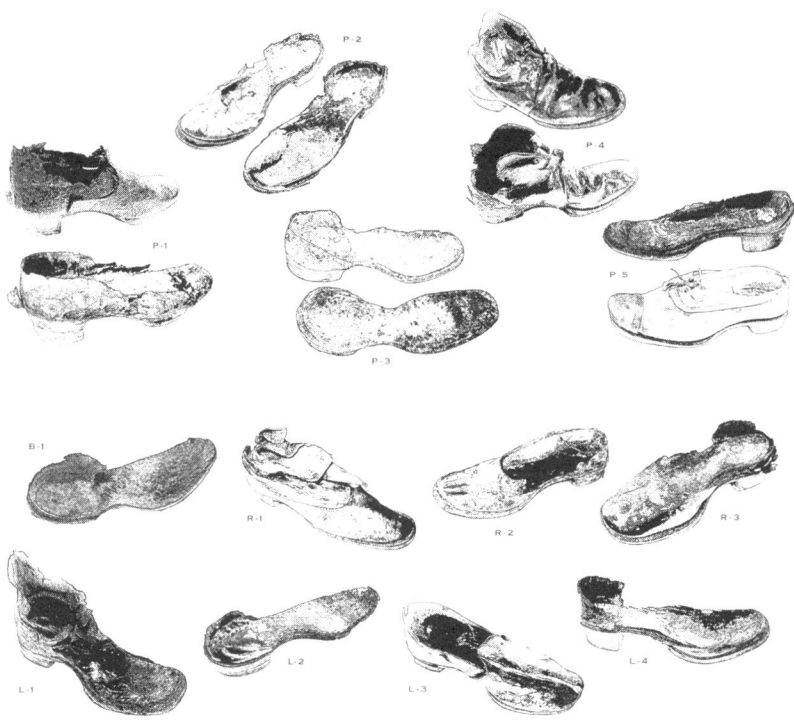

**Five pair and eight single shoes were documented on the wreck, but more may lie hidden. Conceivably thirteen or more pair existed but only six or seven men served as crew. The presence of a fine leather loafer and a wing-tip-style shoe may suggest that passengers really were on board the *Hume* when it foundered.** *Drawings by the author*

have left state officials with fewer staff to properly consider permits so conse-quently most are quickly denied. Uproar from sport divers, like in the wake of the *Rockaway* project when all artifacts from the wreck were recovered for the sake of archaeological study, has made officials skittish to allow any recovery. Past lawsuit losses, such as over the *Lady Elgin* in Illinois and the *Rosinco* in Wisconsin, have resulted in the various states taking a stance when they can exert authority. In addition, the fact that a Michigan team would be surveying an Illinois wreck could cause jurisdictional issues. Indeed, Il-linois' state archaeologist Joe Phillipe denied the permit, although Illinois law could not keep the team from surveying the wreck. Phillipe indicated that the artifacts should be "left where they are to best preserve their in-tegrity for future study." Considering that MSRA would be conducting a professional survey 120 years after the sinking, it seemed the "future" had already arrived. Plus, sport divers were already beginning to regularly visit the site. Although most divers respect the law, artifacts would undoubted-ly be handled, moved, and possibly pilfered. The *Hume* would not remain pristine for any other future archaeological studies. The response from the Illinois Historic Preservation Agency seemed rather shortsighted.

Instead, MSRA had to study everything while underwater, which added much time, cost, and increased danger. Although 150 feet is certainly divable on air, divers used tri-mix to keep a clear head for doing detailed work, usually spending about thirty minutes on the bottom and up to forty-five minutes in decompres-sion. Over the summer of 2010, MSRA, with the assistance of the Lakeshore Museum Center, conducted one of the most comprehensive "in-situ" shipwreck surveys in the Great Lakes on the wreck of the *Thomas Hume*. The team focused its efforts documenting the individual artifacts rather than the ship's construction since so few shipwrecks contain such a wealth of cultural materials.

Artifacts in the stern that would have fallen below when the cabin broke off during the sinking include a large cast iron cook stove, plates, utensils, lan-terns, frying pans, water pitchers, and crockery. Tools in that vicinity include a hammer, caulking chisel and mallet, paintbrush, and what appear to be lumps of paint, indicating that the crew undertook repairs while on board. The dis-covery of a cast iron toilet marked one of the earliest known cases of such a luxury on a working schooner. A derby hat found among the artifacts may have belonged to the captain, who would have kept quarters in the cabin. In fact, the wall of what would have been his berth revealed the remnants of what might have been a mirror, another luxury.

Study of the artifacts in the fo'c's'le proved amazing. The bunks have bro-ken up, probably from the inrush of water, but a number of personal items remain on a sturdy, triangular shelf at the bow. A small box stove that would have provided heat for the crew in the fo'c'sle, lies on its side on the platform, surrounded by a large number of fabric garments. The panels of these garments remain intact, but the threads that held them together have decayed. These items include shirts, vests, pants, knit hats, socks, sweaters, and a supple leather dress glove. A button near the fabric of a heavy wool jacket is inscribed with the name "Nicol the Tailor." Nicol was a famous maker of expensive men's clothing. An open mesh garment proved a curiosity until

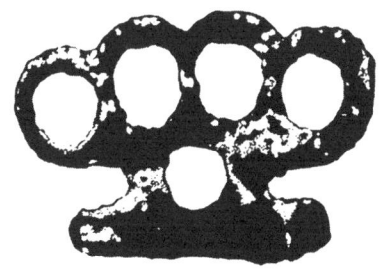

A "brass" knuckle (actually iron) found in the stern quarter of the *Thomas Hume* suggests how the captain may have maintained authority on the vessel or how the crew may have defied him. *Drawing by the author*

the discovery of a similar garment pictured in a 1902 Sears catalogue advertising the "coolest undershirt made." The team also recorded a total of eighteen shoes, five in pairs and eight singles. There is a chance that more remain hidden. The presence of one rubber boot sole, inscribed with the logo "Goodyear's Manufacturing Company," explains why so many shoes exist on the wreck and why no human remains were found. The crew would have likely donned rubber boots during the storm, leaving their shoes below deck, and would have gone overboard when the ship sank.

Fabric clothing is rare to find intact even in fresh water because bacteria usually consumes natural fibers. In the case of the *Hume*, this might be explained because the clothing exists in a confined space where there is little water movement. Also, when divers surfaced from the dive in the fo'c'sle, their suits had streaks of a greasy substance that smelled like petroleum. This may represent a residue of caulking oakum that might inhibit bacterial activity in that area.

Several other artifacts found in the fo'c'sle proved insightful. Two Indian Head pennies and several small denomination Norwegian, Austrian, and Dutch coins indicate the immigrant makeup of the crew and suggest that Midwestern businesses may have accepted foreign currency at that time. As expected, all coins exhibit dates prior to 1891 when the *Hume* sank, offering further circumstantial proof of the wreck's identity. An iron cobbler's form suggests that someone on board was either transporting it to Muskegon or, more likely, repaired shoes during the trip across the lake. Several shoes have patches on the soles, perhaps repaired by the cobbler/crewman. A brass watch fob and locket inscribed New York, 1874, suggest that its owner carried the piece for almost twenty years. A leather apron and pair of leather thigh guards, typically worn by members of a shore-based dockwalloper (lumber-handling) union, indicate that at least one crewmember participated in the handling of cargo, something not previously thought possible in light of the union. While conclusive proof of the vessel's identity was never found, a wealth of circumstantial evidence

**Artifacts pictured include a hat, lamp parts, and crocks.** *Photograph by Robert Underhill*

confirmed it to be the *Thomas Hume*.

On May 21, 2011, the 120th anniversary of the *Thomas Hume*'s loss, the exploration team held a public event. Attendees toured the exhibit at the Hackley and Hume historic home site, then moved on to the Muskegon Art Center for the debut of the documentary film, *Unsolved Mysteries: The Shipwreck Thomas Hume*, and a concert by folksinger Lee Murdock. Murdock's song "I'm Still Here," written for the event, personified the shipwreck. The song's last line, "[I] hope my story will outlive my hulk's decay," indicates powerfully how archaeology is important to document a shipwreck before the remains completely decay, something that will eventually happen, even in fresh water.

Through studying the *Thomas Hume*, the team positively identified it, determined why and how it sank, and extracted important information about shipboard life and the shipping of lumber. In light of the vast amount of data gathered from the shipwreck, a conclusion could be drawn about whether the note found in the bottle three months after the disappearance was real or a hoax. The note, written by supposed passengers Grover and Maynard, indicated that the *Hume*'s hold was rapidly filling with water while on the St. Joseph course. Artifacts on the wreck substantiate the note. Since seamen rarely carried luggage and were not wealthy, then the large numbers of shoes—including a casual leather loafer, a wing tip, and a brogan all the same size—and the large amount of clothing—including a "designer" jacket and a dressy leather glove—suggest the possibility of middle-class passengers. The 1880 census confirmed that a single druggist, Wilbur Grover, lived near Elkhart, Indiana, the place where the note indicated he had friends. His name did not appear anywhere in the 1900 census, taken nine years after the accident. The location of the wreck offers the greatest evidence of the note's authenticity. It is located midpoint between Chicago and St. Joseph—right on the St. Joseph course as the note indicated. In all likelihood, Wilbur Grover and Frank Maynard took passage on the *Thomas Hume* and perished alongside the *Hume*'s crew.

When considering the last words of the passengers, a conclusion can be drawn about the *Hume*'s sinking. Rough seas likely forced the *Hume* south off its normal course. Captain Albrightson probably tried to sail toward the closest point of safety at St. Joseph, but the vessel undoubtedly took on too much water and the wind probably caused it to capsize. One last piece of evidence supports this conclusion. Days after the accident, on May 31, the *Muskegon Morning News* quoted a Mr. Lindboltz of the Seamen's Union who had spoken with Saxe Larson, a former *Hume* crewman. Apparently Larson sailed on the *Hume* several times that spring and noticed that "it leaked badly." In fact, Larson said he was supposed to sail on the *Thomas Hume* on May 21, 1891, but he "didn't make it to the boat in time." Suffice it to say, Larson lived. Did something really delay him or did Larson decide it would have been too risky to sail that day? Unfortunately, archaeology can't solve every mystery.

Side scan sonar has been, and may remain for the foreseeable future, the best tool of choice for locating shipwrecks. Acoustical signals bounce off any objects that project above the lake bottom and send a return signal to a computer on board the search boat.

# CONCLUSION

The twenty stories of legendary shipwreck discoveries in Lake Michigan presented here represent just a small fraction of all the vessels lost. These shipwrecks were found in a variety of ways, from purely accidental to methodical search efforts. Some were found by commercial salvors, others by independent sport divers, and still others by nonprofit organizations. In reviewing the stories of what took place after these shipwrecks were located, spanning the years from 1895 when the *Cayuga* was found to 2010 when the *Thomas Hume* was surveyed, it becomes clear that treatment of a new discovery has changed immensely over more than a century, ranging from complete commercial salvage, to souvenir recovery, to professional archaeology. In the 1980s, state governments began to realize the value of the historic treasures that rested on their bottomlands and became involved in the management and preservation of those cultural resources. Illinois, Wisconsin, Michigan, and Indiana, all bordering Lake Michigan, as well as the other Great Lake states, have established laws to protect its shipwrecks and most have taken legal actions to prosecute suspected violations of those laws.

The State of Wisconsin, through employed personnel, has taken the lead in documenting Lake Michigan shipwrecks, nominating them to the National Register, and prosecuting infringements in the law. This may well stem in part from the loss of the *Alvin Clark* as a result of its recovery: Wisconsin also has two very active volunteer nonprofit organizations, the Great Lakes Shipwreck Research Foundation and the Wisconsin Underwater Archaeological Society that work independently and with state assistance to document and interpret shipwrecks.

Although the State of Indiana controls the smallest fraction of Lake Michigan, it took an early stance in employing archaeological staff to deal with historic shipwrecks. Like Wisconsin, this may have been as a reaction to the destruction and looting of several shipwrecks like the *Material Service*.

After several years of inactivity in the wake of losing archaeologist Gary Ellis to the private sector, Indiana initiated a project in 2011, sponsored by the Lake Michigan Coastal Management Program and the Division of Historic Preservation and Archaeology, to continue the efforts to manage the state's submerged cultural resources. It has recently become active in managing its submerged resources with the appointment of a consulting archaeological firm to document and interpret its nearly dozen and a half discovered shipwrecks. In 2011, the Indiana DNR sponsored another project to relocate these wrecks, search for previously unidentified sites, and conduct research, archaeological survey, and public outreach. The DNR hired the services of Commonwealth Cultural Resources Group to develop a management plan focused on conservation and preservation of these resources. Archaeologists at CCRG conducted surveys on nine sites first documented through the Submerged Artifact and Vessel Evaluation Program (SAVE) and are involved in educating the public about these submerged cultural resources. Through this program, the wreck of the *Material Service* has been nominated to the National Register of Historic Places. Perhaps, it will soon be listed.

Right after the establishment of the Abandoned Shipwreck Act, the State of Illinois made an effort, through a partnership with the nonprofit Underwater Archaeological Society of Chicago, to manage its historic shipwrecks through its support of the *David Dows* and *Wells Burt* surveys. However, the two, high-profile, contentious cases fought in its courts, involving the *Sea Bird* and the *Lady Elgin*, may have colored Illinois' interest in historic shipwrecks. The state has not undertaken any further shipwreck projects since and now, after the owner of the *Lady Elgin* insisted the wreck be removed from the National Register, has no shipwrecks on the register. The UASC continues to take the lead in dealing with the state's many shipwrecks, with no support from the government.

Although the State of Michigan owns the most bottomlands in Lake Michigan, it has had little involvement in dealing with its shipwrecks, instead leaving that work to various independent nonprofits such as the Michigan Maritime Museum, the Association for Great Lakes Maritime History, the Michigan Shipwreck Research Association, the Manitou Passage Underwater Preserve Committee, the Southwest Michigan Underwater Preserve Committee, and the Committee for the proposed West Michigan Underwater Preserve. The *Hennepin* stands as the only shipwreck in the Michigan waters of Lake Michigan listed on the National Register. It was nominated by private citizens (the author and her partner William Lafferty), not state employees as is typical of the listings in Wisconsin and Indiana. The State of Michigan has a much larger presence in shipwreck management in Lake Huron since partnering with the National Oceanic and Atmospheric Administration in the management of the National Marine Sanctuary at Thunder Bay, which grew out of the early preserve at Thunder Bay. However, the state leaves shipwrecks in its other portions of Lake Huron as well as Lakes Erie and Superior to be dealt with by private individuals and groups.

A movement that began taking place about a decade ago seems clearly designed to offer divers an alternative activity to pilfering artifacts from shipwrecks. Various government and nonprofit organizations began partnering with the Nautical Archaeology Society (NAS), a non-government, nonprofit organization based in the United Kingdom that works to further education in nautical archaeology. The NAS recognizes the nonrenewable nature of shipwrecks; supports recording, preservation, and responsible management of them; respects national and local legislation and does not endorse intrusive archaeological work unless justified by archaeological imperatives and conducted by professionals. Through local chapters in the Midwest and partner organizations, the NAS has begun certifying divers in the techniques of noninvasive underwater archaeology and in so doing has diverted divers from behavior that might be considered destructive. Now, divers more typically dive with a camera, tape measure, slate board, and pencil rather than crowbars and explosives. Times have certainly changed. It is hoped that divers will continue to operate within the spirit of the laws and leave shipwrecks and their artifacts on the bottom for study. Artifacts should only be recovered under permit if they are professionally conserved and remain in the ownership of the states for the public to see and learn from.

After considering the losses and discoveries of the many ships presented in these pages, it becomes clear that shipwrecks often live on after sinking. They are objects of conquest for those who want to solve mysteries; they become tourist attractions for recreational divers; they generate revenue for lakeside communities; they become laboratories for archaeologists and historians; they provide the data that can solve the mysteries of their sinkings; and offer the evidence that allows writers to pen the final chapters of their careers. Most assuredly, the sagas of these important lake ships did not end when the waves of Lake Michigan washed over them.

# INDEX

# BIBLIOGRAPHY

**Introduction**
Davison, Gary, interview by the author, August 2010.
Davison, Jeff, interview by the author, August 2010.
"DESCO Corporation," accessed February 3, 2012, http://www.descocorp.com/company_history. htm.
Olson,Robert interview by the author, January 1999.
"PADI," accessed May 3, 2012, http://www.padi.com/scuba/about-padi/padi-history/Default.aspx.

**1. CAYUGA**: Double Trouble
*Buffalo Evening News,* April 10, 1890, May 10, 11, 1895.
*Buffalo Enquirer,* May 10, 1895.
*Buffalo Evening News,* May 11, 1895.
Donner, Mary Francis, *The Salvager.* Minnesota: Ross and Haines, Inc., 1958.
Feltner, Dr. Charles and Jeri Baron Feltner. *Shipwrecks of the Straits of Mackinac.* Michigan: Seajay Publications, 1991.
Grownow, Steve, Maritime Exchange Museum, correspondence with the author July, 2012. *Marine Review,* various dates, 1889-1900.

**2. CARL D. BRADLEY:** Tragedy and Triumph
Albrecht, Doug. "Saddened Rogers City Mourns its dead" *Bay City Times,* May 9, 1965.
Clary, James, email correspondence with the author, telephone, April 2008.
Erickson, David, interview by the author, Rogers City, Michigan, November, 2008.
Lafferty, William, and Valerie Van Heest, *Buckets and Belts: Evolution of the Great Lakes Self-Unloader.* Michigan: In-Depth Editions, 2009.
Lewis, R. David, interviews by the author, telephone, March-July, 2008.
Mays, Frank, interview by the author, Rogers City, Michigan, November, 2008.
Van Heest, Valerie. "Rogers City Remembers." *Michigan History Magazine,* January/February 2009: 32-41.

**3. FRANCISCO MORAZAN:** Accidental Attraction
*Benton Harbor News Palladium,* December 6, 1960
*Holland City News,* November 30, 1960
*Traverse City Record Eagle,* December 2, 14, 1960, January 3, 1961, August 17, 29, 1968
Van Heest, Jack, former South Manitou Island tour guide, interview by the author, Holland, Michigan, December 3, 2011.

**4. ALVIN CLARK:** Death and Resurrection
"Alvin Clark Beyond Repair," *The Daily Globe,* Ironwood, Michigan, May 21, 1994.

Avery, Thomas. *The Mystery Ship from 19 Fathoms* (AuTrain, Michigan: Avery Color Studios 1974.

Bloom, Bernie, interview by the author, telephone, April 2008.

Brain, Bud, interview by the author, May 2008.

Ewer, Robert (grandson of Michael Cray), interview by the author at his home in Coloma, Michigan, May 2008.

Hayward, Joyce. "The Sad Saga of the Alvin Clark," unpublished presentation script.

McCutcheon, C. T. "Lessons from a Great Lakes Schooner." *Wooden Boat*. May/June 1983.

McCutcheon, C. T. *Diving Times*. "The Alvin Clark," June/July Vol 6, No. 3 1983.

*Wisconsin State Journal*, September 2, 1969.


### 5. **MATERIAL SERVICE:** Disaster and Detonation

Czachor, Larry, telephone interview by the author, June 19, 2012.

Drew, Rick, email correspondence by the author, June 19, 2012.

Ellis, Gary, telephone interview by the author, July 10, 2012.

Lafferty, William, and Valerie Van Heest. *Buckets and Belts: Evolution of the Great Lakes Self-Unloader*. Michigan: In-Depth Editions, 2008.

*Logansport Reporter,* July 29, 1936.

Petrulus, Al, telephone interview by the author, June 21, 2012.

Pearson, Keith, telephone interview by the author, June 21, 2012.

*Sheboygan Press*, July 29, 1936.


### 6. ROCKAWAY: Loss and Gain

Jepson, George P. "Great Lakes Schooner - The Heartland Sails into the Industrial Age." *Wooden Boat*, May/June 2009.

*Holland City News*, November 21, 1891.

*Muskegon Dailey Chronicle*, June 2, 1881.

Personal observations of the author when diving the wreck of the *Rockaway* in 1988 and 1995.

Pott, Kenneth. "Wreck of the Rockaway: The Historical Archaeology of a Great Lakes Scow Schooner." Thesis, Western Michigan University, June 2001.

*South Haven Messenger*, November 1891.

United States Life-Saving Service. *Annual Report of the United States Life-Saving Service*. Government Printing Office, Washington D.C. 1892.


### 7. DAVID DOWS: White Elephant

"A Launch at Toledo." *Cleveland Herald*, April 2, 1881. *Buffalo Evening News,* August 7, 14 1908.

*Chicago Tribune*, November 30 and December 1, 1889.

Clary, James, interview by the author, May 2012.

*Cleveland Herald*, April 22, 1881.

*Detroit Free Press*, November 30,1889.

Mansfield, J. B. (Ed.). *History of the Great Lakes*. 2 vols. Chicago, 1899; rpt. Cleveland, 1972

McMannamon, John. "Historical Profile of the David Dows." Chicago Maritime Society, 1989.

Miller, John F. "The David Dows." *Telescope* ,October 3, 1921: 43-45.

Personal observations of the author when diving the wreck of the *David Dows* in 1988 and 1992.

"She's the Queen." *Toledo Blade*, April 21, 1881. "Swept by Icy Gales." *Chicago Tribune*. November 30, 1889.

"The David Dows," *Toledo Blade*. May 17, 1881.

"The David Dows Founders Near Chicago," *Detroit Free Press*, November 30,1889.

*Toledo Blade*, April 21, 1881, May 17, 1881, August 22, 1898.


### 8. WELLS BURT: Impetus for Change

"A Night's Horrors," *Chicago Tribune*, May 19, 1883.

"An Unknown Schooner," *Chicago Tribune*, May 22, 1883.

*Buffalo Evening News*, June 25, 1904.

*Chicago Tribune,* May 26, May 28, 1883.

"Friday's Furries," *Chicago Tribune,* May 20, 1883.

"Lake Marine," *Chicago Daily Tribune,* July 2, 1884.

"Launch of the Wells Burt," *Detroit Free Press*, July 13, 1873.

"Marine News," *Chicago Tribune*, May 24, 1883.

McManamon, John, and Valerie Olson. *The Wells Burt Project: A Report of the Survey of a Submerged Nineteenth Century Schooner:* Chicago: Underwater Archaeological Society of Chicago, 1989.

Personal observations of the author when diving the wreck of the *Wells Burt* in 1988, 1989, 1992.

"The Storm," *Chicago Tribune*, May 23, 1883.

"Traps on the Lake," *Cleveland Herald*, June 5, 1883.


**9. SEA BIRD:** Fiery Fights

*Chicago Times*, April 10, 1868.

*Chicago Tribune*, April 10, 1868.

Gabois, Robert. "The Seabird An Historical Essay." Unpublished Manuscript, Chicago, 1994.

Heyl, Erik. *Early American Steamers. USA:* E. Heyl, 1969.

Trask, Kerry A. "Fire in the Lake." *Anchor News*, a publication of the Manitowoc Maritime Museum. (September/October 1991).

*Manitowoc Pilot*, April 17, 1868.

*Milwaukee Sentinel*, April 10, 11, 1868.

*The Chicago Times*, April 10, 11, 19, 1868.

*The Daily Milwaukee News*, April 10, 1868.

Personal observations of the author when diving the wreck of the *Sea Bird* in 1990.


**10. LADY ELGIN:** Tragedy and Trials

Aetna Letterbook, June 23, 1860 - March 5, 1861.

"A Military Company Disbanded," *Milwaukee Daily Sentinel*, March 8, 1860.

*Buffalo Morning Express*, August 29, 1851. *Chicago Journal*, September 8, 1860. *Chicago Press and Tribune*, September 8, 10, 1860. *Evening Patriot*, March 12, 1860.

Excursion to Chicago," *Milwaukee Daily Sentinel*, August 27, 1860.

"Further Particulars," *Milwaukee Daily Sentinel*, September 11, 1860.

"Governor Randall and the Union Guards," (Milwaukee) *Evening Patriot*, March 12, 1860.

Harry Zych, d/b/a/ American Diving and Salvage Co. v. The Unidentified, Wrecked and Abandoned Vessel, believed to be the SB Lady Elgin v. The Lady Elgin Foundation. No. 89 C 6501. United States District Court for the Northern Division of Illinois Eastern Division, 1990.

Hess, Peter, Telephone Interview by Author, February 2010.

Illinois Historic Preservation Agency. Photographic records of artifacts recovered from the *Lady Elgin.*

Johnston, Paul, Ph.D. *Report on the Wreck of the Lady Elgin* prepared for the Illinois Historic Preservation Agency. Unpublished, 1992.

Johanssen, Robert W. *Stephen A. Douglas* USA: Illini Books, 1997.

Labadie, C. Patrick. Lady Elgin National Register of Historic Places Submission, May 14, 1993.

"Later," *Evening Tribune* (Manitowoc), September 10, 1860.

"Later from the Wreck," *Chicago Journal*, September 8, 1860.

"The Loss of the Lady Elgin - An Appleton Man's Escape, "*Milwaukee Sentinel*, September 4, 1892. *Milwaukee Daily Sentinel*, November 17, 1851 and September 11, 1860.

*Milwaukee Sentinel*, September 10, 1860.

*Milwaukee Daily Sentinel*, September 19, 1860.

People of the State of Illinois, ex rel., Illinois Historic Preservation Agency, et al. v. Harry Zych, doing business as American Diving and Salvage Co., Lady Elgin Foundation, Inc., an Illinois not for profit corporation, and Cigna Property and Casualty Insurance Company, a Connecticut corporation. No. 92 CH 8493. Circuit Court of Cook County, Illinois, County Department-Chancery Division. 1995.

Personal observations of the author when diving the wreck of the *Lady Elgin* in 1992 and 1993.

"Still, Later, Details," *Milwaukee, Daily Sentinel*, September 10, 1860.

*The Daily Tribune* (Manitowoc WI), September 10, 1860. *The Daily Milwaukee*, March 17, 1860.

"Terrible Calamity," *Chicago Daily Journal*, September 8, 1860.

"The Scene at Winnetka," *Chicago Press and Tribune*, September 10, 1860.

Scott, Col. Robert N. *The War Of The Rebellion A Compilation Of The Official Records Of The Union*

*And Confederate Armies, Vol. 1 Series 3, Correspondence, Orders, Reports, and Returns Of The Union Authorities.* Washington: Government Printing Office, 1883.

U.S. Customs Department. Permanent Enrollments issued in District of Buffalo Creek, New York, May 24, 1853, November 5 & 25, 1851, May 24, 1853, May 41855. Chicago, Illinois, July 6, 1860. In files of Civil Records Branch, U.S. National Archives, Washington D.C.

Van Heest, Valerie. *Lost on The Lady Elgin.* Michigan: In-Depth Editions, 2010.

(Wisconsin) *Daily Patriot*, March 12, 1860.

**11. UC-97:** To the Victor

"A German Sea Serpent with its Fangs Pulled," *Chicago Daily Tribune*, August 17, 1919.

A&T Recovery. Accessed Nov., 2010, http://www.atrecovery.com/athome.htm, November 2010.

Bukowski, Doug, "Chicago's Other U-Boat,"*Chicago Tribune*, January 28, 1998.

Halsey, John. "The Three Brothers." *Michigan History Magazine*, November/December 1996.

Hirsley, Michael. "Odd Crew Search for Sunken Sub." *Chicago Tribune*, April 16, 1978.

Mullen, William. "Old Sub Again a Target Practice." *Chicago Tribune*, December 7, 1967.

Wise, James E. "The Sinking of the UC-11." *Naval History*, Winter, 1989.

"U.S. Shells Sink German U-Boat in Lake Michigan," *Chicago Daily Tribune*, June 8, 1921.

**12 ROSINCO:** Unfortunate Occurrences

Boyd, Dr. Richard, Jefferson Gray, Russell Green and Dr. John Jensen. "The Wreck of the Luxury Yacht *Rosinco* : An Early Twentieth Century Time Capsule." *Wisconsin's Underwater Heritage,* a publication of the Wisconsin Underwater Archaeology Association, Vol. 11 No. 2 (2001): 1, 6-8.

Boyd, Dr. Richard, Jefferson Gray, Russell Green, and Dr. John Jensen. National Register of Historic Places Nomination 2001.

"Edward T. Stotesbury," Wikipedia,, accessed June 6, 2012, http://en.wikipedia.org/wiki/Edward_T._ Stotesbury.

"*Georgiana III* : A Sea-Going Motor Yacht," *The Motor Boat*, Vol. 23, No. 24, 1916, 20-22.

Gray, Jefferson, interview by the author, July 11, 2012.

*Kenosha Evening News*, September 19, 1928.

"Philadelphia In The World War 1914-1919." New York: Wynkoop Hallenbeck & Crawford Co. 1922.

"Race to Mackinac Trophies," Chicago Yacht Club, accessed June 6, 2012, http://www. chicagoyachtclub.org/viewCustomPage.aspx?id=140&cid=141.

"Section Patrol Craft Photo Archive Georgiana III (SP 83)," NavSource Online, accessed June 6, 2012, http://www.navsource.org/archives/12/170083.htm.

"USS *Georgiana III* (SP-83), 1917-1918," Department of the Navy-Naval History and Heritage Command, accessed June 6, 2012, http://www.ibiblio.org/hyperwar/OnlineLibrary/photos/ sh-usn/usnsh-g/sp83.htm.

William, Helen, and Georgiana Coxe. 1910 Census.

*Wisconsin Rapids Daily Tribune*, September 19, 1928.

**13. LOTTIE COOPER:** Surf to Shore

*Evening Telegram*, March 21, April 12, April 24, May 18, 1894.

*Manitowoc Tribune,* April 6, 1876.

*Milwaukee Sentinel*, April 29, 1876, August 30, 1884.

*Sheboygan County News,* March 28, April 11, 1894.

*Sheboygan Evening Telegraph*, April 9, May 26, June 18, 1894.

*The Sheboygan Press,* December 2011.

Tidewater Atlantic Research, Inc. "A Phase III Historical and Underwater Archeological Investigation to Identify and Document the Remains of a Vessel in the Inner Harbor at Sheboygan, Wisconsin." Washington, N.C.: 1993.

**14. THREE BROTHERS:** Shifting Sands

*Chicago Inter-Ocean*, September /October, 1911.

Depolo, Jamie "A Preservation Effort Takes Shape." Futures, a publication of Michigan State University, (Winter/Spring/Summer 2000): 16-21.

"Had Narrow Escape," (Traverse City) *Record Eagle,* September 29, 1911.

Halsey, John. "The Three Brothers." *Michigan History Magazine*, November/December 1996.

*Milwaukee Sentinel*, September/October, 1911.

Moccasin, Marla, *Record-Eagle* August 26, 2003.

Personal observations of the author when diving the wreck of the *Three Brothers*, September 1996

"Steamer Beached," (Traverse City) *Record Eagle,* September 28, 1911.

Vrana, Kenneth, interview by the author, April 10, 2012.

Wreck Report of the South Manitou United States Life-Saving Station, September 1911.


**15. H. C. AKELEY:** Convoluted Circumstances

*Chicago Tribune*, November 15, 1883, and December 11,1883.

*Cleveland Herald*, Friday, April 29, 1881.

Ewing, Wallace K., Ph.D. "A Directory Of People In Northwest Ottawa County From Tri-Cities." Accessed May 21, 2012, http://sllib.org/wp-content/uploads/2012/05/HISTpeople.pdf.

Gilbert, Bob. "Albert James Myer Contributions to Meteorology," accessed May 21, 2012, http://www.civilwarsignals.org/1st/myer/weather/myerpostwar.html. Halbert E. Paine. Wikipedia, accessed May 21, 2012, http://en.wikipedia.org/wiki/Halbert_E._Paine.

*Marine Record*, November 15, 1883.

Patch,Barbara (descendant of Captain Edward Stretch), email correspondence with the author May 2012.

Personal observations of the author viewing video footage by MSRA divers of the wreck of the *H. C. Akeley* in 2002.

*Port Huron Daily Times*, November 15, 1883.

*The Daily InterOcean*, November 16, 1883.

United States Life-Saving Service. *Annual Report of the United States Life-Saving Service*. Government Printing Office, Washington D.C., 1884.


**16. MICHIGAN:** A Hero's Welcome

*Allegan Gazette,* February 14, 20, 21 and March 7, 23, 1885.

*Allegan Journal,* February 27, 1885.

*Cleveland Leader,* March 24, 1885.

Hilton, George. *Lake Michigan Passenger Steamers:* Stanford University Press, 2002.

*Holland City News,* February 14, 28 and March 7, 14, 23, 1885

*Grand Haven Tribune,* February 12, 18, March 6, 1885, and July 26, 1906.

*(*Grand Rapids*) Daily Democrat*, February 9, 14, 18, 20, 23 and March 11, 13, 18, 23, 31, 1885. *Milwaukee Sentinel,* February 9, 1885.

Personal observations of author studying video by MSRA divers on the wreck of the *Michigan* in 2005.

*Saugatuck Commercial Record,* March 6, 1885.

Sheldon, George, 1880 United States Census, 1880.

Van Heest, Valerie. *Icebound: The Adventures of Young George Sheldon and the S. S. Michigan*. Michigan: In-Depth Editions, 2008.


**17. ANN ARBOR NO. 5** Rewriting History

Brown, Grant. *Ninety Years Crossing Lake Michigan: The History of the Ann Arbor Car Ferries*. Ann Arbor: The University of Michigan Press, 2008.

Bultema, John Sr., interview by author, Muskegon, Michigan, August 2005.

Bultema, John Jr., interview by author, Muskegon, Michigan, August 2005.

Cussler, Clive, interviews by the author, 2006-2010.

Jaworski, Jed, interview by author, South Haven, Michigan September 2005.

Love, Robert, interview by author, Holland, Michigan, July 2005.

Personal observations of the author when diving the wreck of the *Ann Arbor No. 5* in 2006.

Vande Vusse, Robert, interview by author, Holland, Michigan, June 2005

Wilbanks, Ralph, interviews by the author, 2004-2010.


**18. HENNEPIN:** Revolutionary Development

"All Rescued as Hennepin Sinks," *Saugatuck Commercial Record*, August 18, 1927.

Anon, "Stone Handling Plant of the Lake Shore Stone Co., Belgium, Wisconsin."

Cross, Albert W., "Recent Developments in Great Lakes Self-Unloading Bulk Cargoes." New York, N.Y. : Society of Naval Architects and Marine Engineers, 1938.

Eichenberger, R. W., "The Self Unloading Vessel." Society of Naval Architects and Marine Engineers, Great Lakes Section, June 10, 1948.

*Engineering News,* January 19, 1905.

Lafferty, William. "Technological Innovation in Great Lakes Shipping: Leathem D. Smith and the Rise of the Self-Unloader," in Victoria Brehm, ed., "A Fully Accredited Ocean: "Essays on the Great Lakes. Ann Arbor: University of Michigan Press, 1998.

Lafferty William, and Valerie Van Heest. *Buckets and Belts: Evolution of the Great Lakes Self-Unloader.* Michigan: In-Depth Editions, 2009.

Nordholt, John B. Jr. and James S. Nordholt. Webster Industries, Inc., "One Hundred Years of Trial, Travail and Triumph. Tiffin, Ohio, The Newcomen Society of North America, 1977.

Penton, Henry D. and Herbert C. Sadler. "Self-Unloading Bulk Cargo Vessels on the Great Lakes."

Personal observations of the author when diving the wreck of the *Hennepin* in 2008.

Transactions of the Society of Naval Architects and Marine Engineers, 1924.

"The Hennepin Sinks on the way to this Port," *Grand Haven Tribune,* August 22, 1927.

Verplank, Vern. Oral History, Loutit Library, Grand Haven, MI.

## 19 PIZZAZZ: Lessons Learned

Chris-Craft History, http://www.chriscraft.com/history/history-timeline.

Marr, Tim Sr., interview by the author, July 2009.

Marr, Tim Jr., interview by the author, July 2009.

Pearson, Keith, interview by the author, July 2009.

Richards, Erin, "Coast Guard Rescues 13 from capsized charter boat," *Milwaukee Journal Sentinel,* August 27, 2011.

## 20. THOMAS HUME: Mystery Solved

A&T Recovery. Accessed November, 2010, http://www.atrecovery.com/athome.htm.

*Buffalo Enquirer*

*Chicago Daily Tribune*

*Der Nord-Westen* (Manitowoc, Wisconsin)

*Detroit Free Press*

Hackley & Hume Papers from 1859 to 1955. The Michigan State University Archives.

*Herald Palladium*

*History of Muskegon County, Michigan, with Illustrations and Biographical Sketches of Some of Its Prominent Men and Pioneers.* Chicago: H. R. Page & Co., 1882.

Manitowoc *Pilot*

*Marine Record,* November 8, 1883.

*Muskegon Chronicle*

*New York Times,* October 30, 1878.

Personal observations by the author diving the wreck of the *Thomas Hume* in 2010.

Plumb, Ralph G., *A History of Manitowoc County,* Manitowoc, Wisconsin: Brandt Printing and Binding Co., 1904.

Strange Disappearance of the Thomas Hume," Accessed, November 2010, http://perdurabo10.tripod.com/ships/id147.html.

*The Daily InterOcean.*

"Van Heest, Valerie, and William Lafferty. *Unsolved Mysteries: The Shipwreck Thomas Hume.* Michigan: In-Depth Editions, 2011.

# ABOUT THE AUTHOR

A veteran shipwreck explorer, an award-winning author, and a museum exhibit design professional, V. O. Van Heest has spent a lifetime documenting and preserving historic shipwrecks and sharing those stories through lectures, museum exhibits, articles, and books in ways to educate, entertain, and inspire. This work has resulted in the receipt of multiple literary and production awards, as well as an Historical Society of Michigan award for promoting and preserving the state's maritime history.

Van Heest has written for a variety of magazines and appeared on major television news networks, including CNN and Aljazeera America, as well as the Discovery and Travel Channels and is a regular presenter at museums, libraries, and film festivals sharing the dramatic stories of ships gone missing on the Great Lakes. As a founding director of the nonprofit Michigan Shipwreck Research Association, Van Heest spearheads the organization's search for ships lost off western Michigan, which has resulted in the discovery of more than a dozen shipwrecks.

## ALSO BY V. O. VAN HEEST

### FATAL CROSSING:
**The Mysterious Disappearance of NWA Flight 2501 and the Quest for Answers**
*Winner: Silver Medal, Independent Publisher Book Award, Regional Nonfiction*

### UNSOLVED MYSTERIES: The Shipwreck *Thomas Hume*

### LOST ON THE LADY ELGIN
*Winner: INDIE Book Award for Nonfiction History*

### BUCKETS & BELTS: Evolution of the Great Lakes Self-Unloaders
*Winner: State History Award from the Historical Society of Michigan*

### ICEBOUND: The Adventures of Young George Sheldon and the SS *Michigan*
*Winner: State History Award from the Historical Society of Michigan*

# ABOUT THE BOOK

V. O. Van Heest's newest book, *Lost and Found*, takes readers deep into the human side of twenty of Lake Michigan's most famous shipwrecks. Not only does this very well-researched book present details of the initial loss of the boats, but of the dramas that unfolded after the boats settled on the bottom of the lake. Van Heest uses vast diving experience and extensive contacts in the Great Lakes diving community to present the heretofore untold personal stories of men and women touched by the tragedies.

   - Neel R. Zoss, Author of *McDougall's Great Lakes Whalebacks.*

"Beginning with the early pioneers of scuba diving in the Lake Michigan region, V. O. Van Heest takes the reader along on an historical tour de force of ships gone missing and their subsequent discoveries often more than a century later. Though many of these discoveries dealt with a tremendous amount of controversy, some of them leading to high-profile and contentious legal cases, Van Heest travels the "high road" in presenting the tales in a fair and even-handed manner."

   - Craig Rich, author of *For Those in Peril* and *Through Surf and Storm.*

This book delivers true tales of Lake Michigan ships lost, discovered, and explored, as well as the history of state and federal shipwreck legislation and preservation efforts made to guarantee the rights of all to explore shipwrecks. V. O. Van Heest has provided the most engaging, comprehensive overview of the events that shaped the past and will shape the future of Lake Michigan's rich maritime history. Enjoy!

   - David Trotter, renowned Great Lakes Shipwreck hunter and explorer
     and the subject of the book, *Shipwreck Hunter* by Gerry Volgenau.